Family Abolition

"M. E. O'Brien tells us exactly how the family has delivered human survival throughout modern history even as it has served the needs of capital accumulation, cis-hetero-patriarchy, and the colonial state. Here is an accessibly written distillation of two centuries worth of reproductive class struggle; a revived vision of revolutionary 'beloved community' for an age of climate catastrophe and permanent pandemics. Spread this book around, and start communizing care!"

—Sophie Lewis, author of *Abolish the Family*

"M. E. O'Brien has gifted us a stunningly urgent and timely book that not only sustains our 'freedom dreaming,' but also our concrete efforts at enacting a world where the concept and mechanism of family does not have to be complicated by coercion, domination, and the privatization that creates untenable labor conditions. Through an exhilaratingly accessible narrative, O'Brien moves effortlessly between history, current sociopolitical specificities, and future possibilities to show that communized care is not a far-off fantasy, but rather, a vibrant necessity for current day life-making."

—Lara Sheehi, Assistant Professor of Clinical Psychology, George Washington University

"A bracing account of the crisis of the family and an important history of struggles to transcend it. O'Brien is a sensitive and astute guide to the material realities and the impossible ideal of the family—that site of dependency and love, intimacy and violence, coercion and care. This is an essential guide to the critique of the family form and a radical vision of care beyond it."

—Katrina Forrester, Associate Professor of Social Sciences, Harvard University

"An important work of queer theory which examines family abolition from a generative—not punitive—mindset, asking how can we create a future where we all receive the essential care that is currently doled out only to some of us by the crapshoot lottery of birth?"

—Hugh Ryan, author of *When Brooklyn Was Queer*

"Bringing impressive erudition to a vast subject, O'Brien takes a debate to new frontiers, illuminating how a family in perpetual crisis fuels racism and violence. From Oaxaca to Minneapolis, *Family Abolition* shows 'insurgent reproduction' preparing a world of 'red love.'"

—Peter Drucker, author of *Warped: Gay Normality and Queer Anticapitalism*

"Incisively traces the warps and strictures of our embattled history and culture, unleashing a searing yet hopeful paean towards a different set of possibilities. A precious book for anyone trying to understand our current crises and how to transform ourselves and our communities towards justice and wholeness for all."

—hannah baer, author of *trans girl suicide museum*

"Compact but expansive, *Family Abolition* is an incisive work of history, theory, and imagination. O'Brien locates family abolition as an insurgent tradition deep within revolutionary movements around the world. It is an inspired call to action and a call to community: Come, let us abolish the family—together."

—Dan Berger, author of *Stayed on Freedom: The Long History of Black Power Through One Family's Journey*

"An immensely useful book that will help us not just understand the violence of gender and family relations, but also take action to establish new methods of caring for one another and building survivable social relations ... A tool for transformation, skillfully drawing on insurgent histories and contemporary struggles to increase our capacity to build new ways of being together."

—Dean Spade, author of *Mutual Aid: Building Solidarity During This Crisis (and the Next)*

"A vision for the future that draws on insights from both the history of the workers' and Black liberation movements, and contemporary struggles worldwide. Both meticulous in its historical account of insurrectionary moments (that unsettled our assumptions about how to care for one another). And daring in providing a strategy for replacing private households with 'beloved community', founded around Red Love. Highly recommended to anyone committed to both care and revolt, or bored of household chores."

—Jules Gleeson, writer, comedian, historian, co-editor of *Transgender Marxism*

Family Abolition

Capitalism and the
Communizing of Care

M. E. O'Brien

First published 2023 by Pluto Press
New Wing, Somerset House, Strand, London WC2R 1LA
and Pluto Press Inc.
1930 Village Center Circle, 3-834, Las Vegas, NV 89134

www.plutobooks.com

British Library Cataloguing in Publication Data
A catalogue record for this book is available from the British Library

ISBN 978 0 7453 4382 2   Paperback
ISBN 978 0 7453 4386 0   PDF
ISBN 978 0 7453 4384 6   EPUB

This book is printed on paper suitable for recycling and made from fully
managed and sustained forest sources. Logging, pulping and manufacturing processes are expected to conform to the environmental standards of the
country of origin.

Typeset by Stanford DTP Services, Northampton, England

Simultaneously printed in the United Kingdom and United States of America

Contents

This book is dedicated to the militants of
the George Floyd rebellion.

Acknowledgments

This book depended on a considerable amount of help.

Significant portions of Part I of this book appear in an essay in *Endnotes*. This was made possible by the tutelage and support of John Clegg over several years. The *Endnotes* editorial collective as a whole gave detailed feedback on every paragraph of that essay, improving my own analysis and thinking. The editorial collective is largely anonymous, so I will not list them here. Jules Joanne Gleeson also edited the full draft as a volunteer and comrade.

A more succinct version of Part III appears in an essay in *Pinko*. Here the *Pinko* editorial collective all contributed to my analysis and writing. At the time, the collective included Lou Cornum, Max Fox, Jasmine Gibson, Rami Karim, Tiana Reid, virgil b/g taylor, Addison Vawters, and myself. The current list of collective members can be found at pinko.online/about.

The initial idea for extending these essays into a book came with the support of my editor at Pluto Press, David Shulman. During extended periods when I had little confidence in my own abilities as a writer, David encouraged and nurtured my efforts. David also facilitated the process of submitting the book proposal to Pluto as well as editing the manuscript itself. Anonymous reviewers of my proposal at Pluto were quite helpful in their critical feedback. Thank you to the entire team at Pluto.

Part I was restructured thanks to the careful feedback of a writing group entitled The Longfellow—named for the neighborhood in Minneapolis where rioters burned a police station to the ground during the George Floyd rebellion. The Longfellow also provided feedback on my concluding chapters. The members of that group who gave direct feedback were Ashley Bohrer, Max Fox, Aaron Jaffe, and Wilson Sherwin.

Other friends and comrades read later versions of the book. Hannah Zeavin has been among the book's most ardent and impassioned fans. She offered excellent feedback and encouragement on the entire book. Ariel Ajeno and Abigail Schott-Rosenfield volunteered to edit the book in response to a public plea. They each carefully read the entire book and provided exceedingly helpful and detailed responses. Katrina Black, Misha Falk, and Tegan Jaye-Luzhin also offered, but my rewriting schedule prevented me from taking them up on their generosity. With the exception of Pluto staff and contractors, no one who assisted in this book was paid. All these contributions as volunteers were far more than I deserve.

While drafting this book, I have been descending into the netherworld of psychoanalytic theory and training. Though I was unable to incorporate psychoanalytic insights into this book—that will have to wait for future publications—I had the tremendously good fortune of encountering a circle of wonderful people excited about creating a rich dialogue between psychoanalysis and family abolition. They are the editors of *Parapraxis*. At the time of this writing, the editors are Hannah Zeavin, Alex Colston, Noor Asif, Wendy Lotterman, Michelle Rada, Zoé Samudzi, and myself. Among other activities, we convened a six-month seminar on "The Problem of the Family." The two hundred some participants and presenters of this seminar have greatly expanded my understanding of the family-abolitionist dimensions of psychoanalysis. Through the efforts of Hannah Zeavin, I was able to present part of this book at the June 2022 Annual Meeting of the American Psychoanalytic Association, and the comments of the attendees and fellow panelists were productive and challenging.

I had several other opportunities to present aspects of the argument of this book to various audiences, and greatly appreciated their feedback. Two sections were presented in successive years at a gathering in Washington State colloquially known as "Commie Camp." I presented at two Red May Seattle panels, in 2020 and again in 2021. In 2022, I joined a panel entitled "Abolish the Family?" hosted by the London-based Learning Cooperative and Red Clinic. I also co-led, with Sophie Lewis, one session of a workshop on envisioning revolutionary family abolition at the Amant Foundation in Brooklyn.

Other writers on family abolition were essential to making this book possible. Sophie Lewis has been an essential comrade, friend, and discussant. Their writing informs my thinking throughout. Kade Doyle Griffiths, Jules Joanne Gleeson, and Madeline Lane-McKinley are all similarly the incredible combination of sharp family-abolitionist theorists and dear personal friends. The work of Tiffany Lethabo King has also been crucial to developing this book.

Outside of reading and responding to drafts, many personal friends, family members, and comrades provided me with emotional care, social reproductive labor, encouragement, and love. My supportive family members include Olivia, Theo, my co-parents Sonar, Tra, and Navah; my parents Kim, Steve, Debra, and Jon; and my sister, Nadia. I am also deeply grateful for my dear friends. In addition to those many dear friends listed here, I would like to include Adele, Alexandra, David, Katrina, Kriti, Lizzie, Lucretia, María, Rowan, and Tiffany, as well as my bffs Eman and Nathan.

All faults of this book are exclusively my own.

Introduction
The Oaxaca Commune

In June 2006 three thousand police officers attacked a teachers' protest in the Mexican city of Oaxaca. The teachers had been on strike for a month, occupying the central square of the city. The police and teachers battled for hours over the course of the day, leading to over a hundred hospitalizations. In the aftermath of the confrontation, hundreds of social movement organizations gathered to form the Asamblea Popular de los Pueblos de Oaxaca (APPO), an organization that became the central coordinating body of hundreds of protests and occupations over the coming seven months. In August, insurgent women seized control of multiple radio stations, going on to use them as communication hubs for the movement. At the end of one radio broadcast of an occupied station, the newscaster concluded, "Transmitting from the Oaxaca Commune." Insurgents took up the name, referencing the Paris Commune of 1871.[1]

The militants of the Oaxaca Commune erected hundreds of barricades throughout the city. They used the barricades to defend their neighborhoods against nightly attacks by police and paramilitaries. Many workers were on strike, living full time at the barricades. Many not on strike spent their nights on the barricades after their day's work was done. Insurgents communicated with each other from one barricade to the next using radio and began to identify themselves by the name of their barricade.

These barricades became sites of what I call *insurgent social reproduction*, the transformation of the daily tasks of household labor into means of sustaining militant protest. Barucha Peller writes, "The barricades were places where the people of Oaxaca slept, cooked and shared food, had sex, shared news, and came together at the end of the day."[2] Women on the barricades redistributed seized goods, conducted educational workshops,

1

gathered supplies, socialized together, and shared life. Peller goes on, "People belonged to the Commune simply because they took part in this reproduction of daily life—from cooking at the barricades, carrying coffee to the barricades from homes or businesses, carrying news between barricades, to making molotovs at barricades, stacking rocks or simply sharing stories."[3]

The women of the Oaxaca Commune were engaged in a moment of *family abolition*. They were rebelling simultaneously against both abusive husbands and racist, anti-indigenous, and anti-worker state forces. They were challenging the social role to which they were relegated as women, as wives, as mothers, upending norms of gender and sexuality. Their collective labor made the rebellion possible. Rather than the atomized isolation of private households, during the rebellion people lived collectively on the barricades. What had been women's work in the home became the daily practice of reproducing the insurrection. Through the barricades, the women of the Oaxaca Commune created a new, collective life that overcame the divisions between private and public. They were refusing the private household as a link in the circuits of racial capitalism.

For these women, rejection of the family was not a move toward isolation or abandoning of caretaking relationships. They brought their children with them to the barricades. They were not simply rejecting maternal caretaking but radically transforming it. They were expanding the care labor of their private homes into a mass insurrectionary movement for the transformation of society as a whole. In creating the collective life of the barricades, they were constituting a new basis for shared social reproduction and shared intimacy. They were transforming the isolation of domestic life into a means of communal, revolutionary survival.

The daily life of the barricades and the city's other occupations became a site of escalating gendered struggle. Many husbands, frustrated their wives at the barricades were no longer serving them in their home, forced their wives to abandon the occupation. A participant recounts:

There were comrades who complained that since August 1, my woman doesn't serve me. There were many women who suffered domestic violence for being at the occupations and marches, sometimes their husbands even attempted to divorce or separate. The husbands didn't take well to the idea of women abandoning the housework to participate politically. They didn't help in the sense of doing the housework, such as taking care of kids or washing clothes, so that the women could continue being at the station.[4]

This reassertion of the family as a system of private, male-dominated households contributed to the defeat of the Oaxaca Commune. The women could not act as both frontline militants and obedient wives. The family was a tool of counterinsurgency.

The women of the Oaxaca Commune rebelled against a system of private households, male-dominated kinship arrangements, and a gendered division of labor. All these are dimensions of the family form that characterize most people's lives under racial capitalism. Families typically exist as private households in segmented isolation from each other, divided by architecture, resources, public policy, and custom. Each family works separately, helping to reproduce capitalist society from one generation to the next. Families raise children and offer them their first socialization in heteronormative gender norms and labor market discipline. Through maintaining a stable family, individuals gain legitimacy, social acceptance, and respectability. People's kinship arrangements and households are judged by the extent to which they manage to obtain an ideal of the family rooted in a long history of white supremacy and capitalism.

Through the Oaxaca Commune, women sought to overcome the family form; their efforts in turn made the scale of the mobilization possible. Many popular rebellions share this quality. When large numbers of working-class people move into open rebellion, the boundaries of the family begin to break down. The private household gives way to the collective life of shared, insurgent social reproduction. Those subjugated within the private family seize the opportunities of new ways of living and loving together. Rather than rigid gender roles, people may begin to care for each other as comrades. Replacing private family kitchens or takeout from local restaurants, people may gather around protest kitchens, canteens, and group meals. Care for children, the injured, and others unable to work becomes a shared concern of collective projects of survival. Family abolition is a horizon of human freedom, one briefly visible on the barricades of the Oaxaca Commune.

FAMILY AS LIMIT

The family is a limit to human emancipation. The family's horrors are vast, its abuses widespread, its logic coercive. The family is a joy for some, a necessity for most, and a nightmare for too many. Behind its closed doors, the household is a gamble. Children born into abusive households have no recourse from harmful parents. Those trapped in abusive couple relationships may see their means of escape gradually cut off by manipulative and controlling partners. Those working-class adults who wish to be a part of a child's life are forced into degrees of economic precarity to keep their children fed and cared for, trapping parents further within awful jobs. The family policing system targets poor, Black, Indigenous, and migrant families with new forms of state violence in the name of protecting children, leaving the violence of the white, propertied family form untouched.

The family is also a limit to our imagination. Many of us grow up in private households and struggle to envision anything else. We can barely conceive of real alternatives to the family. Shared households are often a necessary survival strategy for proletarians, yet most working-class families come under frequent pressure from changing labor market conditions, state policies, or state violence. These pressures make it hard to form and hold together families, but even harder to maintain chosen, nonnormative living arrangements. Many imagine and pursue a household that is entirely chosen and a radical alternative to the normative family, but attempts at holding such arrangements together often fall apart over decades of the stresses of trying to find and maintain work, to pay rent, to deal with medical emergencies, or to face aging. Others flee shared households altogether, often to find isolation and loneliness. Beyond some variation on the private household, what could possibly provide the care that we all so desperately need?

The family is also a limit for many mass social movements and revolutionary struggles. Social revolutions that left untouched the

4

tyranny of the home prevented a deeper social and cultural change that could extend into everyone's lives. So long as the private household is maintained, no revolutionary process can overcome class society. Many reform protest movements run into major internal crisis when they are forced to grapple with conflicts and contradictions often relegated to the family. Countless organizations and parties have been destroyed because they were unable to adequately address sexual assault, intimate partner violence, the unequal gendered division of labor, or the demands of child-rearing. The family is a limit, and the real movement for collective liberation must abolish it.

FAMILY ABOLITION

Family abolition is a fraught phrase. Right-wing critics accuse proponents of family abolition of trying to destroy gender, market relations, and civilization. Progressive opponents of the idea suggest it is an ultra-left fantasy likely to alienate people, foreclosing the mass constituency necessary for social democratic demands. Some astute skeptics of family abolition point to how Black, Indigenous, and people of color (BIPOC) rely on family relations to survive the racist onslaught of the state. Many imagine that family abolition calls for the acceleration of the current neoliberal social forces that make having children or finding a stable home challenging for so many people.

These critiques of family abolition reflect deep anxieties. Many people rely on their family when they are at their most vulnerable—as newborns and children, while sick or disabled, while aging and approaching death. For those lucky enough to have loving family members, such support can be a source of great solace. Even those with unsupportive families of origin may keep them close throughout their lives. Those who raise us have a profound impact on our emotional, physical, and social development. Parenting, in turn, can be an extraordinary space of self-growth and experience of long-term care for another person. Unlike most relationships in a capitalist society, families can offer what feels to be an unconditional and unwavering form of love, at least sometimes.

It is through the language of family that people often articulate their yearnings for care, for affection, for the long-term interweaving of our lives. For those with cruel or harmful families, the idea of doing it better, of forming healing chosen family can be profoundly compelling. Family abolition provokes in listeners' fears of being abandoned, of being without support, of being left alone to face the violent power of the state or the cruelty of work. These are nearly universal fears in an era of neoliberal dismantling of social welfare supports, increasing atomization of capitalist society, racist state violence, and generalized instability. Many imagine family abolition as the Left robbing them of their only means of solace and survival. In their imagination, to abolish the family is to make the world unlivable.

Human life depends on care. We are all inescapably interdependent. In our society, many important forms of care are often concentrated in families. Everyone needs material supports. For some, these are found through a family's access to jobs or property, safe housing, financial support during difficult times, healthy food, mobility, or quality healthcare. But the basis of a rich human life also includes the emotional, interpersonal, and physical support families provide. These are all basic human needs, and the family is where we are most likely to have found them. To those who fear family abolition, abolishing the family sounds as if it involves eliminating access to care; however, the opposite is true.

Family abolition is a commitment to making the care necessary for human flourishing freely available throughout society. Rather than relying solely on one's immediate personal relationships, access to care could be built into the social fabric of our collective lives. Family abolition is the vision that the basis of thriving should not depend on who your parents happen to be, who you love, or who you choose to live with. Family abolition is a horizon of sexual and gender freedom beyond the bigotry imposed by those on whom we depend. Family abolition is the expansion of care as a universal, unconditional social good. Family abolition is not just the positive assertion of care but also a refusal of the harmful relationships of domination that the family form enables. Family abolition is a belief that no child should be trapped by cruel parents; no woman should be afraid of poverty or isolation in leaving her violent husband; no aging, disabled, or sick person should be afraid of having to depend on an indifferent and uncaring family member. Family abolition is the recognition that no human being should ever own or entirely dominate another person, even children. No individual should have the means to coerce intimacy or labor from another, as current property relations enable. Family abolition is the destruction of private households as systems of accumulating power and property at the cost of others' well-being.

As well as overcoming the private household, family abolition is also the radical overturning in how society values particular family forms at the expense of others. A long history of white supremacy, heteronormativity, and capitalist property relations have enshrined a particular narrow vision of the family as the basis of an orderly society. Certain family norms are upheld in law, enforced through state violence, and defended in popular culture. Family abolition is a call for embracing the many forms of care and love through which people can form rich and fulfilling lives. It is for the destruction and overcoming of an ideal that treats some family structures as normal while devaluing or destroying other care relations.

As a meditation on family abolition, this book sets out to offer three linked arguments. First, it details a diagnosis of the ongoing crisis of the family today. Part I of this book engages multiple dimensions of family to understand this crisis, focusing on the family as private household and as a site of violence. Families as private households are embedded in the broader circuits of property, labor markets, and the state. All these link together to reproduce capitalist society as a whole. The family simultaneously is a site of multiple forms of violence. Through the racist, heterosexual normative ideals of family, institutions of racial capitalism assault chosen care relations. In trying to function within racial capitalism, families are pushed to embody a normative ideal set out in public policy and the cultural imagination. Yet this ideal is impossible without the stabilizing foundations of property, whiteness, and empire. Shrouded in privacy and bound by relationships of dependency, families readily enable violence and abuse.

Second, this book is a history of family forms in capitalist society and the changing visions of its overcoming. Part II offers a history of the family and anti-family struggle embedded in the dynamics of capitalist development. Over the last two hundred years, revolutionaries have repeatedly come up against the family form and imagined something more. Family abolition has taken on many meanings in each era of mass struggle: the destruction of bourgeois society and private property, the rebellion against white supremacy, the collectivization of household chores and cooking, the rejection of suburban isolation. All these meanings will be explored throughout this book, along with the particular conditions in capitalist society that gave them each substance.

Third, this book concludes with a specific speculative vision for what family abolition could become in our future. Family abolition entails imagining how a revolutionary transformation of society may enable new ways of approaching things we ask of our families today: raising children, forming intimate relationships, cooking and eating, managing disability and illness, and aging and death. This may be accomplished in many ways. In Part III I offer an imagining of the commune as a social form that arises during the escalation of mass insurgency against capitalism and the state. Like the women of the Oaxaca Commune, making daily life communal can be a strategy of insurrection and survival, a means of abolishing the family.

STRUCTURE OF THE BOOK

Part I lays out the core concepts of the book through examining the crisis of the family in the present. Chapter 1 uses the context of the coronavirus pandemic lockdowns to explore a primary meaning of family as used throughout this text: the family as private household. Private households are embedded in the circuits of the reproduction of capitalist society. However, they are not sufficient on their own to complete the basic tasks of raising children, caring for the elderly, or making it from one day of work to the next. I offer the threefold schema of the family, the market, and the state as the three main means of survival under capitalism, a framework I later use to identify the changing place of the family in capitalist society.

Chapter 2 considers a photograph in the aftermath of racial terror to explore the family as a racial, normative, and social ideal. This chapter considers two dimensions of the family as a source of violence: the external violence inflicted by the family policing system and racial capitalism, and the internal violence enabled by the family's particular combination of coercion and care. This internal violence is a mechanism in socializing gender roles, imposing heterosexual norms, and maintaining male domination.

Chapter 3 turns to another positive meaning of family: the plea for love, for help, and for salvation. Taking as my point of departure George Floyd's call for his deceased mother, I introduce the movement to go beyond the family as the fulfillment of this plea. In the struggle for human freedom, movements periodically point the way to the possibility of moving beyond the family, into less coercive means of interpersonal care. This chapter also grapples with the tensions between abolition as destruction and abolition as transformation, and is written in dialogue with the multiple revolutionary political traditions that raise the call of abolition.

Part II outlines a history of family abolition, one that follows the changing role of the family in racial capitalism. The nuclear family is a recent historical phenomenon, essentially unique to the capitalist era. Its dominant forms and how accessible it has been have changed over the last two centuries. Chapters 4–9 delve into the past, examining the changing meanings of family abolition over the course of capitalist development, explained through the changing role of the working-class family. In each phase, proletarian struggle against the family was the horizon of gender and sexual freedom. Yet the particular meanings and form of this struggle changed over time, as the place of the family in capitalist development changed. Table 1 (overleaf) provides an outline of these historical chapters.

I begin my account of past struggles against the family in chapter 4, with the family politics of capitalist industrialization in Europe, following the arguments of Marx and Engels. Capitalism destroyed the peasant family, pulling new proletarians into the factories of the Great Towns. There, low wages, overcrowding, and factory labor prevented proletarians from forming stable family structures. Marx and Engels direct their family-abolitionist politics, therefore, against the nuclear family form of the capitalist class. Family abolition is a component of the destruction of the institutions foundational to capitalist society, including bourgeois society, private property, and the state.

Table 1

	1830s–1880s	1890s–1950s	1960s–Early 1970s	1970s–Present
Dominant family form	Bourgeois, white, property-owning family	Respectable working-class, white, male-breadwinner family form, made possible by workers' movement		Diversification of family, but persistence of private household
Transforming working-class families	Capitalist assault on peasant and working-class kin relations; crisis of working-class reproduction	War mobilization of World War I and World War II	Growth of office employment opportunities for women	Working-class male-breadwinner family form impossible
Family racial politics	Natal alienation in plantation slavery; genocide of settler colonialism	Coerced heterosexuality through Jim Crow sharecropping and land allotments to Indigenous families; consolidation of whiteness as respectability	Racist state welfare policies against Black and Indigenous motherhood; suburbs as whiteness	Continuing racist state attacks in border enforcement, police violence, and mass incarceration
Family abolition visions	Destruction of bourgeois family in war on bourgeois society (Engels, Fourier, most socialists and anarchists)	Collectivizing unwaged reproductive labor, moving working-class women into wage labor and freeing them from compulsory family (Kollontai)	Radical feminists, queers, and Black women seek to abolish the suburban, isolated family unit toward sexual and gender liberation	New wave of family abolition: trans Marxist, queer communist, Black feminist, and beyond to the commune

Chapter 5 turns to the racial capitalism of nineteenth-century North America, considering settler colonialism and plantation slavery. Anti-indigenous genocide and the natal alienation of slavery attacked kin relations. Concurrently, racial capitalism consolidated the white heterosexual family, both among slave-owning oligarchs and frontier homesteaders. Later in the nineteenth century, the family politics of white supremacy shifted, as Jim Crow mandated heterosexual marriage on Black sharecroppers, and land allotments sought to break up Indigenous life into private, patriarchal families.

Chapter 6 counterposes the oppressive family politics of nineteenth-century capitalism to glimpses of proletarian sexual transgression: sex workers, sodomites, and transfeminine proletarians engaged in rebellion and resistance, emancipated Black people forming nonnormative family relations during Reconstruction, and the thinking of French utopian socialist Charles Fourier.

Chapter 7 traces the rise and consolidation of a particular form of the workers' movement toward the end of the nineteenth century. A strata of workers won access to a kind of family that resembled those of their bourgeois adversaries: based on a single male breadwinner, children in school, and an unwaged housewife. Socialists of the Second International grappled with the place of the family in their thinking, torn between the movement's conflicting commitments to gender equality through full proletarianization and to the stability and respectability of the housewife family form. Briefly, the Bolshevik Revolution opened a vision of family abolition through the full collectivization of household labor.

Chapter 8 turns to the uprisings of the Red Decade, a phrase for the global insurgencies from the mid-1960s to the mid-1970s. The family again came under attack by revolutionaries. Multiple movements contested the suburban, heterosexual, white, housewife-based family form. Here I focus on three specific struggles, focused on the United States: Black women radicals, including as welfare rights organizers; radical feminism; and gay and trans liberationists.

Chapter 9, concluding Part II, returns us to the present. Since the mid-1970s, working-class family life has been increasingly thrown into disarray. This has been a result of a deeper, protracted global crisis in profitability, and the displacement of this crisis onto the working class. The housewife form is no longer viable for any sector of the working class. Further, people are increasingly pursuing new modes of living outside of traditional family structures and its normative regime of sex and gender: queer relationships, gender transitions, living alone, postponing or avoiding marriage, and much else. But these have been concurrent with increased dependency on the private household.

Part III considers resistance to the family. Chapter 10 argues that the struggle to move beyond the family can link multiple constituencies. Progressive anti-family reforms are policy changes that materially expand people's ability to choose their own household arrangements, or undo the regulatory policies that bolster normative families.

Chapters 11–13 move into family abolition as a horizon of a freer society. In chapter 11 I begin by outlining other writers' visions of family abolition. Then I theorize the essential qualities of what I call *communist social reproduction*, based on the maxim, "From each according to their ability, to each according to their need."

Chapter 12 looks to existing protest movements to consider how they practice care and interdependence beyond the market and the state. At protest camps, mass occupations, and other struggles, people form collective practices for social reproduction. Like the Oaxaca Commune, these can point toward the potential mechanisms of family abolition. Chapter 13 speculatively sketches the commune as one possible mode through which new forms of social reproduction emerge in the course of mass insurrection and revolutionary struggle. In the conclusion, I use Martin Luther King Jr's vision of beloved community alongside Marx's notion of *Gemeinwesen* to argue that family abolition can be a guiding ethic of interdependence and care.

Overall, this book is a work of communist theory that draws from multiple political and theoretical traditions. It depends on prior rigorous research in historical materialism, social reproduction theory, family abolitionism, Black Feminism, Black theology, Indigenous Studies, socialist and anarchist politics, Gay Liberationism, Queer Theory, and writing by trans and queer radicals. At multiple points, I also engage relevant dimensions of a specific and somewhat obscure communist theoretical tradition called *communization*. In understanding communization theory, I draw from the work of the French collective Théorie Communiste and the Anglophone journal *Endnotes*. I introduce and outline their work gradually in relevant sections, beginning in chapter 7.

In the spirit of the Oaxaca Commune, let us advance.

PART I

The Impossible Family

1

Private Households

In March and April 2020 large swaths of the global capitalist economy ground to a halt in the face of the coronavirus pandemic. Over the following years, periodic general quarantines shut down work and travel. During these lockdowns, the working class of advanced capitalist countries faced three possible fates: unemployment, continuing to work on-site at their place of employment, or remote work. Millions lost work in the biggest economic plunge since the 1930s. Emergency cash-transfer benefits, eviction moratoriums, and economic bailout packages staved off an even worse social crisis. Those who continued to work outside of their homes, disproportionately Black and migrant working-class people, faced high rates of exposure to COVID-19, with lethal consequences. The last third or so of the workforce switched to remote work for the remainder of the year. These were most often white-collar professionals who had previously worked in offices.

This new experience of home life revealed the labor—both within and beyond the household—required to sustain families. Every day, there is a great deal of work to be done: acquiring and preparing food, feeding everyone in the household, accessing health care and education, cleaning homes and bodies and clothes, supervising children, and tending to the elderly or disabled. Working-class families of color tend to manage such labor with the help of interdependent kin structures beyond their nuclear family, including through relying on grandparents, aunts, and family friends. They also rely on state-subsidized childcare centers and public schools. Affluent parents or those working as busy professionals, more likely to be isolated into a nuclear family household, manage these tasks through outsourcing the labor to others: hiring immigrant nannies and housecleaners, ordering takeout meals, dropping children off at private day care or schools, using laundry services, or placing grandparents in nursing homes.

Outsourcing domestic labor is not new. Bourgeois European families employed servants in large numbers up until World War II, for example, while white propertied American families employed Black women as domestic workers from Reconstruction to the 1960s. Before emancipation, enslaved Black women provided childcare, household labor, and breastfeeding, integrated into the domestic life of white owners.[1] However, today's professional families rely not only on low-wage migrant domestic workers but also on access to a wide assortment of service commodities such as food preparation, laundry, and on-call drivers. Along with the institutions of universal schooling and separated senior residential facilities, these commodified reproductive services have enabled busy professionals to raise families without necessarily relying on the unwaged support of extended family or a housewife.

COVID-19 temporarily shattered these intricate networks sustaining professional families. With schools closed, parents working from home, and most service industry businesses abruptly shut down, parents suddenly found their task utterly impossible. The COVID-19 shutdowns made it clear that caring and educating children every day is completely beyond the capabilities of one or two parents simultaneously trying to maintain a waged job. Along with the concentrated mass death in nursing homes and the social isolation of the nuclear family under quarantine, COVID-19 sparked a crisis of anxiety and doubt among professionals about the nuclear family. The ideological representatives of the propertied class, figures such as David Brooks, began to openly question the wisdom of the nuclear family structure as a viable unit of daily life.[2]

COVID-19 intensified many people's experiences of their family as a private household. Social-distancing practices and the closure of public institutions forced everyone back into their household, trapped and alone with their cohabitants. Within family households, the typical emotional and financial interdependency became much more strained and intense. Raising children, financial support of each other, housecleaning, cooking—all these activities had to be done within the isolated family household to an extent not seen in many decades. Those not currently in a family household found themselves alone or with roommates who might be near-strangers. Those without households—those living and reproducing themselves as individuals—faced an intense level of isolation and loneliness throughout the pandemic. Living with a family was impossible, living without one even worse.

As the pandemic shutdowns continued, people cobbled together other strategies for meeting their material needs. Mutual aid support networks emerged across major cities. In New York City, for example, the intensity and speed of the shutdown left many people without easy access to purchasing food. Volunteer bicycle messengers delivered groceries to people who were scared to leave their homes, or to those living in neighborhoods where local grocery stores began to run out of supplies. In thousands of apartment buildings, people went door-to-door to check on their neighbors. Through these networks, many briefly glimpsed a different vision of care. Mutual aid exceeded the limits of the family, or the inequalities of purchasing services on the market. A flurry of activist books documented this rich moment of mutual aid, recognizing its connection to a long-standing organizing tradition.[3]

But this opening was short lived. Grocery stores reorganized, creating home delivery options and hiring working-class men of color as low-wage delivery workers. Online retailers expanded and filled enough of the gaps in their commodity chains. Once again people retreated to surviving through means more familiar in capitalist society: their immediate kin, marginal state aid, their jobs, and purchasing food and services. Underfunded public schools slowly readjusted to online learning where they were able. Private day camps, tutoring programs, and schools filled the educational gaps for families who could afford it. Low-income service workers were increasingly called back to work, even with the higher risk and mortality. As vaccines became available—in the United States, over the spring of 2021—white-collar workers also returned to the office.

Echoes of the crisis remained. Throughout 2021 the service economy that fills reproductive needs of households did not return to a pre-pandemic normal. Huge numbers of service industry workers, hit hard by pandemic deaths and having enjoyed the respite from degrading work, refused to return to their previous workplaces. Millions of people quit their jobs, creating an unusually tight labor market in the United States. Service industry employers that depend on a desperate, low-wage workforce found themselves unable to fill their job positions. Through the summer of 2021, children's camps—a major childcare provider for professional families—struggled to fill staffing shortages. Parents were forced to collect their kids from camp and to find other options for the reproductive labor of childcare.

These professional families suddenly experienced the advent of what had longed plagued parents who were less well-off: a *care crisis*. Working-class families face compounding factors fueling this lasting and worsening care crisis, including falling wages, fragmentation of marital and other family relations, and cutbacks in public services. These material conditions force working-class mothers to work longer hours of both waged and unwaged work. Different sectors of the working class have experienced this crisis in varied ways. It is no longer affordable for nearly anyone to keep a mother out of the workforce, though this was once a feasible possibility for better-off white working-class families. For Black and migrant mothers, and others in the lower tiers of the working class, however, the housewife family form has never been obtainable. For them, this care crisis has been compounded by state violence, mass incarceration, and the dismantling of poverty-relief services.

The effects of the coronavirus pandemic made it starkly evident that working-class families have always been asked to do too much work. The tasks of daily and generational social reproduction are more than any family can bear alone. Vast hours of work are needed to care for the elderly, to raise and educate children, to keep everyone fed and clothed and housed, all to enable family members to make it to work the next day. Social reproduction theory argues that this people-making within and beyond the nuclear family plays an essential role in the functioning of capitalism, the creation of a viable workforce each day and across each generation.

Everyone needs others, beyond our families, in order to survive. Families depend on outside help, linking the family into broader networks of care. Nuclear families cannot carry the immense burden of work placed on them. In capitalist society, this extended support typically takes the forms of extended family, of services purchased on the market, or through increasingly limited state programs and institutions. Without these supports, families are crushed under the impossible burden of reproductive labor. This necessary dependency of families on outside support reproduces the inequality of market relations, dividing people's material conditions and life chances by class, by race, and by family structure. The care crisis of the coronavirus pandemic illuminated how families function as *private households*, a key dimension of the family laid out in this chapter.

FAMILY AS PRIVATE HOUSEHOLDS

The meaning of *the family* is fraught. As a link in the cycles of capitalist reproduction, the role of the family has changed repeatedly, and its form usually varies drastically given its members' place in class society. Everyone citing the family as an aspirational ideal brings their own political commitments and values to how the concept is imagined and articulated. Debates about the meaning of family quickly become emotionally charged. For one speaker, family may be a primary source of love and care, yet for another it may represent their most intense experience of subjugation and abuse.

This book uses the term *family* in multiple senses, recognizing its myriad uses and meanings in society today. Other scholars and critics of the family have productively emphasized the family as a site of ideological reproduction and socialization,[4] as a rhetorical trope and fantasy wielded to advance various regressive political positions,[5] as an institution producing atomization and isolation,[6] as a system of "bio-genetic kinship,"[7] as a juridical and legal category, as a metaphor of national belonging,[8] and much more. These varied definitions of family make appearances throughout this book. This chapter focuses on one meaning: *family as private household, a unit of privatized care*. Identifying the family as a private household helps make sense of how families situate us within the circuits of capitalist reproduction. In the next chapter, I shift to other contrasting meanings of family, organized by external and internal violence. These meanings of family are woven throughout this book.

A household is made up of people who live together, who share resources together, and who are interdependent on each other in decisions about employment, housing, and schooling. They function partially as a single economic unit. Often the family as private household also consists of formal, legal, and biological kinship units, constituted by marriage, procreation, and genetic ties. These relationships can be especially charged, often people's primary emotional attachments. Households can include multiple generations of a family, but increasingly under capitalism, they are primarily composed of nuclear families: adults and their minor children. A household may also be chosen family, as close friends, complex kinship ties, or members of a shared community housing together. Chosen family function as households in the sense used here insofar as they are intimately economically interdependent and systems of organizing private care, such as relying on each other during periods of unemployment.

The family as a household manages and coordinates forms of labor within the home. Within the household, the family is the site through which people receive much of the care they need to survive. The family raises children, cares for members when sick or infirm, and provides primary support to members who are disabled or out of work. This care takes many forms, including emotional comfort, romantic love, financial aid, and meeting of immediate bodily needs. In our society, these needs are primarily met through the private domain of the family as household. The private family serves as the primary site in capitalist society of interpersonal care and social reproductive labor.

Yet as sites of work, families are unusual. The experience of family life often depends on the illusion of being free of transactions or exchange. Instead of impersonal domination characteristic of market relationships, the power relationships within a family are quite personal forms of intimacy or control. Domineering husbands might command their wives. Parents might command their children. These hierarchies are naturalized and fiercely defended. Unlike most jobs, much of a household's internal labor is often unwaged. Housecleaning, cooking, childcare, and other reproductive care may, in some contexts, be outsourced to wage workers outside the family. Yet when these tasks are done by family members, they are typically performed without pay by feminized members of the household, often mothers or wives. Despite the illusion of being free of internal exchange, one's power within a family is often linked to access to outside resources. Among family members, it is typically adult men who have the best access to outside wages, accrued property, social privilege, or legal legitimacy. Those (often male) family members with the most access to outside resources can leverage them to reduce their personal responsibility for household labor and increase their authority within the family.

Family as private household also helps identify the uneven accessibility of the family form for proletarians. Many people throughout history have social relations they may call their family but are not recognized as such by dominant social institutions. Elements of this mismatch are explored in the next chapter. One aspect of this exclusion from a recognized family is not having the means to form and maintain a private household. Relationships between enslaved people, for example, could never constitute an economic unit of the household. Those living in severe poverty often have too much instability in housing arrangements to maintain a private household. Many working-class people across history could not afford to rent a separate living space for their immediate household, instead forced to live with multiple other nonfamily members. These people may understand themselves as having families, but their immediate relationships do not quite constitute a private household as a unit of privatized care.

THE HOUSEHOLD IN CAPITALIST REPRODUCTION

Capitalism, like other class societies before it, depends on the family as a form of privatized social reproduction. Capitalism relies on a large number of people being able to show up for work each day, and for the workforce to be maintained from one generation to the next. Those people don't just magically appear; they arrive at the workplace, having been raised and cared for by families. For every worker, someone had to gestate and give birth to them, care for them as infants, raise them as children, and teach them the skills to navigate the labor market and find a job. From one day to the next, someone has to wash their clothes, provide them with the means of bathing, and feed them. This is an immense amount of work, dependent on extensive infrastructures of housing, fresh water, waste disposal, and access to basic goods. The reproduction of the workforce requires a whole other form of work that takes place outside of industrial manufacturing, and often outside the wage relation altogether. These are essential points of social reproduction theory.

Capitalism also created and enforced a series of important social divisions in how work is organized largely unknown in feudal societies. These divisions reconstituted the character of the family as a unit of reproduction. Industrial development gradually and increasingly separated the unwaged reproductive labor done in the home from waged labor, which was increasingly done in workplaces located outside the home. New systems of wage labor, private property, and social legitimacy under capitalism separated the privacy of the family house from the public and political sphere. Capitalist development also took up and expanded distinctions between different forms of waged work, such as feminized reproductive labor focused on direct people-making—childcare—and the masculinized labor focused on social control or object-making. In each case, how these divisions were made seemed natural and intractable. But the particular form of these divisions rapidly changed with each era of capitalist development and the particular dynamics between class and capital. The role of the family in class society was remade through these divisions introduced by capitalist production.

The functions of the family as economic units vary between classes. Capitalist families may pass down accumulated property and wealth through inheritance. Households with wealth are structures of ownership and property relationships; spouses generally jointly own whatever assets and debt they have acquired, bonds between children and adults are managed through promised inheritance or monetary aid, power dynamics within the family unfold through access to wealth and control over financial decision-making. For working-class people, families can be important strategies for sharing limited resources and sustaining each other when work is unavailable. The family serves as the primary institution mediating access to the wage for working-class people. Proletarian families may share their wages and debt; some privileged strata of the working class may aid their adult children in accessing a particular form of work, or after their death leave an inheritance of a privately owned home. Each class works to instill in children its particular values and strategies for navigating the world, and to support its children in acquiring the best opportunities available. Class inequality and the class relations of capitalism are reproduced through the family as a system of private households.

Recognizing the working-class household as a segment of capitalist society raises challenging political questions. Social reproduction theory evolved in part through Marxist feminist debates in the 1970s about the specific role of the housewife and the private household in capitalist reproduction. Working women were challenged by what feminist scholars called the double shift, the additional unwaged household work they had to do after getting home from paid jobs. Many women saw the question of household labor as linked to struggles over sex, parenting, relationship abuse, and their efforts to build fulfilling lives. Socialist feminists argued that these struggles over housework were integral to the broader struggle against capitalism. They sought to link fights by women over housework to campaigns by unions and socialist organizations over waged work and state power.

The theoretical side of these debates often narrowly focused on the question of whether unwaged household labor creates *value*, a specific and technical idea in Marxist theory. Unfortunately, these debates often did not explicitly state the political consequences of their positions. Implicitly, the discussion centered on whether household labor was a legitimate issue of struggle by the working class. Should women's demands specifically about household labor be included in socialist organizing strategy? For working-class families, these struggles challenged the internal relationships between family members, upending gender roles within heterosexual relationships. Some activists called for "wages for housework" as a way of drawing attention to the vast, unwaged labor often done by working-class women within the household. This campaign was one of several efforts to politicize and mobilize both housewives and working mothers as political agents, challenging the private domain of the family.[9] All these efforts echoed a long-standing debate among socialists. Was the way to winning gender equality through having all women working outside the home for wages? Could the private, unwaged, atomized labor of housework be transformed into a collective, waged social good? Should those doing unwaged housework within the family demand that their work be respected and valued? How did struggle by housewives and working mothers over unwaged household labor relate to the struggles of Black and brown paid domestic workers, or incarcerated women, or sex workers?

Wages for Housework, the household labor debate, and socialist feminists were arguing that the family was one site in the broader reproduction of capitalism. This book relies on their framework. Alongside the family, two other sites are central to social reproduction in capitalist society: the exchange of commodities and paid work on the market, and the activity of state institutions. Analyzing them together is essential for making sense of the changing role of the family under capitalism.

THE FAMILY, THE MARKET, AND THE STATE

The family, the market, and the state collectively enable the reproduction of capitalist society. Each institution is dependent on the others for its functioning. Though no single institution entirely determines the rest, the market is the primary driver of major historical change. These three institutions interconnect to reproduce all the key aspects of capitalist society, interrelating both on a large scale across history and in the specific minutiae of our day-to-day lives. Food, housing, and physical care are provided by some combination of the unwaged help of family members, buying commodities at a local store, and receiving aid from a government agency. Most workers, in most eras of capitalist society, return to private households when they get off work. Through the interrelationships of this threefold schema of the family, the market, and the state, Part II of this book traces the changing dynamics of the family over time; Part III imagines family abolition as the necessary overcoming of these three capitalist social institutions.

Households cannot survive without outside support, requiring their dependency on the broader capitalist society. Proletarian families depend on one or more members of their family finding a job, the means of selling their capacity to work to an employer. These wages are then partially or wholly distributed to other family members who cannot or do not work. Access to wages shapes how people form families. Capitalism has built into its development certain long-term tendencies that all transform people's access to wages: urbanization, industrialization, the growth and decline of whole industries, and the increasing production of surplus populations who are excluded from formal labor markets. Because the family as a household unit is almost entirely dependent on the income derived from its outside economic activities, the changing dynamics of capitalist industry has enormous consequences for how people are able to form families. Stable employment is a necessary precondition of stable family relationships. Under economic strain and protracted underemployment, families are likely to fracture. As industries rise and fall, families change with them. As the forms of work in capitalist society changes, this in turn forecloses or enables new forms of family life.

In other words, people form families based on available work. Markets, particularly labor markets, have a major but nondetermining impact on family life. By and large, employers do not dictate how working-class people form households. Families will move to find work, select housing they can afford, and decide how many people to send into the workforce, all based on available incomes and labor market conditions. Instead of directly controlling families, capitalists generally depend on proletarians to figure out how to reproduce themselves. In *Capital*, Marx describes the wage laborer as "free in a double sense," free to sell their labor and "free" from any other means of surviving. Many proletarians are also free to form the families they choose so long as they can maintain consistent access to work and are "free" of other means of maintaining stable families if wages and property are no longer available.

Though private families dominate social reproduction under capitalism, there have always been people outside the family unit who survive directly through the market or through relying on state institutions. There are exceptions both to the private family form and to access to wage work. For example, enslaved people were sharply limited in their ability to form and maintain romantic relationships and private households, or to exercise control over who they lived with. Those subject to human trafficking, living in company towns or worker barracks, or incarcerated in prisons, are not able to form families. Instead, their reproduction is immediately embedded in the state or the direct control of capitalists. Access to wage work and access to something resembling the private family form are historically connected.

States have encouraged particular forms of families, policed family life, determined what types of housing are available, provided public schooling, and legally regulated relationships of shared resources, sex, or parenting. All these have huge impacts on the choices that families are likely to make about how to live. At a number of historical moments, states have tried to engineer large-scale changes to family life—such as by intervening in working-class family relations through the intervention of social workers and welfare benefits; promoting the construction of new living arrangements like suburban development; criminalizing abortion, sex work, and gay sex; or propagandizing the benefits or harms of various family structures.

But state efforts to cultivate certain family structures have only a limited effect if they are not linked to large-scale self-organization by families themselves, or to major changes in labor market conditions. State efforts to intervene in fertility rates, for example, have been almost entirely unsuccessful, despite the considerable resources occasionally involved. States generally have primarily an indirect effect on family choices through public policies facilitating or hindering certain kinds of family formation. Families, evaluating available state supports and market conditions, make many of their own choices. The most significant impact states have on families is through violence—such as through the use of mass incarceration, state murder, border enforcement, or public policies that increase mortality risk—that robs a family of one or more of its members.

* * *

Much of this book relies on the formulation that the family is a private household that organizes forms of privatized care. It is through locating the family as a private household in a broader system of capitalist reproduction that we can understand the considerable changes in working-class family life over the last two centuries of capitalist development, the multiple politics of the family pursued by the institutions of racial capitalism and by radical movements, and the crisis of the family today. This framework also provides a crucial dimension of family abolition as an overcoming of the private household. But the family as private household is not the only means of understanding the politics of the family. It must also be read alongside another dimension, discussed in the next chapter: the family as a site of violence, from both outside and within.

2

Family Terrors

On August 8, 2019, the White House released a photo to Flickr, taken during a presidential visit to the El Paso University Medical Center the day before (see image, p. 33). First Lady Melania Trump smiles while holding a baby. On her right is the president, who also grins broadly and gives a thumbs-up. On either side are the baby's uncle and aunt. The baby wears a small plaid bow tie and turns toward his aunt to his left. The baby's name is Paul Anchondo. Four days before the photo was released, he had survived a mass shooting, in which both of his parents were killed. Based on the location of her body and Paul's injuries, his mother, Jordan, likely died while shielding her baby from gunfire. The Trumps were photographed with this baby because the other survivors of the massacre recovering at the hospital refused to meet with them.

The shooter was a twenty-one-year-old white supremacist named Patrick Wood Crusius. He drove ten hours from Dallas to the Walmart in El Paso in order to target Mexican migrants. There he murdered twenty-three people and left twenty-three others injured. He had previously posted a manifesto to the message board 8chan detailing the planned massacre, stating that "the attack is a response to the Hispanic invasion of Texas."[1] In the manifesto, Crusius proposed dividing the country into segregated racial territories. The manifesto included fears of automation, critiques of corporate America, and concern about environmental destruction—all points popularly associated with the Left, but also with purchase in Far-Right white supremacist circles. Crusius stated that he hoped the shooting, and others like it, would lead "Hispanic" migrants to leave the United States and reverse their demographic growth. His implied mechanism is clear: the shooting was intended as an act of strategic terrorism, an attempt to create an environment of racist terror that would force migrants to leave the country, fearing for their lives.

Crusius had company. Though there are no known co-conspirators, he acted in a long American tradition of white supremacist terror, both state-sanctioned and extralegal. Since the 1980s, white supremacist insurgents in the United States have pursued a strategy of promoting mass terror attacks against civilian targets, like the massacre in El Paso. White supremacist groups have sought to foment racial war, hoping to reverse the gains of the mid-twentieth-century African American civil rights movement. To avoid state repression, they have pursued a strategy of "lone wolf" actions, encouraging individuals like Crusius to plan and execute attacks on their own.

In recent years, insurgent white supremacists have received the boon of elite endorsement. National news commentators like Tucker Carlson share Crusius's concern with the "Great Replace-ment," a vision of immigration and demographic changes leading to a white minority. This narrative has been previously deployed by white supremacists for decades. President Trump shared his own implicit endorsements for racial terror: in his grin and thumbs-up in the photo with Paul Anchondo, in a tweet con-demning Crusius for being a "coward" and "giving himself up" so easily to authorities, in extensively espousing a fear of immi-grant "invasion," among other sympathetic overtures to America's white supremacist movement. American, elite-supported white supremacist terror is not confined to the recent Far Right. It is a thread throughout American history continuing to the present. Racial terror is a crucial dimension of today's police violence and mass incarceration. American history is littered with sustained, massive campaigns of brutal racial violence against civilians: the long history of American slavery and anti-Native genocide, the brutal counterrevolution against Black organizing during Recon-struction, the labor regime of Jim Crow segregation, in addition to periodic race riots against immigrant and Black communities.

White supremacist, fascist rhetoric has long made the white family as central to its worldview and political project. White supremacist writing and speeches make frequent reference to the "14 words," coined by David Lane of the terror group The Order and derived from Hitler's *Mein Kampf*: "We must secure the existence of our people and a future for white children." Nazi-allied Vichy France chose the slogan "Travail, famille, patrie" (Work, family, homeland). Renaud Camus's book *Le grand remplacement* (*The great replacement*), cited as influential by Crusius in his manifesto, argues that France is being destroyed by Muslim migrants. Camus defines the French as determined "by birth and by ancestors, by one's family."[2] He compares France today housing migrant children to a "old spinster raising other people's children."[3] Defense of the white family is central to the fascist imagination. Children and mothers, in this fantasy, are the vulnerable innocents who must be defended through righteous violence. Throughout US history, this rhetoric of defense of the white family appears prominently in the rollback of Reconstruction, in mass lynching efforts, in anti-Native genocide, and in today's racist ideology.

Credit: Andrea Hanks/The White House

The photo taken at the El Paso University Medical Center depicts the First Family. Donald and Melania Trump beam as a twisted caricature of proud and enthusiastic parents. Here they embody a fantasy at the heart of whiteness, settler colonialism, anti-Blackness, and capitalism: possessing a child stolen through racist violence. Typically, American presidents are seen as embodying some fantasy version of the ideal, respectable American family. When accused otherwise, such as Bill Clinton's infidelity, for example, maintaining legitimacy depends on reestablishing the image of a normative family arrangement. Like the bourgeoisie's family ideal, most American presidents have managed to keep their family dramas and transgressions out of public attention. Trump and his family turned these expectations upside down. Instead of embodying a normative family under the loving patriarch, they offered an image of vast and unchecked pleasure. The father of infinite pleasure touches deeply on long-standing desires and tropes of white American masculinity. The components of President Trump's relationship to family reflects a different dimension of a particular racial and gendered fantasy: his apparent disinterest in caring for his children, his incestuous sexualization of his daughter, his extensive practices of nepotism and mafia-like familial loyalty, his amassing of a real estate empire through his father's patronage, and his plastering of his family name as an international brand.

The Trumps offended many of their elite peers because they made the horror of their family too overt. They were condemned for failing to mask their improprieties. As noted in the previous chapter and explored more later, the historical creation of the bourgeois family instituted a division between public and private, shrouding the violence of the family behind the closed doors of the home. This logic of privacy obscures the violence of the white, property-owning family from public view. A "proper" family is one that is able to erase and ignore the broad structural domination on which it depends, and successfully masks its internal relationships of coercion and abuse. The Trumps make the usually hidden violent racial, gendered, sexual, and capitalist logics of the family too evident. With Donald's grin, his thumbs-up, and the surviving baby in Melania's arms, this photo depicts the often-invisible carnage of the white family ideal.

This photo also offers us an image of a second family, one under attack by racial terror. Jordan Anchando died saving her child. Flanking the Trumps are Paul's aunt and uncle. His extended relatives grieved together, and together had to find ways of raising this orphaned baby. As an orphan, Paul Anchondo—whatever

34

the politics and aspirations of his multiracial extended family members—is permanently barred from a particular normative family experience.

Poor people often cannot secure the material conditions or freedom from persecution necessary to be able to constitute a domestic life resembling the fantasy of the stable, "respectable" nuclear family. Over generations, Black people, indigenous people, poor people, queer people, and migrants—all overlapping and interconnected groups—have struggled to care for each other, protect each other, and love each other in the face of racial capitalism. This collective struggle is part of the efforts of the multiracial working class to form relationships of care and solidarity in a hostile world. Often, people have used the language of family to describe these relations, however nonnormative they may be in practice. Sometimes, marginalized people go to great lengths to try to force their complex care relations into the ideal of the normative family.

The two families in this photo are both broken, both failures at any normative ideal. One celebrates its failures, capitalizing on them, perversely enjoying the ability to do and say anything. The other grieves, shattered by trauma and violence. These two families share an intimate, inner relation, mutually constituting each other in the long history of racial violence. These two families are bound together in the social order and fantasy of the family. Both the violent destruction of some care relations and the valorization of the normative white family are two interdependent sides of the same process and institution. Where these two dimensions are often kept a psychic distance from each other, this photo is unusual for illustrating both sides simultaneously, and in so doing evoking the internal and external violence on which the normative family relies.

This chapter considers two forms of violence integral to the family as understood throughout this book: first, the family as a white supremacist normative ideal, imposed through violence, state policy, and cultural norms; second, the terrors within the family, the violences it enables and obscures, the regimes of gender and power it reproduces. External imposed violence and hidden internal violence, together they constitute family terrors.

THE FAMILY IDEAL

The depiction of America's First Family evokes another meaning of family: *The family is a normative ideal, structured through race, sexuality, class, and gender.* The family as normative ideal is a white supremacist image, a fantasy space of terror that defines the human, the innocent, and the sexually pure. The family as normative ideal binds together three principal dimensions: a cultural image and psychic fantasy; a particular, privileged form of the family household characteristic historically of the capitalist class and whiteness; and a regulatory regime created by government policy. In the family ideal, the material class and race politics of how people are able to form families is bound together with social status, cultural fantasy, and government policies.

The family ideal is taken up, pursued, or rejected by households, linking the meanings of family between the last chapter and this one. People partially excluded from this family ideal may reject it by forming households organized through a contrasting set of values and countercultural commitments. Or those excluded may yearn to achieve it, imagining it could afford them stability and support in a chaotic and difficult world. Families as household units consolidate forms of social legitimacy or social stigma in the eyes of their neighbors, their creditors, their employers, the courts, and state agents. Whether a family is cast as legitimate through obtaining this ideal or stigmatized in failing to meet it has major consequences for the material well-being of that family. Gaining this legitimacy typically depends on how well the family is able to gain control over property, either in the form of capital, real estate, or particular privileges of more stable working-class life.

The family ideal is a cultural construction, a myth cobbled together from a collection of popular cultural images from film, television, literature, and magazines. It is prominent in the constructions of social scientists and psychologists. It figures in childhood development and fantasy life, as what a proper family should be. Critics of the family have often focused their attack on this fantasy ideal. Since the rise of bourgeois society, this family ideal is imagined to be white, to be centrally organized around a long-term heterosexual relationship, to own a stand-alone house, to have an unwaged housewife, and to have children enrolled in school. It is likely nuclear, with grandparents, aunts and uncles, and adult children living elsewhere. It keeps its pleasures and abuses adequately hidden from public view, adequately repressed and unacknowledged. This family ideal is closely associated with other conceptual constructions: pristine white femininity, innocent children, true love, the home as refuge and solace. It embodies stability—for individuals, for a neighborhood, for a nation. This family ideal pervades our culture, shaping the ways many people judge themselves and their neighbors, appearing throughout media and literature.

This image of the family ideal is closely related to the broader ideological projects that the concept of family serves. It appears in fascist and Far-Right imaginaries with consistent frequency. It is integral to the rise of the Evangelical Christian Right in the United States, who combine it with white nationalism, homophobia, anti-choice sentiment, and a deep-set sexual conservatism. But the family ideal has served many other projects across the political spectrum. Aspiring to some variation of a normative family has widespread appeal in substantial sectors of the working class. The normative family ideal is a seductive politics, drawing people into a conservative worldview. Many commentators have noted how integral a normative family ideal is to nationalist projects of all sorts.[4] The nation only became fully conceivable on the basis of an imagined community of stable families.

THE FAMILY POLICING SYSTEM

Deviations from the family ideal are treated with skepticism or ridicule, denounced as pathology, or violently attacked. This racist family ideal is contrasted with racialized and queer others against which it is defined. Such ideological edifices depend on binary oppositions, and alongside producing this family ideal they defined its opposite, those whose bodies and desires are considered deviant: the very poor, queers, sex workers, Black people, Indigenous people, "foreigners," and the colonial subject. The racial and eugenic construction of sexual deviancy is inseparable from its opposite, the normative family. Numerous racist and queerphobic fantasies of the gender and sexual politics of these demonized others are linked together to help collectively shape the normative ideal of the family. Black studies scholars like Patricia Hill Collins, Tiffany Lethabo King, and Hortense Spillers have all critiqued the family as racist ideal, as regime designed to distinguish between the privileged and the excluded.[5]

The racist family norm today is forcefully institutionalized through child protective services (CPS). Dorothy Roberts identifies CPS as a *family policing system*, a massive state apparatus of public and private agencies operating in conjunction with law enforcement that aggressively intervenes in Black family life. A majority of Black American children experience at least one CPS investigation growing up. A quarter of a million US children—disproportionately poor, Black children—are taken from their households every year. A majority of the children removed are not based on claims of abuse, but rather neglect, defined primarily as the conditions of poverty. The family policing system claims to protect children but does not provide families with the support services to deal with the crisis of poverty, drug use, or housing instability. Instead, it further destabilizes and undermines care relations between Black people.[6] CPS operates a system of harming children, regulating family norms, and terrorizing Black life, and does little to actually address the causes and harms of child abuse.

The family policing system of CPS is embedded in the long history of violent state regulation of family norms. Through migration and border policy, mass incarceration, and police murder, some people are barred from forming family-based households altogether. The kinship and mutual care systems people form in the midst of racialized poverty are then treated as pathological by the state, such as in condemning independent Black mothers as a cause of ongoing poverty. Poor, brown, and Black families are invaded, surveilled, and disciplined. When these families fail to measure up to a standard rooted in property ownership and whiteness, welfare workers will separate children and parents, incarcerate, and punish. The regulation of families is also embedded in eugenic histories, including the sterilization, medical experimentation, and criminalization of reproduction of disabled women, women in Puerto Rico, African American women, Indigenous women, and others.

Recently, the US Right has made major advances in criminalizing abortion access and gender-affirming care for trans children, using the state to impose narrow sexual and gender norms.

The family ideal is bolstered through state through juridical and legal recognition. This family ideal is a regulatory regime, a set of interconnected administrative policies and legal codes encouraging and subsidizing heterosexual marriage, the construction of single-family residences, parental authority, and family-based property ownership. These government policies, in turn, were shaped by particular strategies of class rule, often through attempting to consolidate particular relationships of race and gender. Other forms of state regulation and policing of families reappear as a thread throughout this book. Chapter 5 looks to the separation, institutionalization, and mass deaths of Indigenous children in boarding schools in the United States and Canada, the practice of separating families that is integral to slavery, and the corresponding idealization of white bourgeois family life. Chapter 6 traces nineteenth-century state efforts to police and repress sex work and sodomy in the growing cities, and to impose white family norms on formerly enslaved people. Chapter 8 considers organizing by Black women in the 1960s against the policing of sexual relationships and kin relations by welfare departments and social service workers.

PRIVATE TERRORS

The family policing system claims to protect and save children. Like mass incarceration as a false solution to violence, the family policing system takes a real social problem of child abuse and neglect and grossly misconstrues its causes, exacerbates the problems it claims to address, and instead produces harm. The claim to save and protect children has been central to the fantasy of the family norm, to the fascist imaginary, and to state policy, even when pursuing policies that lead to the mass death of children. Actually conceiving of a system that protects children, that provides the basis for care and flourishing for all, will require analyzing how the private family form structurally enables child abuse. The external terror of the state, settler colonialism, and fascist violence all help consolidate the normative family based on whiteness and property. This normative family form, obscured from view, is a private domain of control and subjugation.

The normative, white, property-owning family, unlike their poor or Black counterparts subjected to state surveillance, is one founded on privacy. The private space of the bourgeois home is one separated from the public world of production and governance. This division was made possible through dynamics unique to capitalist society. This division was first widely available to capitalist families, who used the resources available through capital accumulation and colonization to create a protected sphere of family relations. Isolating the family into a private world in turn helped create new racialized concepts of femininity, of women needing to be isolated and protected. It also inaugurated new approaches to child raising that placed a huge emphasis on the child's psychological and spiritual development but also subjugated them to new intensive forms of control. For much of early capitalist history, private households depended on control over property, a power only available to elites. Only later did it become available to others.

Privacy, private interests, private property—these are integral to the family ideal, intimately linking it to the family as private household. The family draws a boundary between outside and inside. *The family looks out for its own. Family has each other's backs. Family first.* The sense of support from family can greatly benefit those who have it, while shutting out those who do not. The structure of the family, defending its interests, lends itself to nepotism, insularity, and competition. Families pursuing their interests intensify other forms of inequality and further atomize the social world.[7] Working-class family households, particularly in communities of color, cannot easily wall themselves off in isolation. But if they gain in class status and property, families are likely to isolate themselves, cutting themselves off from neighbors and possibly extended family members to better assure the reproduction of their class standing. This exclusive, competitive character of many families is built into the conditions of their survival under capitalism.

As a fantasy, the normative family ideal obscures a dark underside integral to its history and logic. The nepotism, incest, and crass ambition of the Trump family's public presentation has always been the unstated and unacknowledged dimension of the bourgeois family. Freud and psychoanalytic theory drew out the underlying fantasies that held together the psychic bonds of the bourgeois nuclear family, a tangle of sexual desire, taboo, and the threat of violence. That disavowed psychic landscape emerges periodically in cultural depictions of the family, sometimes even as a desired aspiration, exemplified by the Trump family.

Violence and sexual abuse within the family are not only fantasies; they are often quite real. This private world of the family enables other terrors—the direct domination of children, women, disabled people, and the elderly. Child abuse is a pervasive reality. Most children facing sexual, physical, and emotional abuse face that in their own households by a family member. Children are more likely to be traumatically harmed, raped, or killed by a family member in their household than anyone else. In 2020 over 1,750 children died in the United States from abuse in their families. Reported rates of child abuse include one in seven children.[8] Even in households without physical violence, children are widely seen as the possession of their parents and are subject to their parents' unilateral authority.

Women similarly face violence and death in the family. Adult women are much more likely to be beaten or murdered by boyfriends or partners than anyone else in their life. One study by the Centers for Disease Control and Prevention (CDC) found that 55 percent of women murdered in the United States were killed by current or former partners, compared to 16 percent by strangers. Black women and Native American women were the most likely to be killed by partners.[9] One in five US women have been raped, and the majority of them by an intimate partner.[10] Worldwide, about forty-seven thousand women were killed by their partner in 2020.[11]

Abuse within the family is made possible through the structure of the private household itself. Functioning as a private economic unit, members of the family can become stuck in its internal order. Living in an isolated and separated home, a goal for many families, prevents others from seeing or intervening in family dynamics. There is a clear division in many families between behavior presented to the outside world and what is acceptable behind closed doors, creating the conditions for otherwise socially unacceptable violence. Even when clear to others, the norms of family privacy make intervention extremely difficult. Serious male abusers rely on the structural privacy and ideological justification of family authority, sustaining their family politics with the aid of other men in close-knit social peer groups.[12] Women are most likely to be murdered by their husbands or boyfriends when they try to leave, emphasizing the role of violence as a means of enforcing familial unity.[13]

Even in less abusive households, the family serves as a primary site of enforcing gender and sexual norms and behaviors. Family are structured through gender roles, often organized around a socially acceptable primary sexual relationship. These gender roles are often hierarchical, based on degrees of authority both inside and outside the home. Gendered division of household labor remains starkly uneven, only slowly shifting with the entry of women into the workforce.[14] These roles both enforce male authority at the expense of women's time and well-being, and trap all participants in narrow and alienated gender expectations. Children learn to be boys and girls under the guidance and control of their parents. They observe and internalize the gender norms modeled by their parents. It is in their family that children first experience the imposition of binary gender and the coercive expectations of heterosexuality. Familial judgment often delays queer or trans people from being able to come out. Family attitudes encourage most household members to constrain themselves a bit, to try to conform, to subordinate those parts of ourselves most likely to be scorned. It is through families that heterosexuality becomes an organizing logic of social life.

COERCION AND CARE

Understanding the violence of the family form requires seeing not only its coercive, forced character but also the reasons family is pursued and chosen. Within class society, the family is a necessary strategy for survival and care. Violence and mutual support are interwoven throughout family forms. All people rely for their survival on some sort of relationships of care, love, affection, sex, and material sharing of resources. Families are the main means of survival in capitalist society for those not currently able to work. Both the human life cycle, and the dynamics of capitalist labor markets, produce many people unable to work. Children, many disabled people, the elderly, the unemployed, and those shut out of labor markets due to discrimination—all rely primarily on families to have their basic needs met. Such people cannot easily get a job, and as a result they cannot afford the basic necessities of life, often forcing them to stay with their families.

Depending on where and when those unable to work are living, they may have access to alternatives to family aid provided through state institutions. But state supports are usually restricted, depend on a particular combination of class forces, and at best operate as adjunctive supports to the family and the market. For most people, in most class societies and most places, the family as household is the only realistic place to survive when you cannot work. For people not able to work, the family is fundamentally coercive. If one cannot easily leave, one cannot choose to stay. If moving away from your family would drastically lower your standard of living, you are likely to try to endure a great deal before attempting exit. The lack of an escape route leaves these people particularly vulnerable. They are most likely to be subject to domination by family members who are best able to access outside labor markets: generally able-bodied adult men. Fathers may be the head of the household by sexist tradition, culture, psychology, or norms. But that authority is bolstered and maintained materially, in part, through the unequal gendered access to the labor market. Those without outside support are more vulnerable to abuse and dependency within the family.

Even for those with supportive and non-abusive families, the private household can be economically coercive. People who are able to work outside the home, sharing information and referrals through family ties, can be integral to finding and maintaining work. For nonworking and dependent family members, even loving relationships can be a source of humiliation, frustration, and low-level conflict. With the tight real estate markets and high rents in my home city of New York, for example, couples move in together much more quickly than they would if they could easily afford housing separately. After separating, some couples continue living together because living apart is cost prohibitive.

Yet the family is also, for many people, the primary experience of love, care, and support. The same vulnerability and dependency that forces many to rely on their family members can also mean the family becomes the site of the deepest gratitude, love, and the meeting of basic human needs. Many people stay with their families not only out of some coercive economic necessity but because they feel loved by their family members. They love their families, and that love fills deep-set human needs. Particularly for people of color who may face hostility and violence from racist institutions, the family can be a primary experience of political solidarity. Wage workers often depend on their family members to comfort them from the abuse they may face from an employer.

The family often fills basic needs that could not easily be met elsewhere. Unlike most friends, the family may be there for a lifetime. Unlike service workers, the family may care without pay, out of genuine and real affection. Unlike roommates or neighbors, the family may provide a place to live for months or years of unemployment. Unlike most dates, a spouse may grow to love and accept even the most shameful and secret parts of a person. Unlike a boss, a family is not likely to cast you out for an unproductive day or a single conflict. Though families can judge, attack, and exclude, for most people the family is the closest we ever come to experiencing unconditional love and support. The family as a social form joins together care and coercion, dependency and love, abuse and affection. These relationships can be sources of genuine care, but the necessary ties of dependency leave them constantly open to abuse. This is the dual character of any family structure in class society. The family offers precisely that which is most precious and most needed in human life. Yet it is also where someone is most likely to be brutalized, raped, or forced into a long-term relationship of violent subordination.

BONDING VIOLENCE

Two terrors, outside and inside. From outside the assault of the racist state, tearing at people's ability to care for each other. Alongside the long history of extralegal racial terror, state actors enforce white supremacy through their day-to-day jobs as social workers, border patrol agents, or parole officers. These agents of their state gain their power amid the horrors of racialized poverty, surplus populations excluded from stable wage labor, and the erosion of working-class life. Yet children *are* often in real danger in their families. The family hides its own internal terrors. The private family operates as a space of gender and sexual coercion and control, providing the opportunity for abuse and coercion. These two forms of violence may appear in direct opposition—those claiming to protect children on one hand, and the widespread reality of child abuse on the other. But the family form bonds these two forms of violence together. This bond operates through the binary logic of the family ideal, by naturalizing and normalizing some families while treating others as pathological. It operates historically (and at times presently) through the eugenic racial policies of immigration, natalism, and uneven access to repro-ductive health to attempt to promote and defend the white settler family while discouraging or fracturing other household forma-tions. It works in zoning, marriage and divorce law, and taxation, encouraging nuclear family formation while making other kinship relations more precious and difficult. Some families are strength-ened, protected from scrutiny, empowered in their normative status, while others are subject to surveillance and violence.

The bond between these two forms of violence is also on display in the photo with which this chapter opened. Paul Anchondo's parents have been murdered; he has become a prop in a photo opportunity for a president who supports white terror. The destruction of his family here helps produce and reify another, monstrous family. The First Family of the Trumps embodies not quite the proper normative family of the bourgeois imagi-nation, but its perverse and disavowed truth. Without the baby, President Trump could not offer such a compelling image of an all-powerful white father of the state, the racist imagination, and an unconscious familial fantasy. From this fantasized position of the primal father, Trump can openly sexualize his daughter, brag about rape and sexual assault, and be the embodiment of a new upsurge of revanchist, heterosexual, patriarchal authority. Two violences, bond together, begetting each other. Family abolition, to be anything, must be both the radical refusal of state and fascist violence against care relations, and the remaking of care relations to challenge internal abuse.

3

Lines of Flight

In the spring and summer of 2020, the United States saw an uprising. More Americans marched in a protest than in any previous mass mobilization in history, with estimates ranging from fifteen to twenty-five million people marching in over two thousand cities.[1] The protests included weeks of rioting, with curfews in two hundred cities.[2] In the protest's originating city, Minneapolis, protesters burned down a police station. By early June nearly a hundred thousand state and federal troops were deployed in US cities across twenty-one states to quell riots.[3] Police arrested fourteen thousand people.[4] The disruptions followed years of unevenly mounting protest under the banner of Black Lives Matter against the police murder of African Americans.

The event that triggered the insurrection was the murder by Minneapolis police officers of George Floyd on May 25, 2020. Many new to the movement cited the video as prompting their steps toward collective political action. For nine minutes and twenty-nine seconds of the video, police officer Derek Chauvin kneels on George Floyd's neck. Floyd says, "I can't breathe" twenty-seven times, then "I'm about to die … they are gonna kill me," before he dies on camera.[5] The video struck deeply into the psyches of many who watched it. Many viewers noted the emotional intensity of Floyd's begging for his mother. As one popular protest sign, mural, and social media message repeated, "All mothers were summoned when he called out to his momma." "Momma," he called out as he was choked to death, "Momma, I'm through."

George Floyd's mother was Larcenia Jones Floyd. Her friends and family called her Miss Cissy. She died two years before George; the anniversary of her death was less than a week away when George was murdered. By all accounts, George loved his mother deeply. He had her name tattooed on his stomach. She raised her children as a single mother in a neighborhood called the Bricks, a Black working-class area of Houston, Texas. They lived in a public housing complex, where Larcenia was a leader and activist in the resident council.[6] While George was a child, his mother worked at a fast-food stand. Larcenia's parents were sharecroppers in North Carolina, living under the racial terror system of Jim Crow. She had thirteen siblings, all of whom graduated from high school. One of her ancestors, Millery Thomas Stewart Sr., was born enslaved on tobacco plantations in North Carolina. When he was eight years old, the Civil War ended slavery. By his twenties, he had acquired five hundred acres of land, but it was soon seized by white farmers.[7]

Having been unable to fulfill his aspirations of college and professional sports, at twenty-four years old George Floyd returned to live in the same public housing complex where he grew up, and where his mother still lived. There, Larcenia saw George arrested repeatedly for drug possession. In 2007 he spent four years in a privately run prison three hours from Houston. Larcenia taught her children the pervasive reality of white supremacy. In an interview, George's brother Philonise Floyd recounted: "My mom, she used to always tell us that growing up in America, you already have two strikes, and you're going to have to work three times as hard as everybody else, if you want to make it in this world."[8] George Floyd's family was fragmented by mass incarceration, racial terror, and the legacy of American slavery. Far from a normative white, propertied household, Floyd's family reflects many dimensions of the racist state violence and poverty that shape the domestic lives of Black Americans. Growing up with a single mother in a poor, segregated neighborhood, and then lacking the stability and resources to establish a household of his own, George Floyd's life was marked by exclusion from a family ideal. But in calling to his deceased mother, George Floyd offers a third, radically distinct meaning of family: *a plea for help*. For Floyd at his most horrifically vulnerable, I take his comments to mean that he saw in his mother the meaning of salvation, aid, and care. I hear in his call a turn to his love for his mother to save him, to comfort him, to be with him. In his plea, many people recognized something of themselves, of their own fears and despair, their own desire to help and comfort.

Family abolition, as offered here, includes the destruction of private households as economic units reproducing the system of class inequality that relegated Floyd's family to poverty. It is a call for the overcoming of a normative ideal built on racism and homophobia, and an end to the violent assault against care relations. It is a policy demand to undo the regulatory regimes that support some normative families by punishing others, families like Floyd's. Family abolition includes the dismantling of personal domination and property that enable child abuse and interpersonal violence. Family abolition is the dimension of collective liberation as it unfolds in our personal lives, alongside other abolitions—of property, of capital, of police, of the state. Yet family abolition is not just a call for destruction and overcoming; it is also a positive embrace of the love at the heart of the best families. Floyd called to a woman who had cared for him against the cruelty of the world. Family abolition must be an affirmative response to George Floyd's plea to his mother. That tie of love is at the heart of justice, of the struggle for a free world. The affirmation of family abolition is the demand that this love be a universal and unconditional basis for a social order that extends to include everyone. Yes, we all deserve love. Yes, we all deserve help. Yes, we all deserve to survive. Yes, we will defend each other. Yes, we will keep us safe.

BREAKING OPEN

The family of the present is impossible. It is torn between the violence and precarity of racial capitalism, the excessive demands of daily labor, and collective yearnings for freedom. Part I of this book sketches multiple dimensions of the family: the family as private household in crisis, the family as binding an oppressive ideal and internal violence, and the family as the plea for help against terror. All weave together to form the impossible tangle of the family. Family politics join together these impossible contradictions: violence and work, race and gender, domination and love.

We are in the midst of multiple global crises: deep economic stagnation and intensifying working-class precarity; the ecological horror of mass species death and climate change; and the rise of fascist politics, religious fundamentalisms, and intensifying state authoritarianism. Every year the climate catastrophes escalate. In the summer of 2022, a heat wave gripped India, Europe, and the United States, causing over twenty thousand deaths in Europe alone and multiple mass wildfires. Droughts dried up rivers in the American Southwest, Europe, and China. Nearly concurrently, heavy rains caused flooding across Pakistan, the American Southeast, Bangladesh, and elsewhere in China. Fascist-sympathetic administrations have taken power across much of the world and are rising forces everywhere. Even in the wealthiest countries, most people live constantly on the edge of destitution. The world is broken. The survival of everything we care about is in question.

Many people imagine the family as a refuge, as this strategy of survival. For many people, family members may be the only support available against the brutalities integral to capitalist labor markets, ecological catastrophe, and state violence. The family is imagined as the heart of a heartless world, the soul of soulless commodification of everything, and numerous other clichés that occasionally ring true. Many love their families and feel loved by their families, and love is not easy to find.

But the family, too, is in crisis. From within, queer and trans children are challenging the bigotry of their parents. Wives and girlfriends are rejecting interpersonal abuse and the gross unequal division of household labor. People are choosing to marry later, to have fewer children or none at all, to divorce or separate often, and to live alone for much of their lives. From without, Black, brown, and migrant families face the perpetual crisis from the assaults of the racist terror state in the form of police murders, mass incarceration, and deportation. Families cannot carry the impossible expectations of household reproductive labor. Working-class family life is in crisis, from the protracted economic strain of chronic underemployment, welfare austerity, and stagnant wages. Property has always been integral to the illusion of family stability. Now that illusion is unavailable for most, and precarious for nearly all.

The family, as a norm, as an institution, as an aspiration, has already catastrophically failed numerous people. Many already experience the family as a trap of hopelessness: homeless queer youth, people fleeing abusive partners, others stuck in dissatisfying and lifeless relationships, or millions of the people choosing to live alone. Even for those who love their immediate relatives, families are grossly inadequate to meet our collective needs for survival and care. Private, individual households as economic units can barely function, made stable only through property and privilege, shattered quickly by unemployment, conflict, and violence. As ecological and economic crises deepen, our world will see a chaotic and uneven decline, including state failure, labor market breakdowns, and mass hardship. Growing numbers of families will find themselves excluded from work, trapped in refugee camps, or forcibly spread across continents. Under such conditions, the normative nuclear family may be viable for no one, and all other household kin arrangements may come under extreme strain. In periods of increasing chaos, many people may turn to broader collective units to survive. These survival needs beyond the family could easily be met in fascistic ways through religious cults, clientelist political parties, or walled-off neighborhoods. This book is toward an aspiration that we can do better.

We are poised in a historic moment where many, in various forms, are questioning old family ideals. Racked by the devastating effects of COVID-19 and the generalization of the care crisis, even the privileged are doubting the wisdom of the nuclear family. Far from the front lines of the rebellion, some are questioning whether this is the only way to live. Experimental speculations with alternative living arrangements have become popular with the propertied classes, drawing on long-standing queer, Black, and migrant proletarian survival strategies to try to imagine the possibility of collective meaning and joy to atomized and isolated lives.

BEYOND THE FAMILY

Amid the intensifying crises of human survival, we must collectively do everything we can to save each other, to make something with each other that can carry us through, that can heal this world. We need something else, something more, as the expression and substantiation of our love and care for each other. Black feminists evoke this possibility when they point to solidarity as a practice moving beyond the nuclear family's logic of racial property. Alexis Pauline Gumbs suggests this going beyond through "radical mothering."[9] Queer and trans youth pursue this possibility through what many call "chosen family," however difficult these arrangements may be to maintain. This possibility is yearned for, but not achieved, in efforts toward deliberate alternative living, cooperative housing, and rural communes. It is there in Sophie Lewis's articulation of the struggle of "real families against the family."[10] It is substantiated in mutual aid during catastrophe and in the cooperative strategies that poor people use to survive. Scholars and activists have been discussing "radical kinship" in its myriad forms. It is in Martin Luther King Jr.'s vision of "beloved community."

The family was challenged repeatedly in every era of proletarian rebellion, including today. This resistance sometimes takes the form of a passive refusal. Adolescents run away from home, single people avoid dating, couples delay marriage, mothers insist on working outside the home over their spouse's objections, fathers don't stick around to raise their kids, or wives flee bad relationships. All these choices are heavily constrained by labor market conditions and external social forces, but they are also choices people may make at great personal cost.

This moving beyond the family is found through the collective movement of mass struggle. The millions of people moved by George Floyd's plea to his mother to take the streets or burn police cars were taking up the kernel of love in some families and making it into something greater. Throughout the history of mass uprisings, new forms of care are evident. During rebellions like the Oaxaca Commune, on barricades and occupations, people forge new collective approaches to childcare, food preparation, living arrangements, and new practices of intimacy and care. In the peaks of resistance, there are also moments of collective care on the streets, in the midst of riots and protest, that point our way beyond the narrow logic of the family. People form new relations of solidarity and love in the intensity of uprisings. In these moments of insurgency, the tasks of caring for each other take on new meaning, new urgency, and new forms.

In the coming decades of social chaos and ecological crisis, we may also see growing mass resistance to the family. As more and more people come out as trans, or refuse to settle for bad relationships, or refuse the subtle coercion of the couple form, people will flee their families in search of better practices of care. As future waves of mass rebellion periodically spread, we may see the reemergence of a revolutionary horizon beyond class society. If history is any indication, these rebellions will necessarily entail mass challenges to the family, and articulated yearnings for something more, something better, something loving, something free. All these efforts to move beyond the family are moments that point us to a revolutionary horizon. They draw from and embody certain elements that draw us to family life: long-term and intergenerational relationships of care, interdependency, and solidarity. Yet these efforts also unleash that care into new forms, new practices, and new relationships. The forms of love present in the best families are not destroyed in the struggle to move beyond the family, but are broadened, generalized, and made universal.

Family abolition is the care we all need abundantly available beyond the family. This care could extend through the whole of society, made possible through deep revolutionary change. Family abolition is the expansion and generalization of relations of care and consensual interdependency. Family abolition is a commitment that no one should be without support, that everyone should have the freedom to find ways of loving and caring without coercion. The coercion of the family takes many forms, including interpersonal violence and the blackmail of providing necessary care only when certain conditions are met. A free society is one where people are able to form intimate relations without these forms of coercion. Family abolition is a commitment that who you love should not determine the material conditions of your life.

This abolition of the family cannot happen in a society dominated by capitalism and racist states. It can only occur as one dimension of a broader collective liberation. Overcoming of the coercive family form is one essential dimension of human emancipation. Revolutionary struggles points us to other linked forms of collective liberation: destroying the basis for prisons and police, overcoming private property and wage labor, constituting new bases for collectively managing social life. Family abolition is the dimension of this liberation as it unfolds in our interpersonal relationships, in how we reproduce ourselves, in how we love and are loved. Only in this shared movement can family abolition be a form of expanded freedom. So long as the family is the sole alternative to the state or the capitalist market, we will all find ourselves bound to some variation of its particular mix of coercion and care. Family abolition must necessarily be the concurrent overcoming of all the expressions of class society: wage labor, private property, the capitalist state, white supremacy, settler colonialism, and anti-Blackness.

In place of the coercive system of atomized family units, the abolition of the family would generalize what we now call *care*. Care of mutual love and support; care of the labor of raising children and tending to the ill; care of erotic connection and pleasure; care of aiding each other in fulfilling the vast possibilities of our humanity expressed in countless ways, including forms of self-expression we now call gender. Family abolition would be the way to address the profound, pervasive care crisis of capitalist society. Care in our capitalist society is a commodified, subjugating, and alienated act, but in it we can see the kernel of a non-alienating interdependence. The abolition of the family must be the positive creation of new institutions and practices of love, reproduction, and erotic life. Family abolition is not a slogan to rally around, nor a platform that will easily win people over. It is an attempt at theorizing the logic of social reproduction in a free, communist society. This book offers family abolition as a chance for us to all imagine a better, more free life.

ABOLITION, PRESERVATION, AND DESTRUCTION

If *the family* calls up a cacophony of associations, *abolition* has its own multiple meanings. As with the word *family*, I mean something both quite specific and a bit obscure by the word *abolition*, and still seek to engage its other connotations. I draw from two great traditions of abolitionist thinking: the Black freedom struggle in the Americas, and revolutionary Marxist thought.

The Black freedom struggle battled against slavery in the Americas, including Brazil, the Caribbean, and the United States. Rather than advocating for reforms that may improve the liveli-

54

hood of enslaved people or somehow humanize enslavement, abolitionists were clear that the only way forward was the full eradication of slavery. Abolitionists struggled to end the legal basis of slavery, to destroy the institution of slavery entirely, and to end the social relations that make human bondage possible. Abolitionism was ultimately embodied in the great slave uprisings of the nineteenth century, including the Haitian Revolution and the US Civil War.

This meaning of abolition was taken up in the last half of the twentieth century by the ongoing Black freedom struggle. Beginning in the 1970s, the United States began to incarcerate a rapidly growing share of its population, disproportionately Black and poor. The prison system became a major dimension of institutionalized white supremacy destroying Black life. Prison abolitionists argued for the end of the institutions and practices that made mass incarceration possible, what they called the prison industrial complex. Primarily driven by the movement of currently and formerly incarcerated people, embodied in groups like Critical Resistance, and articulated by Black communist activist intellectuals like Angela Y. Davis and Ruth Wilson Gilmore, prison abolitionism grew through the 1990s and 2000s to become one of the leading revolutionary visions. Since prison abolitionists saw the prison system as intimately linked to other institutions of racial state violence in what they called the prison industrial complex, abolitionist visions soon emerged in the struggle against police violence. With Black Lives Matter and the George Floyd uprising, police abolitionism became the dominant vision for young revolutionaries in the United States. Fully overcoming the prison system and police violence will require the overcoming of private property and class society.

There are ways this abolitionist lineage differs in some ways from family abolition. While most prison abolitionists would gladly support burning prisons to the ground after freeing everyone inside, family abolitionists generally do not advocate setting out to destroy all families. Family abolitionism does not seek to obliterate the social basis through which people may romantically partner, or raise children, or care for each other. For those who want to be freed from their families, by all means we all must enable their escape. But for others the family may be their best source of support. Nearly everyone in families does not have many better options. Family abolitionists are not setting out to rob people of the support and care they currently find in their families.

The second abolitionist tradition is less well known in the United States: revolutionary socialism, particularly as it is articulated through Hegelian Marxism. For the German philosopher G. W. F. Hegel, the concept of abolition, of *Aufhebung*, is central to his understanding of transformation. *Aufhebung* has multiple contradictory meanings: to suspend, to annul, to cancel, but also to preserve, to lift up, to save, and to keep. Hegel seemed to delight in these contradictory meanings and played off them in his thinking. In philosophical writing, *Aufhebung* is most often translated as *to sublate*, or as a *positive supersession*. It here suggests both destroying something and preserving part of that thing in a new, transformed form. In their early writing Marx and Engels used the word *Aufhebung* extensively. In their work, it is typically translated as *to abolish*. Marx and Engels called for the abolition of the state, property, and—with some ambivalence explored in the next chapter—the family. The abolition of property was not simply to destroy all possessions but to transform how goods are produced, distributed, and consumed toward the common good. The abolition of the state was not just the destruction of all governing institutions (though perhaps it is that as well) but also the transformation of governance through the radical democratic action of the working class and the dissolving of the state into the social body as a whole. Marx argued this was best embodied in the assemblies of the Paris Commune. In each case, abolition is neither simply destruction nor only transformation. What remains of property or the state takes on a radically different form, unrecognizable from what came before.

Most family abolitionists stand with those working to defend kinship relations against the attacks by capitalism or the racial state, reflecting elements of *Aufhebung* as a political tradition. Instead of destroying the family, we must abolish it by preserving what is crucial to it—human love, connection, care, community, romance—without binding these qualities to the particular form of the household within capitalism. Abolition means radically transforming these qualities, freeing them from relationships of coercion, abuse, isolation, and property. Abolition is a powerful way to describe moving toward the simultaneous destruction of the basis of coercion, and the unleashing of new forms of care. To abolish the family means to free our capacity to care for each other.

The tension between these two meanings of abolition can be confusing and misleading. But they may not be entirely as opposed as they seem. The Black freedom struggle of abolitionism has always included not only the destruction of forms of racist oppression but also the creation of new ways of being. As well as working to destroy slavery, anti-slavery abolitionists had positive visions they pursued: winning full citizenship and social rights for formerly enslaved Africans in the Americas, gaining the material basis for people to be able to reproduce themselves and economically survive, as well as the social basis to flourish and thrive. Anti-prison abolitionists argue that prisons do not make us safe; instead, as the popular slogan puts it, "we keep us safe." They have shown the need to talk about and pursue the basis of true safety: racial justice, economic redistribution, and community-based transformative justice. These positive visions of a free society are as central to this abolitionist tradition as the need to destroy institutions of oppression.

Other links between the two currents of abolitionism are worth further research. Two of the great abolitionist thinkers of the Black radical tradition—W. E. B. Du Bois and Angela Y. Davis—are both Marxists who spent periods of their life studying Hegelian philosophy and were almost certainly aware of the word's Hegelian and Marxist connotations. Marxists of many stripes have been an active part of the US prison and police abolitionist movements. Not only do Black radicals in the United States draw from Hegelian Marxism, but the Hegelian notion of abolition may also owe much to the Black radical struggle in the Americas. Susan Buck-Morss argues that the Haitian Revolution fundamentally overturned how European philosophy grappled with questions of bondage and freedom.[11] Hegel developed his conception of the master-slave dialectic, she argues, while reading daily news reports of the anti-slavery uprising in Haiti. Buck-Morss does not reflect on the possible interplay between anti-slavery abolitionists and Hegel's use of *Aufhebung*. Wilson Sherwin interweaves prison and police abolition theory with anti-work critique, calling for the political necessity of work abolition.[12] We need much more work thinking these multiple abolitionist traditions alongside each other.

My own interest in family abolition is inspired and influenced by anti-prison and anti-police abolitionist organizing. At a formative time in my own political development, I had the chance to be a part of New York City's Critical Resistance chapter. More than any other organizing I've encountered, the practice and theory of my abolitionist comrades grappled deeply with the interrelationship between racist state violence, intimate interpersonal abuse, and the brutality of poverty and class society. Their advanced thinking is foundational to my understanding of family abolitionism. To be of service to today's movements, family-abolitionist politics must reflect a thoroughgoing engagement with the abolitionist tradition of the Black freedom struggle.

* * *

Part I of this book sought to outline multiple definitions of the family—as a private household within the circuits of capitalism, and as a site of binding multiple forms of violence—concluding here with the need for lines of flight, for an escape from the coercion of the family form. These three chapters provide an overall conceptual framework used throughout the book. Part II turns to the history of the family and those who resisted it, a history deeply embedded in the developmental dynamics of racial capitalism. Keeping these frameworks in mind will help make sense of the many twists and turns family politics undergo from industrializing Europe, to American slave plantations and the settler frontier, to the rebellions of the twentieth-century workers' movement. These concepts will also prove useful to theorize the future overcoming of the family in Part III.

PART II

A History of Family Abolition

4

Industrialization and the Bourgeois Family

"Once the earthly family is discovered to be the secret of the holy family," Marx wrote in 1845, "the former must then itself be destroyed in theory and in practice."[1] Marx is here inaugurating a powerful revolutionary rethinking of the family. Feuerbach had argued God and religion were expressions of human alienation. In his "Theses on Feuerbach," Marx argues that this alienation finds its roots in the material relations of society, linking criticism and revolutionary action. Understanding this earthly family, as a social institution of class society and as a form of human alienation, requires our commitment to this family's destruction.

Marx is intertwining two points crucial for thinking critically about the family. First, institutions of class society such as the family are rooted in a material history of the alienated social relations of class society. Second, fully understanding this history demands of us their revolutionary abolition. Subsequent eras of capitalist development would transform what revolutionaries meant, exactly, when they spoke of family. The writing of Marx and Engels, read literally, says little on later communist debates on the family. But on these two points, Marx offers us the conceptual coordinates necessary for not only understanding his own era but also tracing subsequent permutations. For locating the family as a social institution of capitalist society explains the twists and turns in the meaning of family among revolutionaries. It is in the dynamics of capitalist development that we find the causes driving ongoing transformation in the forms of domestic life. But explaining these changes is not enough. Understanding how the family is embedded as a link of capitalist reproduction calls on us, as Marx makes clear in the final thesis on Feuerbach, to abolish it: "The philosophers have only interpreted the world in various ways; the point, however, is to change it."[2]

In *The Manifesto of the Communist Party*, first appearing in 1848, Marx and Engels make public their family-abolitionist commitments. Engels wrote an initial draft critique of the family, but Marx took it much further in his drafting of the final passage. They call for the "Abolition of the family" as the "infamous proposal of the communists."[3] In the following paragraphs, they mock the romanticization of family bonds by the capitalist class, sketch the devastation of working-class kinship ties under modern industry, and confirm their commitment to destroying the capitalist family as founded on property. Two works by Engels, bookending his career, expound on how the family form has transformed due to the developing relations of production of class society. In 1845 Engels published *The Condition of the Working Class*, documenting the consequences of industrialization on proletarian life. Just over forty years later and after Marx's death, Engels wrote *The Origin of the Family, Private Property and the State*, in which he argues that the historical emergence of private property created the monogamous, nuclear family form characteristic of the capitalist class.

This chapter examines the work of Marx and Engels to understand the rapidly changing family dynamics in nineteenth-century industrial capitalism. Their writing helps identify the crisis of working-class reproduction that gripped industrializing Europe, concurrent and inseparable from the consolidation of the bourgeois family form. Together, the destruction of working-class family relations and the ascendency of the bourgeois family are an important moment in the capitalist history of the family. Methodologically, this book takes from Marx and Engels their understanding that the changing logic of the family can be explained and understood through the historical dynamics of class society. This chapter later turns to the vision Marx and Engels offer of family abolition as the destruction of bourgeois society. This vision has resonance far beyond their context of nineteenth-century Europe.

ENGELS IN MANCHESTER

In 1842 a young Engels arrives in the thriving industrial center of Manchester. He spends the next two years there trying to make sense of the life of the new urban proletariat of England. He talks to people, he reads reports, he walks the streets. He tries to share his horror at the proletarian condition:

> Heaps of garbage and ashes lie in all directions, and the foul liquids emptied before the doors gather in stinking pools. Here live the poorest of the poor, the worst paid workers with thieves and the victims of prostitution indiscriminately huddled together, the majority Irish, or of Irish extraction, and those who have not yet sunk in the whirlpool of moral ruin which surrounds them, sinking daily deeper, losing daily more and more of their power to resist the demoralizing influence of want, filth, and evil surroundings.[4]

The stories go on. Fathers died on battlefields and in factories, their children left behind to slowly starve in barren rooms. Six to a bed, every room full and stifling. Disease tears through whole neighborhoods, leaving tens of thousands dead. A class consumed by alcohol, by prostitution, by moral decay. Engels offers us charts documenting what would one day be called the unequal distribution of premature death: "In Manchester, according to the report last quoted, more than fifty-seven per cent of the children of the working-class perish before the fifth year, while but twenty per cent of the children of the higher classes, and not quite."[5] Engels recognizes that the working class cannot survive these conditions: "How is it possible, under such conditions, for the lower class to be healthy and long lived? What else can be expected than an excessive mortality, an unbroken series of epidemics, a progressive deterioration in the physique of the working population?"[6]

Engels rightfully doubts the bourgeois reformers and early social workers attempting to implement various efforts to strengthen the working-class family to address the crisis of social reproduction. Social reformers of his day widely believed that the adoption of bourgeois moralism by the working class, including some closer semblance of the bourgeois family, would provide the necessary antidote to poor health conditions. These advocates imagined the norms of the bourgeois family could save the working class. Marx and Engels rejected such a solution, both on the grounds that it did not address the root causes in industrial employment and that bourgeois moralism was always a sham. They argued that the defeat of the capitalist class and the winning of socialism was the only way out. Unlike many of his contemporaries observing the horror of working-class social life, Engels solidly put the blame on the ruling class.

Implicit in Engels's work was the beginning of an overall framework for thinking about the family as a unit of capitalist society. He sketched the beginnings of a coherent analysis of working-class social reproduction under the conditions of capitalism. Engels identified the links of social reproduction in industrial capitalism: it is the new industrial capitalists who force peasants into the great cities; the new factories that have vast needs for cheap labor, disposable labor, child labor; the production of surplus populations to keep wages down; the resulting extreme urban poverty and horrible living conditions; and the government controlled by capitalists unwilling to intervene to meet people's basic needs for sanitation, housing, or health care.

INDUSTRIALIZATION AND THE CRISIS OF WORKING-CLASS REPRODUCTION

Engels shared with other contemporary observers a realization that the industrial working class was dying faster than they were having children. In the middle decades of the nineteenth century, the English working class could not replace themselves. The conditions that Engels documented—disease, overcrowding, workplace accidents, hunger, child mortality—made making it impossible for proletarians to raise their children to adulthood. Only the constant in-migration of dispossessed peasants led to an increase in the urban population. Ruling-class commentators, early social workers, and socialist advocates all joined in condemning the conditions faced by the industrial working class, recognizing what we may today call a crisis of social reproduction. Research has since backed up their fears. Rates of infant mortality were high, and life expectancy for working-class people plummeted with urbanization. For about half the working class, including unskilled and semiskilled manual workers, wages were mostly sufficient for the daily replacement costs of workers, but not for their generational replacement.[7]

Many shifts in work over the early nineteenth century had produced the conditions Engels observed. The growth of factories drew children, unmarried women, and men to work outside the home. Married working-class women engaged in subcontracted manufacturing work for pay within the home, known as the putting-out system. Factories grew rapidly in industrializing countries throughout the nineteenth century, dependent on the mass entry into waged factory labor of previous artisanal workers and peasants. Early in the century, over half of manufacturing workers in many industrial sectors were pre-adolescent children, such as in English cotton in 1816. As late as the 1840s, 15 percent of French textile workers were preadolescent.[8] The majority of children employed in England and France were hired through cross-generational factory work teams, subcontracted through working-class men. Children were often managed through a male family member or friend of the family, in loose extended relations that served to discipline children through male violence, but limited managerial authority. With the industrialization of the United States, American immigrant industrial workers faced similar conditions. From crowded tenements of the Lower East Side where women stitched dresses while raising their children to the factory slums of Pittsburgh, industrialization saw the parallel disintegration of working-class reproductive survival.

During the period Engels was documenting, proletarian wages were far too low to constitute anything that resembled the bourgeois family. Where capitalism had destroyed the basis of peasant families, the conditions of industrial production made it difficult for proletarians to cohere any semblance of stable family life. Industrialization was undermining the recognizable working-class family as a defined unit of social reproduction. Instead, there was chaos that panicked bourgeois observers. The brutality of industrialization fragmented working-class family relations. Working-class people still depended extensively on kinship networks for accessing work and housing, in disciplining within work teams, in sharing resources, or in their migration decisions, but they lacked the means to cohere stable nuclear families.

Under "Modern Industry," Marx and Engels write in the *Manifesto*, "all family ties among the proletarians are torn asunder, and their children transformed into simple articles of commerce and instruments of labor."[9] These observations were based on real and dramatic pressures industrial labor was putting onto working-class life. Under the conditions of factory labor, kinship ties between proletarians could no longer serve as a ready-made, naturalized system of obligation, care, and domination. Children would work on factory teams often headed by men to whom they were distantly or vaguely related. Proletarians lived in households with multiple families and generations. Proletarian women sold sex to survive. The conditions of wage work loosened and fragmented natal bonds and kinship ties, and remade them in increasingly heterogeneous ways. Coercive gendered violence occurred in workplaces, the streets, and homes, but it was not exclusive to kin-based fathers. For Marx, Engels, and many bourgeois reformers, the family was nonexistent among the industrial working class.

The crisis of working-class reproduction that Engels observed in Manchester continued throughout the history of capitalist development until the present day, moving geographically as industrialization spread. The conditions documented in *The Condition of the Working Class in England in 1844* became a reality in the industrial centers of Germany, and soon elsewhere in Europe. Parallel phenomena emerged in subsequent countries undergoing mass industrialization, whenever a mass workers' movement was not yet able to force a decent standard of living. From the factories of tenement neighborhoods of New York at the beginning of the twentieth century, to the Global South manufacturing export zones of the twenty-first century, wherever factories were built, generations of workers faced overcrowding, slums, workplace injury, infant mortality, and pervasive desperation.

MARX, ENGELS AND THE LUMPENPROLETARIAT

Engels's fears of the moral decay of the industrial poor echoes the hostility of the later socialist movement to the urban poor. When these later theorists sought canonical justification for anti-poor diatribes, they turned to the language of Engels and Marx in their writing on "the lumpenproletariat." For Marx and Engels, the category of the lumpenproletariat is still ambiguous. In his 1851 text *The Eighteenth Brumaire of Louis Bonaparte*, Marx gives the most widely read account of the members of the lumpenproletariat:

> Alongside decayed roués with dubious means of subsistence and of dubious origin, alongside ruined and adventurous off-shoots of the bourgeoisie, were vagabonds, discharged soldiers, discharged jailbirds, escaped galley slaves, rogues, mounte-banks, *lazzaroni*, pickpockets, tricksters, gamblers, *maquereaus*, brothel keepers, porters, *literati*, organ-grinders, rag-pickers, knife grinders, tinkers, beggars—in short, the whole indefinite, disintegrated mass, thrown hither and thither, which the French term *la bohème*.[10]

This list is remarkable for how bizarre it is: the proliferation of roles and names with few common threads or unifying charac-teristics. Many, but not all, of those listed are criminals. Others are informal workers, trying to survive as they are able. It is not entirely evident even Marx knew what brought all these people together. Elsewhere, Marx calls the lumpenproletariat "a mass sharply differentiated from the industrial proletariat, a recruiting ground for thieves and criminals of all kinds, living on the crumbs of society, people without a definite trade."[11] Writing in 1850 in *The Peasant War in Germany*, Engels describes the lumpenproletariat as the "living symptom of the decay of feudal society."[12] The end of feudal society left large numbers of "people without a definite occupation and permanent domicile."[13] The lumpenproletariat were dispossessed peasants who had been remade by industrial urban life. Engels contrasts them with people who still held "sound peasant nature," who "had not as yet been possessed by the venality and depravity of the present 'civilised' lumpenproletariat."[14] The lumpenproletariat in these passages is a heterogeneous array of criminals and informal laborers from which mercenary armies are recruited. These individuals belong to the new industrial cities and capitalist society, drawn from the breakdown of feudal life. But little clearly marks them as entirely separate from the industrial proletariat. Marx believes the lumpenproletariat are recruited to be deployed against strikes and workers' uprisings, but little actually distinguishes them from the rest of the working class.

Read alongside *The Condition of the Working Class*, it becomes clear that the "depravity" Engels describes in *Peasant War* was an increasingly universal as a condition of proletarian life. In much of Marx's and Engels's writing about the life of industrial workers, these same themes of criminality, sex work, social fragmentation, and moral degeneracy are widespread and inescapable. They saw capitalism as driving the entire class into grueling poverty, waged workers and surplus alike. With rare exceptions of accounts of specific intense political confrontations, Engels and Marx are not yet making a clear separation between the working class and the poor; both are still all among the proletariat.

This lack of a clear separation between the lumpenproletariat and the industrial working class is evident in one of Engels's most morally charged concerns: sex work. Engels fears urban poverty was torquing the gender and sexuality of proletarians. All manner of unspoken sexual horror lurks in *The Condition of the Working Class*. He cites prostitution repeatedly, a symptom of moral degeneration and sexual corruption. He hints at the threat of incest and homosexuality in overcrowded housing conditions. Yet rather than sex workers being radically unlike other proletarians, Engels saw sex work as an inevitable outgrowth of the conditions of urban life under industrialization. For most of the nineteenth century, many working-class women spent time engaged in sex work prior to marriage, a practice common enough that it did not radically distinguish them from their neighbors or kin.

During each phase of family abolition described in this book, the place of the lumpenproletariat shifts. In the urban centers of industrializing Europe in the mid-nineteenth century, respectability did not yet extend to any strata of the working class. The lumpenproletariat were dangerous not only because they were occasionally recruited as strikebreaking thugs, but also because they appeared to be the universal future for the working class. Engels feared that capitalism was transforming the entire class into degenerate poor—arguably laden with the eugenic connotations of degeneracy—replacing any semblance of working-class family with queerness, sex work, and premature death. He hoped a socialist movement could rescue the working class from this fate.

THE BOURGEOIS FAMILY

Even as industrial capitalism was destroying some forms of family, it was simultaneously bolstering a new one: the bourgeois family. Capitalists of the industrializing world forged a new form of family that differed from the old European aristocracy. Rather than extended kinship relations, they increasingly narrowed into the nuclear family structure. Rather than open decadence, they celebrated privacy, purity, abstinence, and monogamy. Rather than overtly negotiating marriage as an extension of political alliances, they imagined themselves committed to romantic love.

The fundamental basis of this new family form, as Engels argues in *The Origin of Private Property, the Family and the State*, is the accumulation and expansion of private wealth. As Marx and Engels write in the *Manifesto*: "On what foundation is the present family, the bourgeois family, based? On capital, on private gain. In its completely developed form this family exists only among the bourgeoisie."[15] This bourgeois family, Marx and Engels argue, finds its "compliment in the practical absence of the family among proletarians, and in public prostitution."[16] The new family of capitalist wealth is the necessary counterpart to the destruction of proletarian kinship ties. For Marx and Engels, this new capitalist family form is fundamentally a form of hypocrisy. While bourgeois ideology celebrates chastity and monogamy, in practice it only demands these virtues of women. While the bourgeoisie celebrates romantic love, this is merely a veneer for monied advancement. Where they celebrate the innocence of children, their affluent lives depend on industrial child labor. For Engels, all these forms of hypocrisy are a function of property relations. The capitalist family form becomes the basis of establishing the proper line of inherited wealth, and a vehicle for further accumulation.

In the *Manifesto*, Marx and Engels also identify the integral role of property in constituting the bourgeois family, a theme taken up again by Engels in *The Origin of the Family, Private Property and the State*. Bourgeois men enforced monogamy on their wives to assure that their children were their own; this maintained the proper lines of inheritance. Property plays other roles in bourgeois family relations that were only implied in their writing: the promise of inheritance and gifts of property were the means by which bourgeois parents exerted lifelong control over their children, reproduced their class standing in their children, and constituted their own class position. The bourgeois family was a vehicle for amassing and maintaining wealth. The family was made coherent by property ownership, as well as acting as a form of property of their own. Children belonged to their parents, as wives belonged to their husbands.

In his later writing, Engels was concerned with the oppression of women within the bourgeois family. Capitalist families produced new cults of feminine virginity, true love, and innocent childhood. The bourgeois household created the private sphere—detailed in Part I—subjecting women to a new form of domination:

> This situation changed with the patriarchal family, and even more with the monogamian individual family. The administration of the household lost its public character. It was no longer the concern of society. It became a *private service*. The wife became the first domestic servant, pushed out of participation in social production. ... The modern individual family is based on the overt or covert domestic slavery of the woman; and modern society is a mass composed solely of individual families as its molecules.[17]

Engels contrasts this gender domination within the propertied family to the gender equality he sees among the working class. He argues that the absence of property enables the working class to obtain genuine "sex love." The equalizing force of poverty among proletarians means the absence of male domination or monogamy:

"Here, there is a complete absence of all property, for the safeguard-
ing and bequeathing of which monogamy and male domination
were established. Therefore, there is no stimulus whatever here
to assert male domination."[18] Engels suggests the gender relations among proletarians pointed to the socialist future of gender
equality. Though this shows Engels's awareness of the intimate
links between property and gender inequality among the capitalist class, it also speaks to his general obliviousness to what later
became a central concern of socialist debates about gender: gender
domination within the working class. It would take later moments
of the socialist movement for gender relations between proletarians to come into focus. Instead, Engels and Marx share a politics
of family abolition as an overcoming of the bourgeois family form.

MARX'S AND ENGELS'S FAMILY ABOLITION

In summary, capitalism was producing both the destruction of
proletarian kinship ties and the basis for a new family form among
the capitalist class. It is in this conjunction between the destruction
of one set of kinship ties and the consolidation of another family
form that we can best make sense of Marx's and Engels's vision of
family abolition.

Communists, Marx and Engels say, are widely accused of want-
ing to abolish the family, to create a community of women shared
in common, and to destroy "the most hallowed of relations": that
between parents and child.[19] Marx and Engels neither confirm
nor deny these charges. Instead, they argue capitalism has already
destroyed the family among the working class through the conditions of industrial production and urban poverty. Communists,
they imply, needed no position on working-class family life because
capitalism had already destroyed it. The capitalist class, celebrating
the family in endless "clap-trap," is responsible for these conditions. Since the bourgeois family relies on property, it will "vanish
with the vanishing of capital."[20] Communism, in overcoming private property and capitalist social relations, would automatically
abolish the bourgeois family.

When Marx and Engels condemned the family, they specifically
imagined the family as a component of bourgeois society. In his

early writing, Marx's primary focus is not yet the capitalist mode of production or its laws of motion. Instead, his critique is aimed at the new character of what he called *bügerliche Geselleschaft*, translated variously as *civil society* or *bourgeois society*. Through his early articulations of *bügerliche Geselleschaft*, Marx linked both the material conditions of capitalism to its social, juridical, and state forms. Bourgeois society is the dissolving of old, feudal relations of status and property in addition to the formation of new material and institutional arrangements suited to private property and the accumulation of capital. Marx's understanding of bourgeois society integrated both the new economic relations of wage labor, free exchange, and generalized market dependency, and the social institutions integral to the rule of the capitalist class. The state, the church, and the family resembled elements of their feudal counterparts but were radically remade in the new crucible of bourgeois society. In the face of bourgeois society, communism is a politics of abolition, a "real movement that abolishes the present state of things."[21] This abolition that would free humanity from the alienation of the family form, among other features of bourgeois society, as Marx argues in the *Economic-Philosophic Manuscripts of 1844*: "Religion, family, state, law, morality, science, art, etc., are only particular modes of production, and fall under its general law. The abolition of private property, as the appropriation of human life, is therefore the abolition of all estrangement—that is to say, the return of man from religion, family, state, etc., to his human, i.e., social, existence."[22]

For Marx and Engels, family abolition is a necessary dimension and an inevitable consequence of the abolition of bourgeois society and private property. Communists do not need to directly challenge the family as a strategic priority, nor is there anything positive to salvage in the ideology of the family. In arguing this nuanced and specific position, Marx and Engels are distancing themselves from other tendencies of the socialist movement—both from those like Proudhon who defended and sought to reclaim the dignity of the peasant family, and those like Fourier who argued for a direct assault on the family as a primary communist task.[23] For Marx and Engels, since the bourgeois family is based on property, its abolition in the *Manifesto* takes the programmatic form of the "Abolition of all right to inheritance."[24] Though elsewhere they critique the specific goal of abolishing inheritance while leaving untouched private property in general, in the *Manifesto* they locate inheritance as integral to the logic of bourgeois family relations. For Marx and Engels, the abolition of the family is the destruction of the bourgeois family, inherent in the overcoming of private property.

AFTER THE FAMILY, HETEROSEXUAL MONOGAMY?

In their early writings, Marx and Engels left unspecified the nature of kinship or love after the abolition of the bourgeois family. It would be neither the form of the family ideal of the bourgeoisie nor the generalized prostitution of proletarians known under capitalism. In *The Origin of the Family, Private Property and the State*, Engels argued that communism would have little use of hypocritical bourgeois morality. Destroying the bourgeois family and the capitalist social order would provide the foundation for true love, for marriage based exclusively on "mutual affection."[25] With questions of property and material survival removed entirely from intimate relationships, humanity could discover its natural and inherent sexuality. Communist sexuality would be subject solely to the decisions of the citizens of the future, unconcerned with the opinions of those today.[26]

The call for liberation here is clear, but alongside it Engels advanced other more suspect claims. Abolishing property and the bourgeois family would free humanity to pursue its intrinsic sexuality, a family form freely chosen by the future, that of monogamy: "Prostitution disappears; monogamy, instead of meeting its demise, finally becomes a reality—for the men as well."[27] According to Engels, monogamous marriage would find its true realization in communist love: "Since sex love is by its very nature exclusive—although this exclusiveness is fully realized today only in the woman—then marriage based on sex love is by its very nature monogamy."[28]

Freed of the tyranny of property, humanity would also be freed of the sexual excesses of capitalist prostitution. Marx and Engels correctly recognized the devastation of capitalist poverty on working-class social relations. Yet they were unable to see the positive dimension of sexual freedom among proletarians in the new cities. From their argument that communism would make possible true monogamy, it is only a few steps to the aggressive sexual conservatism of later socialists. Such socialists saw both gender deviancy and homosexuality as bourgeois capitalist perversions. But for Marx and Engels, there could not yet be a clear division between the perversions of the deviant poor and working-class sexual respectability, because the latter did not yet exist. Abolishing bourgeois society and the bourgeois family, Engels argued, was the necessary condition for constituting the basis for an authentic marital life. Marx and Engels themselves expressed contempt and mockery toward the nascent homosexual rights movements, exchanging letters thick with insulting anti-homosexual epithets aimed toward their contemporaries.[29] Despite his concerns for women's emancipation and the cruelty of hypocritical bourgeois monogamy, Engels was unable to imagine anything beyond monogamous, heterosexual marriage. Yet the homophobia of Marx and Engels also showed a certain ambiguity. In an 1869 letter, Engels writes to Marx concerning a book by homosexual militant Karl Ulrich:

> These are extremely unnatural revelations. The pederasts are beginning to count themselves, and discover that they are a power in the state ... they cannot fail to triumph. *Guerre aux cons, paix aus trous-de-cul* will now be the slogan. It is a bit of luck that we, personally, are too old to have to fear that, when this party wins, we shall have to pay physical tribute to the victors. ... Then things will go badly enough for poor frontside people like us, with our childish penchant for females.[30]

Their contempt for homosexual emancipation is clear, but so is their own ironic play at lagging behind the coming queer revolution, contemplating the neglect of their own behinds.

Though it had not occurred to Karl Ulrich to call for the queer dictatorship they imply, Marx likely encountered such a sexual utopia in the pages of Charles Fourier. Marx read Fourier closely, as demonstrated when he favorably quotes Fourier when he wrote: "The degree of emancipation of woman is the natural measure of general emancipation."[31] It seems Marx was less sympathetic to Fourier's defense of sexual freedom. The *Manifesto*'s reference to the "free community of women" was likely both a satirical attack on the bourgeoisie's fear of communism, as well as a reference to some of Fourier's vision of a sexually open communal life. In chapter 5 I will delve into this vision of Fourier's of free love, open relationships, and incorporation of sexual pleasure here rejected by Marx and Engels.

First, however, the following chapter considers another dimension of the new bourgeois family form. Marx and Engels described the family politics of the new bourgeois society, one that did not remain restricted to the industrializing cities of the metropole. European bourgeois society extended its reach across the globe. The white bourgeois family form was integral to the colonial project, serving to stabilize colonial administrations, establish permanent settler colonies, and run agricultural plantations. To the racial family politics of North America we now turn.

5

The Family Politics of Slavery and Genocide

Across the Atlantic from Marx and Engels, other parallel regimes of capitalist family politics were taking shape over the course of the nineteenth century. Capitalism in North America was founded on two overarching white supremacist projects: the genocidal displacement of indigenous people with a settler colonial, white society; and the enslavement of African people for plantation agriculture. This chapter focuses on these two interconnected projects of racial capitalism, focusing on Canada to understand settler colonialism, and the American South to grapple with slavery. Both were intimately regimes of the family, through both the attack and destruction of Indigenous and Black kin relations, and the consolidation of a white, property-owning nuclear family model.

Both the United States and Canada promoted the expansion of white family settlements on the frontier. Their nation-building projects rested on the stability of a normative family form. White families were expected to farm homesteads, create settler communities on the frontier, and reproduce new generations. American slavery was overseen by the plantation family. White women were extensively integrated into the management and ownership of enslaved people. As well as practical systems of ownership and domination, the white families of the settler frontier and the slavery plantation are both infused with a romantic nostalgia, reproduced in the two centuries since through popular culture.

Concurrent with the promoting of the white family of property, racial capitalism enforced a brutal kinlessness on Black, Indigenous, and non-white immigrant families. In both the United States and Canada, systems of residential schools severed Indigenous family relations, forced assimilation of Indigenous children into white society, and enabled mass death. Slavery destroyed the ability of Black people to form persistent, stable kin relations. All bonds between enslaved people could be torn at any time by the system of buying, selling, and redistributing enslaved people. Toward the end of the nineteenth century, a new and differing regime of white supremacist family politics took shape. Rather than solely trying to destroy non-white kin relations, this new strategy sought to enforce white family norms onto Black and Indigenous life. In the American South, in the late 1880s and 1890s, this took the shape of the requirement of marriage to rent land under the Jim Crow tenancy system. Through the Allotment Act of 1887, Indigenous people in male-headed families were provided land plots under a system of private ownership. This was a strategy of enforcing patriarchal gender norms, destroying collective management of the land, and freeing up land for white ownership.

WHITE FAMILIES, WHITE NATIONS

Settler nation-building depends on families. Men, drawn from both the bourgeoisie and the working classes of Europe, were the primary staff of colonial expansion. Men crewed exploratory naval ships, filled the ranks of imperial armies, served in colonial bureaucracies, and staffed the contracted corporations that engaged in rapacious exploitation of the colonies. Often, men were the first and primary settlers on new frontiers. But elites understood that building settler nations would require more. Where the imperial project took on a commitment to establish large, permanent white settlements, they needed families. White women and children helped transition frontiers into lasting towns, and towns into nations.

In 1842, while debating a federal bill to support white settlers in Florida during the Seminole Wars, Senator Samuel Stokely said, "The presence of the families would bind settlers to the soil."[1] He was articulating what was usually left assumed: white families were reliable and necessary for long-term settlement. Promoting marriage was a concern of North American settler administrators. Canadian commentators were particularly fanatical about lifelong, white, legally codified marriage as an antidote both to the heterogeneous kin arrangements of First Nations people, and the perceived destitution of American divorce. The prevalence of single men as farm operators was perceived by elites as a threat to nation building. Sarah Carter writes, "Marriage 'fever' was encouraged by the political, legal, and religious leaders of late-nineteenth-century Canada who saw the perpetuation of a particular marriage model as vital to the future stability and prosperity of the new region."[2]

Both the United States and Canada developed an extensive set of laws and policies encouraging the formation of white settler families.[3] Both nations sought to foster white owner-occupied farms on their frontiers, rather than having land exclusively controlled by large corporate entities or small numbers of wealthy landholders. The US Homestead Act in 1862 distributed land to settlers that had been seized during wars against Native American nations. The Act provided twice the amount of land to married couples than single men. In Canada the Dominion Lands Act went further, banning land allocation to single women. In 1910 Frank Oliver explained that for homesteading to be effective, "not a single woman upon it, nor even a single man, but there should be both the man and the woman in order that the homestead may be made fully advantageous to the country."[4] As envisioned by settler colonists and their administrators, Sara Carter argues, "the patriarchal nuclear family ... would be the foundation of society."[5]

White women were integral to both the practical work of settlement, and also the discursive justification for anti-Indigenous violence. "Indian depredation" narratives of white women dominated federal policy toward militarily supporting settlers. News media in both the United States and Canada detailed gruesome accounts of white settler women being raped and murdered by Native Americans. These news accounts used violence against white women to call for the expanded and consistent military presence, rationalized new anti-Indigenous military assaults, and demonized First Nations people. Military strategy helped cohere and expand the borders of these settler nations.

Slavery in the Caribbean and the American colonies similarly began with white men, far from their families, running plantation agriculture with large workforces of enslaved Africans. As the American slave economy evolved over the course of the colonial era, however, settler families became integral to the management of slavery. By the nineteenth century, white women played central administrative roles in managing the massive cotton and tobacco plantations that depended on enslaved African labor. White women oversaw the administering of households and were involved in agricultural management. White women directly owned, bought, and sold enslaved people throughout the history of American slavery.[6]

American popular and elite culture have long had a peculiar romantic obsession with Southern, white, landowning families. Despite their market dependency and extensive engagement with the economics of debt and investment, wealthy slave-owning families often conceived of themselves as similar to the aristocracy of old Europe, embodying a traditional, anti-modern civilization. White women of the South, ensconced in the property-owning white family, were central to an American cult of femininity. Southern belles are imagined as emblems of pure virtue against the threats of Black masculinity and Northern modernity. The defense of white femininity and the white family was deployed as an ideological weapon during the American Civil War, then against Black Reconstruction, and then in support of the racial terror campaigns of Jim Crow. Two of the most acclaimed American films made before World War II—*Birth of a Nation* (1915) and *Gone with the Wind* (1939)—are both romantic and racist defenses of white Southern femininity and the white family through white supremacist violence.

The white settler and white plantation families of North America were both based on property. Like the industrial bourgeois families of Europe, as analyzed by Marx and Engels, these families consolidated norms based on property, constituting and expanding systems of social domination. Abolishing slavery in the United States required a massive and bloody civil war, one driven forward by the mass insurrection of enslaved people themselves. This anti-slavery rebellion would require a wholesale assault on the white, Southern family and its basis in violence, property, and domination. The American Civil War, among its many achievements, temporarily destroyed the material basis of the plantation-owning white family. The counterrevolution by the slave-owning class at the end of Black Reconstruction was the reassertion of the property-owning white family and the valorization of white womanhood.[7]

INDIGENOUS KINSHIP AND GENOCIDE

In spring 2021 Canadian news covered the discovery of mass graves of Indigenous children buried at residential boarding schools. Through the nineteenth and well into the twentieth century, First Nation children were forcibly removed from their families and placed in such residential boarding schools. Over four thousand children died while living at Canadian residential schools.[8] Several unmarked mass graves were discovered over the course of a few months in 2021, containing the bodies of over a thousand children.[9] Similar residential schools operated in the United States.

The boarding schools in the United States and Canada were typically formed and run by the Catholic Church. But they served the military strategy of state consolidation, supporting US and Canadian state interests in counterinsurgency. Removing children from their parents and forcibly socializing them was seen as a strategy of long-term subjugation. Over time, state policymakers became increasingly active, recognizing residential schools as advancing nation-building projects. In 1819, for example, the US Congress passed an act calling for the education of American Indian children, "for introducing among them the habits and arts of civilization."[10] Schools saw instilling sexual mores as central to their civilizing mission, chiefly by segregating boys and girls. The Indian Office reported Indigenous children had "no inherited tendencies whatever toward morality and chastity."[11] Twentieth-century boarding school survivors in the United States reported the severe abuse integral to the institution. They reported that they had experienced "severe beatings or they witnessed the beatings of fellow students by staff; were caused mental harm; were sexually abused or witnessed sexual abuse; were often located hundreds of miles from their homes; were forced to do manual labor; were hungry; and experienced the forced loss of language, culture, tribal traditions and spirituality."[12]

Native Americans have long theorized the immense collective trauma of the boarding schools as a "soul wound."[13] The schools sought to force cultural assimilation to white, settler culture. There children were forced to learn English, forced to convert to Christianity, and prohibited from engaging Indigenous culture. Some children were adopted into settler families. Boarding schools were just one dimension to a protracted anti-Indigenous genocide that took multiple forms across geography and time. Repeatedly central to this effort at cultural genocide was an assault on the heterogeneous kin arrangements of First Nations peoples. Though codified monogamous marriage and the nuclear family were still relatively recent inventions in Europe, white settlers saw the enforcement of Christian marriage codes on Indigenous people as central to their civilizing mission. They sought to destroy the precolonial kinship relations of First Nation life, and with it a diversity of gender and sexual practices.

Across the Americas, white explorers, colonists, and missionaries encountered an immense range of ways of approaching gender, sexuality, family, romantic partnership, child-rearing, and collective identity. This diversity of kinship forms threatened the imagined naturalness, universality, and social order of the European, bourgeois family. First Nations people included a broad range of nonbinary gender identities, such as the *winkte* of the Lakota, *lhamana* of the A:shwi, *nádleehí* among the Diné, *agokwe* and *agowinini* among Ojibwe people, and many other genders later grouped together under the identity of two-spirit.[14] Missionaries and settlers consciously sought to exterminate such gender diversity. Anti-indigenous genocide efforts foregrounded same-sex eroticism, often articulated through nonbinary gender identities. Even in First Nations where gender and sexual diversity was oppressed, Europeans still saw it everywhere. For example, though Aztecs repressed same-sex eroticism, Spanish Conquistadors still found their comparative tolerance to be an abominable culture of rampant sodomy.[15]

Sarah Carter calls the marriage practices of "Aboriginal people of Western Canada ... complex, diverse, flexible and adaptable."[16] The lack of consistent codes of lifelong heterosexual monogamy shocked European commentators. Jesuit missionaries wrote extensively on their horror at encountering women who could choose to marry and divorce, who had sex for pleasure, and other examples of "the wicked liberty of the savages."[17] In 1884 in Quebec, a judge remarked that "the relations of male and female in savage life" differed so dramatically from Christian marriage they would be better called "concubinage."[18]

Prior to the US invasion of California, Spanish missionaries engaged in a particular kind of family politics. Spanish conquest of California began in 1796 integrating mass rape as a strategy of military conquest.[19] Unlike their Anglo counterparts, Spanish colonial strategy was not primarily about establishing large settler populations. Instead they sought to promote and manage mixed-race and Indigenous procreation, seeking both a labor force and a population adequate for military defense.[20] Franciscan missionaries in the region forced Indigenous people to live in restricted settlements toward forcing adoption of European lifeways, with a particular focus on reproduction and the family. This included public beating and torturing women for engaging in abortion, murdering women accused of witchcraft, and forcing (or prohibiting) marriages and sex. Antonia I. Casteñeda describes one incident:

> Father Olbes at Mission Santa Cruz ordered an infertile couple to have sexual intercourse in his presence because he did not believe they could not have children. The couple refused, but Olbes forcibly inspected the man's penis to learn "whether or not it was in good order" and tried to inspect the woman's genitalia. She refused, fought with him, and tried to bite him. Olbes ordered that she be tied by the hands, and given fifty lashes, shackled, and locked up in the *monjero* (women's dormitory).[21]

American and Canadian settler societies, in contrast, primarily sought full control over the land controlled by Indigenous nations. Their primary orientation was toward genocide—the obliteration of Indigenous people as independent, sovereign, and distinct from settler society. This could done be in three ways: extermination (through disease, mass murder, and producing the conditions for mass death), subjugation (through military defeat, displacement to unfavorable land, and counterinsurgency), and assimilation to white settler culture. All three entailed logics of sexuality, gender, and the family. Extermination and subjugation, settler states found, was easiest through targeting Indigenous children; assimilation depended on instilling white family values.

Colonial-era Anglo settlers primarily used irregular warfare in their military conflicts with Indigenous nations, deliberately murdering, kidnapping, and enslaving children and other noncombatants. The governor of the North Carolina colony said that in the case of war, settlers must "enter into and destroy all the [Cherokee] Towns of those at War with us, make as many of them as we should take their Wives and Children Slaves, by sending them to the Islands."[22] With independence, the United States launched protracted genocidal wars against Indigenous nations as a strategy of westward expansion. When the US Army struggled to win against Indigenous military forces, they would instead target and slaughter women and children remaining in settlements, such as in the 1780s in the Ohio Country and repeatedly over the next century of military conflicts.[23]

The efforts of residential schools to destroy parental relationships between Indigenous people—and with them the transmission of Indigenous lifeways—continued in varying forms throughout the twentieth century. From the 1960s into the 1980s, child welfare workers in Canada separated over twenty thousand First Nations children from their families, relocating them into predominately white families, a practice called "the Sixties Scoop."[24] Parallel violence unfolded in the United States. More than a quarter of Indigenous children in the United States were taken away from their families by the end of the 1960s. The Bureau of Indian Affairs considered Indigenous parents "inherently and irreparably unfit."[25] The massive scale of child welfare relocation of Indigenous children reflects the persistence of genocidal policies, and the particular attack on Indigenous family relationships. White Americans and the settler state related to Indigenous kinship primarily through their goal to control land. But concurrently, another white supremacist family politics had taken shape in the Americas, through the enslavement of Africans as sources of labor. This lent itself to a different form of assaulting and managing reproduction and kinship.

NATAL ALIENATION UNDER SLAVERY

On the slave plantations of the Caribbean and the American South, enslaved people struggled to maintain their kin relations in face of *natal alienation*—the practice and constant possibility of slave owners' separating enslaved parents and children. For Black studies scholars like Orlando Patterson and Saidiya Hartman analyzing the family politics of slavery, natal alienation has become a central focus. These scholars identify natal alienation as constitutive of anti-Blackness and of the racial politics of American society. The counterpart to the consolidation of the white, slave-owning family was the sustained assault on Black kin relations among enslaved people.

Natal alienation was just one component of a broader attack on Black kin relations built into slavery. Slave owners bought and sold enslaved people regularly, showing little regard for biological kin relations, committed relationships of romantic intimacy, or any conceptions of the family among either Black or white people. Several Black radical theorists have grappled with the topic through Frederick Douglass's account of being separated from his mother. Angela Davis describes this fragmented family life under slavery: "Mothers and fathers were brutally separated; children, when they became of age, were branded and frequently severed from their mothers. ... Those who lived under a common roof were often unrelated through blood."[26]

Under the conditions of chattel capitalist slavery, male supremacist violence could be exercised unilaterally and only by slave owners. Enslaved Black men and women working in the fields were subject to the torture and tyranny of slave owners. This shared lack of authority constituted a form of immiserated gender equality. As W. E. B. Du Bois writes, "[The enslaved man's] family, wife and children could be legally and absolutely taken from him."[27] Davis, again: "Excepting the woman's role as caretaker of the household, male supremacist structures could not become deeply embedded in the internal workings of the slave system. ... The Black woman was therefore wholly integrated into the productive force."[28] In contrast, white American women were still seen as belonging to a protective domestic sphere. White farm wives would never have been seen harvesting crops, no matter how poor or desperate Northern families became.

Davis's take on this history ultimately valorizes the heroic efforts by enslaved people to form kinship ties, recuperating the persistence of the Black family even under such brutal conditions. Though many Black radical theorists share Davis's honoring of the relationships of care formed between Black people under slavery, recent scholarship has become more skeptical of framing this in terms of family bonds. Tiffany Lethabo King traces this turn to what she identifies as family abolitionism in Black theory in the work of Saidiya Hartman, Hortense J. Spillers, and Frank Wilderson.

Slave-owner wealth expanded when enslaved women had children. This embedded the dynamics of generational reproduction as components of capital accumulation and the work process. Most enslaved people could not effectively assert any form of parental rights, as the selling of enslaved people was completely beyond their control and often broke up families. Enslaved children were raised by whoever was on hand and available, often enslaved elders too old to work in the fields. In reviewing court law, Hartman finds the definition of motherhood for enslaved people encompassed only that which served slave owners. Enslaved people were subjected to "enforced kinlessness"—their relations were outside the law.[29] Enslaved women were further subject to the violence of sexual assault, rape, and forced reproduction. The work of enslaved women played integral involuntary roles in the domestic reproduction of slave-owning families, as nannies, wet nurses, mistresses, elder care attendants, cooks, and cleaners. The only families enslaved people could have were temporary bonds of care under conditions that constantly worked to destroy and fragment those ties.

In "Mama's Baby, Papa's Maybe: An American Grammar Book," Spillers claims the violent attack on Black relations throws into question the very notion of family. Spillers argues "the confusion of consanguinity" resulting of slavery "throws into crisis all aspects of the blood relations." She writes, "I would call this enforced state of breach another instance of vestibular cultural formation where 'kinship' loses meaning, *since it can be invaded at any given and arbitrary moment by the property relations*."[30] Though one could "call this connectedness 'family,'" it is fundamentally unlike the family of the master and of property. "'Kin,' just as gender formation, has no decisive legal or social efficacy." Spillers, King argues, is questioning whether the connections and relationships established by enslaved African people can or should be understood as "familial." King links Spillers's disinterest in recuperating family to Hartman's characterization of enslaved people as "stripped of genealogy and kin," and Wilderson's dismissal of family as "borrowed institutionally," referring to the adoption of anti-Black codes that do not accurately describe Black existence.

The family dynamics of slavery left a persistent mark on American racial politics. Davis, Spillers, and King all draw direct parallels between the assault on Black life under slavery, and the pathologization of Black families in the 1960s and 1970s by anti-poverty policy in the United States. Attempting to make sense of the mid-twentieth-century demonization of Black American mothers, Black feminists argued that the American history of slavery was an essential piece of the puzzle. In both contexts, racial capitalism prevented Black men from securing stable, patriarchal nuclear families. Black mothers were far more likely than their white counterparts to work outside the home, to parent alone, and to openly exercise decision-making authority. All three of these Black feminist authors are writing within an expansive set of debates on the Black family that continued from the 1960s on.[31]

IMPOSING WHITE FAMILY NORMS

Toward the end of the nineteenth century, changes in capital accumulation and government policy transformed the pressures on Black and Indigenous kinship. In both cases, this was enacted primarily through the distribution of access to agricultural land. Rather than solely trying to destroy kinship relations between Black and Indigenous people, the structures of racial capitalism increasingly imposed white family norms. For Black families, this emerged through the consolidation of Jim Crow land tenancy in the 1890s. For Native American people, the federal policy of allotment redistributed reservation land to male-dominated, nuclear families. In both cases, the imposition of a white family norm disciplined and constrained kinship relations.

In the next chapter, I consider the interregnum of Black Reconstruction, the period between the defeat of the Confederacy and the abolition of slavery (completed in 1865) to the withdrawal of US troops from the South in 1877. That was a period of unprecedented sexual freedom seized by formerly enslaved Black people. Following the defeat of Reconstruction, the slave-owning class spent the late 1870s and 1880s violently wresting back their monopoly control of the Southern agricultural economy, land ownership, electoral power, and social life. By the 1890s a new system had emerged, termed *Jim Crow*. Jim Crow dominated Southern life until its defeat by the civil rights movement in the 1950s and 1960s. During the height of Jim Crow—from the late 1880s into the 1910s—Black people were effectively completely trapped in the rural South, violently prevented from migrating to cities or to northern states. Jim Crow had three dominant components: the political disenfranchisement and legal segregation of Black Southerners, the pervasive climate of racial terror sustained by regular and public violence, and a land tenancy system called sharecropping.

It is less often recognized that Jim Crow included a coercive family politics. Since white landowners would only lease sharecropping tenancies to married couples, Black sharecroppers were forced into marriage. The frontier of cotton agriculture was expanding, plots were small, and land was available to new Black families whenever they were ready to marry. Land was denied to single Black adults or those in unconventional family arrangements. As a result of these conditions, Black people married early and could not separate. When and where Black people were able to escape tenant farming, their rates of marriage declined sharply.[32] This is a crucial and underemphasized dimension of Black American history: heterosexual marriage was a forced feature of Jim Crow white supremacy through the concrete mechanism of access to land in sharecropping. Jim Crow was an imposition not only of poverty, racial terror, political exclusion, and legal subordination, but also of a particularly rigid patriarchal family.

Beginning during World War I and continuing into the 1960s, over six million Black people fled the rural South and migrated, largely to major cities in northern and western states. Taking advantage of the labor demand in industrializing urban centers, along with political openings caused by the decline of the cotton industry, they again seized the opportunity for greater freedom. Among these freedoms were efforts to escape the heterosexual, marriage-based family norm. The post–Jim Crow low rates of Black marriage—a major topic of debate among 1960s policymakers and Black activists—may not only be caused by poverty and lack of stable work, but could also be read as a resistance and flight from the family regime of tenant sharecropping. Recognizing that Jim Crow sharecropping mandated heterosexuality is essential for recognizing the element of sexual freedom in the low rates of Black marriage during and after the Great Migration.

Indigenous families faced a parallel system of imposed white family norms, also through access to land. In 1887 the United States passed the General Allotment Act, also known as the Dawes Act. The president could seize reservation land under the nominal control of sovereign Native nations. Canada implemented a parallel set of policies. This land would then be redistributed to individual Native American heads of families, creating 160-acre individual family-owned plots. Rose Stremlau writes of how allotment sought to use the family form to destroy Indigenous property relations:

At its heart then, reformers believed that the Indian problem was a crisis of Indian families. Common title to land and resources enabled Indians' dysfunctional familial behavior, and allotment promised to replace the chaos of Indian communities with the order of nuclear families. Allotment, then, was a means to an end. The allotment debates were not about land; they were about the kind of societies created by different systems of property ownership. Reformers clearly asserted that private property created superior families and better citizens. By the early 1880s, most believed that other efforts toward assimilation, such as education, proved less effective until communal title was destroyed by legislative force.[33]

Many saw allotments as a crucial component to assimilating Native Americans into white, American society. This policy worked to break up collective ownership and management by tribal authorities, and ultimately sought to destroy the reservation system. Whatever remained of the seized land after its distribution to Native American families was then sold to white settlement. In 1881 Native people controlled 138 million acres; primarily through allotment policy, this declined to 52 million acres by 1934.[34]

Allotments enforced a white, nuclear family model among Native people. Allocations were set at 160 acres, regardless of the size of a family or number of generations, encouraging families to configure themselves in a small nuclear arrangement. Land allotments by family were made only to men as heads of households, strengthening male power within Native family life and undermining alternative, matrilineal kinship arrangements. Allotment included policies to force all members of the household to adopt the same last name, forcing people to abandon Native systems of naming. These were self-conscious efforts at cultural assimilation, articulated explicitly by policymakers like Thomas J. Morgan, US Commissioner of Indian Affairs, when the General Allotment Act passed. For Miller, the nuclear family as a system of property ownership was the foundation of civilized society.[35] The 1900 "Annual Report of the Commissioner of Indian Affairs to the Department of the Interior" cited the law as "a mighty pulverizing engine for breaking up the tribal mass" and a means through which to "recognize the individual" and "protect the family."[36] Each allotment became an individual private household, in keeping with the family logic pervasive in capitalist social life. Native people were restricted from consolidating landholdings, preventing a more collective approach to land management.[37]

The nuclear family was developed by the new capitalist classes of Europe and circulated the world with colonialism. It was enforced either through the extermination of other kinship forms such as in slavery or residential schools, or through imposing of its norms, such as in Jim Crow and allotments. The history of the family is also the history of white supremacy and genocide.

FAMILY ABOLITION AND RACIAL DOMINATION

North American racial capitalism was founded on an attack on kinship relations of First Nations people and enslaved Africans. Though adopting a radically dissimilar form, this parallels elements of the undermining of kin relations among European proletarians. In the nineteenth century, capitalism was destroying proletarian families in the factory slums of Europe, on the frontiers of anti-Indian genocide, and in the slave plantations of the US South and Caribbean. On one side of the Atlantic, the kinship ties of the industrial working class of England were fracturing due to the immiseration of factory labor, poverty, and urban over-crowding. On the other, plantation agriculture and settler colonial regimes relentlessly undermined Black and Indigenous kinship.

For both enslaved and waged proletarians, their kinship ties were not recognized by those in power, not respected by law, and did not readily conform to elite social expectations. In each case, proletarian deviancy was understood in opposition to the consol-idation of gender and sexual norms among the property-owning class, who formed sharply structured families based on inheritance and status. The differences between enslaved workers and waged workers are considerable, and the racialized chasm would divide the world proletarian movement. But despite these differences, in both cases the observation of Marx and Engels that capitalism was already destroying the working-class family described a key feature of nineteenth-century proletarian life.

In this context, what would family abolition mean? Clearly both natal alienation under slavery and residential schools are fun-damentally inimical to human life. This racial history calls for a complete rejection of any vision of overcoming the family that rests on an outside authority taking children en masse away from their parents, that consolidates childcare under the centralized authority of racist states, or that has no regard for preexisting relationships of love and care. States forcefully separating children from BIPOC parents continues today in child welfare policy—described in

chapter 2 as the *family policing system*—in immigration enforcement and in mass incarceration. Family abolition must not ever
support such practices, and no self-identified family abolitionists,
to my knowledge, ever have.

But other senses of overcoming the family are relevant in the
contexts of racist assaults on Black and Indigenous kinship. The
vision offered by Marx and Engels—the destruction of bourgeois society and the bourgeois family, through the overcoming
of private property—is powerfully relevant in the racial politics of
nineteenth-century America. Both the American Civil War and
the armed resistance by First Nations people across North America
were massive militant efforts to challenge the rule of white, propertied families. Family abolition could be the destruction of the white
propertied family and its foundation in slavery and genocide.

Parallel to this classical Marxist critique, recent Black and Indigenous scholarship have offered rich visions of moving beyond the
logic of the white family. King's read on Spillers points to the family
as a project of white supremacy and shows how Black life already
suggests its overcoming.[38] Defining the family through the norms
of property, patriarchy, and whiteness, such scholarship suggests
the diverse strategies of care and kin between Black people may
be a radical strategy of freedom beyond the white family. In
recent years, Indigenous scholars have been theorizing alternative forms of kinship, erotic life, and care through concepts drawn
from varying Indigenous legacies. Daniel Heath Justice explores
"kinship—in all its messy complexity and diversity" as evidence
of the vitality and decolonizing imagination of Indigenous liter-
atures.[39] Kim TallBear critiques the settler construction of family
built on ownership, property, and dispossession.[40] She contrasts
this with "making kin," constituting "caretaking relations" that
include the nonhuman. TallBear points to polyamory as a strategy
of resistance to white settler family norms based on ownership and
property.[41] Another substantial body of TallBear's research critiques biogenetic models of kinship, as weaponized to disenroll
people from Indigenous nations.[42]

In "Desiring the Tribe," Lou Cornum explores the tribe as a
modality of imagining an Indigenous queer communism beyond
the nuclear family form. Cornum identifies both the limits and the

promise in efforts to draw from Indigenous kinship relations to articulate a radical critique of colonialism and heteronormativity:

> There is no pristine past and the future is messy. We work to form kinships, not in the bio-bind of blood lines and percent nor in the institutional pacts of marriage and property inheritance. ... It is however because a tribe is difficult to assimilate into the acceptable containers of liberal politics (individual, household, citizenship, representation) that it reorients the entire value system used to dictate how people live and relate to each other, the world.[43]

* * *

In summary, racial capitalism took shape in North America through consolidating a white family of property and through a relentless attack on Indigenous and Black kinship relations. The attack not only destroyed preexisting ties but eventually forced Black and Indigenous people to partially adopt white, patriarchal family codes. The family as an institution joins both sides of this dynamic—it is both the valorization of a narrow form of organizing people together *and* the destruction and undermining of other forms of care. Family abolition must not be another iteration of states violently intervening in preexisting kin relations. Instead, Cornum's gesture toward Indigenous queer communist solidarity informs the speculative theorizing of family abolition explored in Part I of this book. In the next chapter, we will turn to other moments in the nineteenth century when people resisted and challenged the white bourgeois family form.

6

Sexual Transgression and Capitalist Development

In 1871 the working class seized control of Paris. The Commune, as it came to be known, began on March 18. In the neighborhood of Montmartre, a confrontation broke out between the National Guard and the French army. The National Guard, radicalized while defending Paris during the preceding Franco-Prussian War, refused to cede the city to the newly established Third Republic. Men of the National Guard operated the heavy artillery on the hill of Montmartre, the focus of the fighting, yet women also played a pivotal role that day. Waking up early to prepare breakfast, they were the first to spot the invading government troops. These "women of the morning" came to embody what the leaders of the Commune sought to present to the skeptical world: self-sacrificing "housewives," who "stood in the snow for hours, without bread and without heat in their lodgings, forming queues for rations at the doors of the butchers and bakers," "true women of the people" in the words of Gaston Da Costa, an official of the Commune. As the fighting continued throughout the day, these women Da Costa saw as legitimate and upstanding were replaced by their scandalous counterparts—in Da Costa's words, "a horrible phalanx of regis-tered and unregistered prostitutes from the quartier des Martyrs and ... the hotels, cafes and brothels." These "afternoon women" were "true furies ... the sad froth of prostitution on the revolu-tionary wave" who "got drunk at all the bars, and howled their scoundrel joy at this defeat of the authorities."[1]

In a century of mass rebellions, revolutions against the old aris-tocracy, and new experiments in representative democracy, Marx noted that the Paris Commune was unique in offering a vision of a proletarian government. For two months, assemblies of working-class people ruled the city, proposing and implementing a string of major reforms, including suspending rent, supporting workers in seizing control of their abandoned workplaces, stripping police of their powers, establishing free public education, and separating church and state. For Marx, the Paris Commune was the first emergence of the political rule of the proletariat: "It was essentially a working class government, the product of the struggle of the producing against the appropriating class, the political form at last discovered under which to work out the economical emancipation of labor."[2] Though he wavered on whether the Paris Commune was socialist, Marx was clear that it provided the greatest advancement of working-class emancipation to date.

These true furies, the sex workers of the Commune, refused to go away. At one public meeting, a sex worker declared of the *filles soumises* (government-registered prostitutes): "We are at least 25,000! Well then, if they make us into regiments, if they arm us, we will shatter the power of the Versailles!"[3] Louise Michel, a legendary militant leader of the Commune, challenged its leadership for their refusal to allow sex workers to drive ambulances: "Who has more right than these women, the most pitiful of the old order's victims, to give their lives for the new?"[4] In the final week of the Commune, as the Versailles army was invading, women were on the front lines of combat. Parisians of all genders and ages rushed to defend barricades. Upon retaking control of the city, the forces of Versailles proceeded to massacre of somewhere between ten thousand and thirty thousand Communards.

For a brief two months on the streets of Paris, the world glimpsed a revolutionary worker's society. Like in the Commune, sex workers were often found throughout the urban uprisings of the nineteenth century, battling with police across the growing urban centers of Europe. As the proletariat was the new class counterpart of the bourgeois factory owners, sex workers were the counterpart to the bourgeoisie's monogamous family. On the barricades of the Commune, sex workers showed themselves to be militants of proletariat insurrection.

Inspired by the true furies of the Commune, this chapter traces other possibilities of kinship and pleasure lurking in the industrial cities and revolutionary moments of the nineteenth century.

Industrialization and plantation slavery both created a polarized but linked experience, both imposing kinlessness on some while valorizing the bourgeois family for others. But behind and beyond these oppositions, there are other transgressive and rebellious pleasures. This other nineteenth century points us toward paths not pursued, lost in the sexual conservatism of the workers' movement that took shape at the end of the century. Here three threads of sexual resistance in the nineteenth century parallel the sex workers of the Paris Commune: homosexuality and transfemininity in urban life, the heterodox kin forms pursued by emancipated Black people of the American South during Reconstruction, and the theories of French socialist Charles Fourier.

PROLETARIANIZATION AND URBANIZATION

Proletarianization and homosexual identity are intimately linked.[5] In agrarian peasant life, one's livelihood depends on maintaining relationships with one's family and eventually entering into a long-term heterosexual marriage. For peasant farmers, there is no clear division between work and home. Peasant families, working together on farms, are units of work and production. There is comparatively little gendered division of labor. Peasant families, unlike their proletarian counterparts in capitalism, were not directly market dependent. They neither relied primarily on working for wages off the farm nor on selling the food they grew. Instead, they made nearly all of what they consumed on land they controlled. Direct domination within the peasant family was a component of the production process under feudalism. The authority of fathers rests on tradition, interpersonal obligation, and their exercise of violence in addition to other forms of direct domination.

Under rural peasant life, though nonnormative sex may be an illicit and secretive part of a person's life, the material conditions of reproduction marginalize anyone declaring sexual desires or behaviors incompatible with their family or community's norms. Even in capitalist settler colonies like colonial North America, discussed in chapter 5, rural agricultural life continued to be heavily dependent on the heterosexual family as the main unit of farm ownership and management, sharply constraining sexual freedom.

Though settler colonial farms in North America produced and sold to the market, they also continued to produce much of what the family consumed within the farm and the family. Many of the essential goods of social reproduction were not readily available for market purchase in colonial America, and many people remained dependent on their families for their survival.

Capitalist dispossession of rural peasants expelled people into cities and gradually urbanized society as a whole. Robbed of the land, European peasants—and later, peasants globally—were transformed into proletarians, searching for wage work. This process of rural dispossession was the destruction of the peasant family and its rigid codes of sexuality. Industrialization relied on the labor available through this long process of capitalist transition in the European countryside. Industrial manufacturing offered these proletarians wage-labor jobs, concentrating workers into major cities. The influx of former peasants into cities offered the new industrial capitalists their essential, desperate workforce. Marx and Engels were able to identify the violent destabilization of peasant patriarchy under the grueling poverty of urban proletarianization. Yet the counterpart to this destruction of the peasant family was expanding opportunities for sexual freedom in the Great Towns. Wage labor, for those who could access it, directly lessened the immediate dependency on the family, making domestic life partially autonomous from the production process.

From the early modern period into the twentieth century, urban European life was intensely gender segregated and homosocial. Many industries of early capitalist urbanization were entirely composed of men, including seafarers and armies. Factories tended to have heavily gender-segregated workforces. Women were largely unwelcome in most public places, leaving men to socialize only with each other. Wage work was often intermittent, following boom-and-bust economic cycles or seasonal changes. Large numbers of men were concentrated in cities, with periods of unemployment and downtime.

Urbanization was staggered regionally based on the dynamics of capitalist development and industrialization: in England, it occurred over the eighteenth and nineteen centuries. In the United States, urbanization accelerated in the late nineteenth and early twentieth century, with a majority of Americans not living in cities until World War II. In much of the Global South, most people did not move from the countryside into major cities until the last quarter of the twentieth century. Into the twentieth century, African Americans were largely barred from city life, trapped in the brutal conditions of the rural South. Black people were finally able to move out of the rural South beginning with the labor demand of World War I. This triggered the beginning of what became the first and second Great Migrations, as masses of Black Americans moved into cities and northern and western states, continuing into the 1960s.

SEX IN THE GREAT TOWNS

These new urban conditions together created dramatic changes in proletarian sexual life. Newly independent wage workers— first young white men, and later others as proletarianization deepened—could forgo family life altogether, making unexpected and unconventional choices about who to live with, who to have sex with, and who to love. In each era and locale of urbanization, people express common themes in memoirs, interviews, and historical records: the chaos of moving from a farm to the city, the new misery of jobs and their absence, the rush of sexual freedom and the potential to remake oneself. Where bourgeois reformers saw the sex life of urban proletarians as one of sexual degeneracy and deviance, we can also trace a yearning for autonomy, pleasure, and freedom.

Freed of the rigid hierarchies of the peasant family or rural farm life, evading the surveillance of social workers or vice squads, proletarians pursued the pleasures of sex. The great cities of industrial capitalism offered historically unprecedented opportunities for casual sex, for sodomy, for anonymous sex, for gender transgression, for exchanging sex for money, for subcultures organized around sexual activity, and much else. Sex in the Great Towns took a broad variety of forms, both consensual and coercive, beautiful and brutal. Within exclusively male and hierarchal spaces, men had a great deal of sex with each other, not uncommonly intergenerational and often nonconsensual. Men across class paid sex workers of all genders. Later in the twentieth century, the experience of same-sex relationships among urban wage workers provided the basis for new self-chosen identities, including the emergence of gay identity—uniquely focused on sexual object choice, rather than gender—in the mid-twentieth century.

Simultaneous with the increasing availability of wage labor, cities also provided the means of surviving for those whose gender and sexual deviancy were too visible for employers to welcome them into wage labor. While wage workers could pursue sodomy in their off hours, those who expressed their deviancy in their gender were often excluded from wage labor. Gender variation is a universal throughout human history; what has changed, during each period of economic development, were the means gender-variant people had to survive, and their place in the social order. Mass urbanization created new spaces for gender-variant people to survive, not through wage labor but through criminalized hustles possible in cities, particularly sex work. Transfeminine proletarians sold sex, hustled, stole, and managed to eke out survival on the margins of the urban capitalist societies.

A lexicon of cross-dressing emerged, as alongside cisgender sex workers other new creatures emerged on the streets of London, Amsterdam, and Paris, all forms of transfeminine gender deviants: Mollies, Mary-Anns, he-she ladies, queens. They sold sex to the bourgeoisie, ran from police, fought in riots, held regular drag balls, worked in one of many brothels specializing in male-assigned sex workers scattered across London. In a well-publicized trial in 1870, Stella and Fanny came to represent the city's thousands of transfeminine sex workers. They were accused in court of "the abominable crime of buggery," using the women's toilets, disturbing the peace, years of sex work, and "chirruping" theatergoers at the Strand. They collected around themselves a rich world of "sisters," other queer trans feminine people with whom they engaged in hobby crafts and romantic intrigue.[6]

Alongside these queer subcultures, young women found wage labor in the industrial cities—first white women in the nineteenth century, and later Black American women in the twentieth—they seized on the freedom and independence to pursue romantic pleasure. There are many accounts of young female factory workers living far from home, frequenting dance clubs, pursuing romantic liaisons, having sex for pleasure. Though subject to the sexual predations of bosses, landlords, or bad dates, many young women saw the space away from family provided by wage labor as a great freedom.

Many proletarian women turned to selling sex, to both bourgeois and proletarian men. Due to the enforcement of the anti-sex worker Contagious Disease Acts in England and the campaign for their repeal, there is a substantial historical archive of documents on the lives of sex workers. This archive demonstrates a fluid integration and exchange between proletarian women in industrial labor and sex work, and sex workers embedded in a network of social ties within working-class communities. Sex work provided higher-paying work than manufacturing, and many proletarian women turned to it sporadically, while maintaining strong and positive ties with their family and neighbors.[7] The Contagious Disease Acts were a part of a state campaign precisely to rupture these ties, isolating sex workers as deviants distant from a respectable working class.

This proliferation of sexual and gender diversity was seen by state agents and bourgeois observers as a threat to public order. The open availability of nonmarital sex, paid and unpaid, was denounced as a threat to the monogamous bourgeois family. This moral panic was not just ideological, argues Chris Chitty in *Sexual Hegemony*.[8] State agents criminalized and punished sodomy as part of new strategies of statecraft, seeking to manage the growing and chaotic masses of urban surplus populations. Same-sex relationships were often cross-class, leaving bourgeois men vulnerable to blackmail and robbery. Both anti-sodomy campaigns and libertine sexual subcultures emerged periodically with the waves of capital accumulation.

RECONSTRUCTION AND BLACK LOVE

Black people in the American South pursued their own radical practices of kin and love. Later in the twentieth century, Black Americans would migrate to cities in large numbers, encountering both the poverty and the sexual opportunities familiar to the new factory workers of the prior century. Some of the pursuit of sexual pleasure by newly urbanized young Black women is richly documented.[9] Prior to this migration in the nineteenth century, Black American life remained primarily trapped in rural life in the South. Yet despite being shut out of urban life and free wage labor, for a period in the last quarter of the nineteenth century, Black people leaped at the opportunity to pursue sexual and romantic freedom.

During the American Civil War, enslaved Black people across the South launched waves of rebellions, forcing the US government to make emancipation increasingly central to the war. In the war's immediate aftermath, the South was initially under the military occupation of federal soldiers unsympathetic to the former slave owners. Newly emancipated Black people seized the moment for an explosive period of social, political, and sexual freedom. This period, termed Black Reconstruction or Radical Reconstruction, saw the formation of hundreds of progressive and radical political organizations among the formerly enslaved. Some of those organizations reached out to join the socialist First International, dominated by Europeans and recent European migrants to the United States. Black people voted in large numbers, and formerly enslaved people entered the US Congress and state legislatures. Black movements pursued massive land redistribution of the South.

Among these experiments in radical, abolitionist democracy, newly emancipated Black proletarians also pursued new forms of family and sexual relationships. Under slavery, Black people had long formed a wide range of heterogeneous, unrecognized, and nontraditional romantic bonds. An enslaved couple who informally married might be forcefully separated, and both spouses might then pursue subsequent romantic relationships without the severe moral prohibition associated with marital infidelity by white women. Similarly, the conditions of slavery led many people to choose self-consciously temporary romantic and cohabiting relationships, then extremely uncommon elsewhere in American society. These experiences of temporary or nonmonogamous relationships outside the narrow bonds of heterosexual marriage were a necessary feature of life under slavery, but in the aftermath of emancipation they informed a new period of romantic experimentation.

During Reconstruction, Black people used these experiences and their new freedom to pursue nontraditional, varied, and temporary couple structures. In government records gathered about Black families after the American Civil War, historians find a diversity of relationship and family structures far more expansive than those of their white contemporaries on farms or in factories. The historical evidence of these relationships comes from a particular government-sponsored bureaucratic endeavor following the Civil War: The wives and children of Union soldiers were eligible to receive pension support. Government agents sought to identify the legitimate wives of formerly enslaved Black soldiers to allocate these cash benefits, and had to make these assessments in the absence of legal marriage. The relationships these government agents encountered among Black people shocked them. Black people expressed wide variation in how they defined their heterosexual relationships, unprecedented elsewhere in American life. They distinguished between "taking up" with a partner, in "sweetheart" or "trial marriages," or relationships where partners were "living together" in some variation of nonmarital, temporary, and often nonmonogamous romance. Couples could co-parent in such temporary arrangements, raising "sweetheart children."[10] Such arrangements by other names may be familiar to Americans today but were unheard of among white families in 1870. Black people even formed polyamorous households, as current couples reunited with past lovers, occasionally welcoming them into the household. One soldier, for example, lived with two women, each of whom had been his wife under slavery based on where he was sent to work during the annual harvest rotation.[11]

As these Reconstruction-era government records were specific to war pensions, they do not include documentation of queer or same-sex relationships. In the conditions of Reconstruction, it seems likely that such relationships existed as well. Emancipated people had historically unprecedented means to try to form households around same-sex relationships not available to others still in a rural, agrarian economy: new access to land and housing partially outside of existing institutions, a social environment radically reshaped by personal experiences of rebellion and freedom, and the lack of a rigid, institutionally enforced set of moral codes associated with most rural communities. It is not hard to imagine, under such conditions, that Black people attempted to form households that included wider gender variation than their white counterparts, and more frequent same-sex couples.

In the face of the extensive variation in romantic cohabitation among emancipated Black people, institutions sought to impose the rigid sexual norms of white America. Government agents, preachers, police, and an emerging respectable stratum of Black people sought to aggressively intervene in such informal unions. Legal marriage was mandated for Black couples receiving a range of federal and church services, and soon Black people were investigated and prosecuted for violating marital laws. Marriage was a right some Black people sought, but it imposed a rigid legal structure that pushed against the experimentation, self-determination, and pleasure that emancipated Black proletarians were pursuing. These legal and religious prohibitions on Black sexual life were only partially effective. Reports of the time suggest that many continued to ignore the admonishments by ministers and government officials. The previous chapter recounted what ultimately homogenized and disciplined Black households: the emergence of Jim Crow land tenancy that imposed and required heterosexual marriage.

ON CHARLES FOURIER

The sex workers of the Paris Commune, the chirruping Mary-Anns of London, and the sweetheart marriages of the newly emancipated all gesture toward another kind of communist emancipation, though they could not leave us the documents theorizing a fully fleshed-out vision. Earlier in the century, however, Charles Fourier had linked anti-capitalist politics to sexual freedom in an extensive body of written work. Fourier was a French merchant and clerk, and a major figure in what has come to be called the utopian socialist tradition. He was born shortly before the French Revolution and published most of his work in the early nineteenth century; he died in 1837. Fourier's writing on the evils of the market, the bourgeois family, and collective communes became tremendously influential on socialist politics of the nineteenth century.

Fourier is best known for three theoretical and political contributions: first, he identified early on that the horrors of poverty were a result of the growing market economy and that socialists needed to abolish markets and private property. This new society would guarantee all a "social minimum," a concept of universal material provision that became central to new socialist thinking. Fourier defines the social minimum as essential to the shared well-being of the coming society: "Finally, in this new order the common people must enjoy a guarantee of well-being, a minimum income sufficient for present and future needs. This guarantee must free them from all anxiety either for their own welfare or that of their dependents."[12]

Second, Fourier was a major proponent of women's rights, seeing the subjugation of women as a cornerstone of bourgeois society, the family, monogamous marriage, and the oppressive social order. He advocated extensively for the social, economic, and sexual rights of women, and is believed to have coined the word *feminism*. He generated the theory, later adopted by Marx and others, that the degree of freedom of a society is best measured by the level of women's emancipation. Fourier was also strongly opposed to the bourgeois family. He saw permanent, irreversible, marital monogamy as a fundamental source of misery, social chaos, and despair: "Could anything better than the isolated household and permanent marriage have been invented to introduce dullness, venality and treachery into relations of love and pleasure?"[13]

Third, Fourier proposed that the solution to the horrors of the market and monogamy was a form of commune he termed the *phalanx*, numbering sixteen hundred people in a vast building of the *phalanstery*. Residents would share in the collective activity of a manufacturing specialty, using their shared effort and collaboration to increase productivity. They would further share in reproductive labor, eating together in large collective meals. Fourierist communes were started throughout the United States and Europe in the 1830s and 1840s. Though not as widely studied as his general call for communes, Fourier's vision was deeply informed by his understanding of human sexuality and erotic pleasure. His vision of the phalanx was embedded in his science of the human passions, a "theory of passionate attraction." Through carefully examining the natural instincts, proclivities, pleasures, and developmental capacities of humans, he argued that humanity could design deliberate communities that perfectly calibrate personality types. Rather than relying on compulsion to maintain social order or productive work, these communities could design "amorous work" to skillfully use pleasure, eroticism, and joy as incentives, so that collective and individual benefit align. "Useless as it is today," he wrote, "love will thus become one of the most brilliant mainsprings of the social mechanism."[14] Fourier's theories of human passions were fundamental to his vision of social harmony:

> We are going to discuss a new amorous order in which sentiment, which is the noble side of love, will enjoy an unparalleled prestige and will endow all social relations with a unique charm. How will sentimental love maintain this dominion? Through the fact that the physical impulses, far from being fettered, will be fully satisfied.[15]

Love and attraction would replace domination as the central social bond of society. As well as a social minimum, Fourier advocated for a "sexual minimum," where the physical, erotic needs of all were guaranteed by their community, allowing each person the freedom to pursue full, authentic love:

> When all the amorous needs of a woman are provided for, when she has all the physical lovers, orgies and bacchanalias (both simple and compound) that she wishes, then there will be ample room in her soul for sentimental illusions. Then she will seek out refined sentimental relationships to counterbalance her physical pleasures.[16]

He was confident that humans are naturally polyamorous, bisexual, and erotically joyful. The free love of the phalanx would be among its greatest appeals, and soon no one would be drawn back to the hypocritical horror of the conjugal family.

Fourier allowed himself a considerable degree of outlandish fancy in his writing on sexual freedom. He went to some length describing the integral role that carefully choreographed orgies would play in future communes. As a parody of the Catholic Church, he described a new, voluntary clerical hierarchy based on sexual skill, sexual selflessness, and the capacity to bring sexual pleasure to the least desired in society. As a replacement for the horrors of war, he imagined roving armies of amorous youth competitively demonstrating their erotic prowess on battlefields. Those who were sufficiently awed would signal their defeat by submitting themselves to voluntary erotic bondage and orchestrated sexual punishments for a limited duration. This initial orgy is disrupted by the intervention of same-sex desire: "To break up the skirmish, use should be made of a divisive agent. Since everything is done by attraction in Harmony, mixed or homosexual attractions should be employed. Groups of Sapphists and Spartites should therefore be thrown into the fray to attack people of their own kind."[17] This allows the sexual priesthood to issue their recommendations for the most compatible romantic pairings, as "the goal of Harmony is to establish compound amorous relationships based on both physical and spiritual affinities. Thus while the opening sensual skirmish is indispensable, it is only a prelude."[18]

Fourier, in short, was a delightfully kinky science fiction writer, and an inspiration to imagining pro-queer communes of the future. Fourier's work can provoke in us not only a concrete alternative to the family as a unit of social reproduction, but also an open-ended erotic desire for a better mode of life we have yet to discover. Writing in 1808, Fourier describes the immediate proximity of the complete revolution in all social relations:

Do not be misled by superficial people who think that the invention of the laws of Movement is just a theoretical calculation. Remember that it only requires four or five months to put it into practice over a square league, an attempt which could even be completed by next summer, with the result that the whole human race would move into universal harmony, so your behavior should be governed from now on by the ease and proximity of this immense revolution.[19]

Though like most past revolutionaries, he misjudged how long it may take us to reach his imagined utopia, he is right that communism is always immanent to the present, as the real movement to abolish the existing order of things.

* * *

Recognizing the proliferation of sexual deviancy and family heterogeneity in working-class life of the nineteenth century gestures toward a different kind of gender politics than what the socialist movement ultimately pursued. There was another trajectory out of the crisis of working-class social reproduction, hinted at by Black families seeking to live together outside the narrow respectability of legal marriage, transfeminine Mary-Anns heckling theatergoers, and sailors and factory workers fucking in alleyways. These other queers pursued the abolishing of the working-class family. These proletarian deviants moved toward a different kind of queer communism, one lost over the subsequent decades of the workers' movement.

Engels accuses Fourier of utopian socialism, arguing that Fourier and others like him lacked the understanding of the agent of the proletariat to pursue and win socialism. The Marxist movement would come to view the industrial worker as the pivotal figure in such a transition. But what Engels observed in his years in Manchester was not a unified, homogenous proletarian mass disciplined by factory life, but a cacophony of crime and social chaos. Proliferating proletarian sexual deviances suggest a form of communist agency moving toward Fourier's queer communism, rather than Engels's naturalization of monogamy. Unfortunately, the sexual freedom evoked by the lumpenproletariat and emancipated Black workers would not be the path taken by the socialist movement. The next chapter traces the gender conservatism that would come to dominate the socialist movement through its pursuit of the bourgeois family form.

7

The Family Form of the Workers' Movement

In the last two decades of the nineteenth century, the politics of the family in the industrial centers of capitalism went through a massive shift, one that persisted into much of the twentieth century. These changes were enabled by the changing conditions of capitalist accumulation, new forms of state power, and a substantial infrastructure of working-class organization. With them emerged new patterns of working-class family life. Whereas Marx and Engels saw the monogamous, nuclear family as referring only to bourgeois society, the emerging workers' movement began to advance the family wage as a central demand.

The family wage provided a limited access to a new regime of respectable working-class family life. The characteristic family form of this new workers' movement was the male breadwinner, with a housewife, modeled after the family form of the bourgeoisie. This particular family form was a central aspiration and occasional achievement of the workers' movement's struggle for respectability, state power, and self-differentiation from the poor. In chapter 5 I detailed how this normative family form was imposed on Black and Indigenous life.

During this period of the workers' movement, family abolition and the communist struggle against the family took on new meanings and new directions. Alexandra Kollontai, a leader of the Russian Revolution, led a concerted and large-scale effort to abolish the family. Her thought, and the unfolding family dynamics of revolutionary Russia, reflected both the possibilities and limits of the workers' movement.

THE THESIS OF THE WORKERS' MOVEMENT

This book's historical account periodizes proletarian struggle using a particular concept of *the workers' movement*. One current of communist political thought, occasionally termed *communization theory*, uses this concept to refer to a specific and particular form of proletarian rebellion, limited in time and scope.[1] The concept of the workers' movement was more extensively articulated in this sense by the French communist theory collective Théorie Communiste (TC) in a series of articles from the mid-1970s, the group's inception, to today. Since 2008 an Anglophone collective *Endnotes* has taken up and developed the concept. Throughout this book I use the theoretical framework offered by the various contributors and anonymous editors of *Endnotes* over their five published journal issues. Though obscure, the collected work of the *Endnotes* journal and collective is one of the most challenging and rich readings available of the history of the socialist movement.

For Marx, the proletarian struggle for communism meant seeking to abolish class society, and thus destroy the social relations that constituted the working class. The task of the proletariat as a revolutionary class, for Marx and much of the early communist movement, was its self-abolition. According to TC, *Endnotes*, and my own historical research, in the 1880s and 1890s a new and distinct articulation of working-class struggle took shape that often identified itself as Marxist but offered a contrasting understanding of socialist society. The new workers' movement no longer meaningfully imagined the vision of full communism suggested by Marx, one where wages, money, and the class relation itself have been overcome.

Instead, the workers' movement constituted itself through affirming a working-class identity, based on what we may now call working-class pride. The advocates of the workers' movement argued that their status as the working class provided the shared basis of struggle. This working-class identity offered a means of collective organizing, constituting formal organizations of struggle, and a vision of revolutionary society as the "emancipation of labor," the rule of the working class over the whole of society. The working class can struggle, in this conception, because it is already partially autonomous, able to act independently from capitalist relations. TC criticized the workers' movement as unable to grasp that the very basis of the existence of the autonomous, affirmative working class is only constituted through its relation to capital and within the logic of capitalist development.[2]

Rather than destroying the capitalist system of value, abstract labor, and wages, the workers' movement argued that these forms could provide the basis for workers' emancipation. This new workers' movement sought to create a workers' society. The workers' movement called for a socialist society ruled over by wage workers, where the interdependence and cooperation of the factory become the basis of society as a whole. This vision, shared across the anti-capitalist political spectrum, sought to found a socialist society on the experience of industrial labor. The movement conceived the emancipation of the wage laborer as being the generalization of wage labor across the vast majority of society—making everyone into a worker. This would include the destruction or subordination of the capitalist class and the proletarianization of the peasantry through economic development.[3] The workers' movement's widespread appeal depended on the steady expansion of a particular form of work: wage labor, engaged in productive manufacturing, based in factories. It was on the experience of the factory that the workers' movement conceived of the basis of struggle and the nature of a free society. So long as global capitalism saw the steady expansion of this form of industrial work in both relative and abstract terms, large sectors of the working class, organizing through the workers' movement, could imagine inevitable victory. It was the economic development of industrial capitalism that enabled the shared vision of the workers' movement.

This new articulation rapidly spread to encompass nearly the entirety of European communists, anarchists, and socialists. It was, in this sense, what TC and communization theory call a *horizon*, an implicit vision of revolutionary change shared by otherwise opposed anti-capitalist political tendencies. It describes an essential feature of every major communist tendency of the following decades: Kautsky and the Second International's vision of a gradual democratic takeover of society, Lenin and the Bolsheviks' plan for revolutionary Russia, anarchists and council communists who opposed state socialism, or class-collaborationist postwar social democrats. The horizon of the workers' movement was shared by the most revolutionary and the most reformist, the most democratic and the most authoritarian. It provided the shared assumptions of working-class organizing from the last decade of the nineteenth century until the global rebellions of the late 1960s and the economic crisis of the mid-1970s.

The workers' movement, by basing its vision on the experience of wage labor and factory production, created a long series of internal oppositions and divisions within the proletariat—distinctions that adopted and accentuated the divisions introduced by the capitalist mode of production. TC describes the limits of workers' identity:

> This is the conflictual situation which developed as workers' identity—an identity which found its distinction and its immediate modalities of recognition (its confirmation) in the "large factory," in the dichotomy between employment and unemployment, work and training, in the submission of the labor process to the collectivity of workers, in the link between wages, growth and productivity on a national level, in the institutional representations that all this implied, as much in the factory as at the level of the state, and, last but not least, in the social and cultural legitimacy and pride in being a worker.[4]

The workers' movement created a new identity to contrast and distinguish itself from the poor, the unwaged, the unemployed, or the nonworker. This split the proletariat into two distinct categories still with us today: the respectable worker proud of their work, and the very poor, an unneeded and shameful surplus of society. It was through the workers' movement and its new divisions that the lumpenproletariat became the despised and excluded enemies of the working class. The family was essential to this distinction.

For readers more familiar with queer theory or Black studies than communization, one way of explaining the thesis of the workers' movement draws parallels with recent critiques: it was the invention of a respectability politics for the working class. Marx and Engels saw the proletariat destined to liberate the world, but their theory made little recourse to the dignity of labor or of working-class life. By the 1890s and lasting into the 1970s, a socialist vision took hold that asserted that the working class could govern the whole of society. This working class defined itself as respectable, as capable of governing either through suffrage or a workers' state. This definition depended on an opposition to other sections of the class: those who were very poor, incarcerated, criminalized, deviant, queer, unwaged, or racialized.

THE HOUSEWIFE-BASED FAMILY FORM

The workers' movement forged a new family norm in pursuit of respectability and legitimacy. The family norm had once been available only to the bourgeoisie, but through the advances of the workers' movement it became available to a stratum of white workers. This characteristic family norm of the workers' movement had a number of essential characteristics: the single male wage earner supporting an unwaged housewife, their children enrolled in schooling, their home a respectable center of moral and sexual conformity. The workers' movement struggled for and, for some, won this family form during its period of ascendency. This male-breadwinner family form, coupled with the parallel economic and political victories of the workers' movement, contributed to new stable conditions for sustained generational working-class social reproduction. Even among working-class families unable to economically achieve removing a wife or mother from the labor market entirely, key elements of this family form became essential to an emergent working-class respectability that had been rare in the previous era: not living with other families; seeking single-family dwellings when possible; men assuming control over the household finances; and wives assuming full responsibility of unwaged reproductive labor. The flip side of the isolation and privacy provided by the dwellings of the respectable family was obscuring parental abuse from scrutiny or intervention.

This family form was a tremendous victory in improving the standard of living and survival of millions of working-class people. It created a basis for stable neighborhood organization, sustained socialist struggle, and major political victories. Yet more insidiously, it was also the means by which the workers' movement would distinguish itself from the lumpenproletariat, Black workers, and queers. It would provide a sexual and gendered basis for white American identity and middle-class property owner-ship. The accessibility of this family form expanded dramatically for white American and European wage workers in the 1880s and 1890s, and it became the dominant family form in many stable working-class neighborhoods. Several factors created the condi-tions for the male-breadwinner norm in the industrial centers of the United States and Europe: raised wages, cheaper commodities, centralization of industrial production, reduction in child labor, and new municipal infrastructure.[5]

Trade unions, workers' parties, and liberal bourgeois social reformers, aided by the threat of disruptive working-class insur-gency, won a series of regulations and public infrastructure developments that dramatically improved working-class life. Trade union agitation and organization won significant wage increases and a growing wage share, enabling an overall improvement in the standard of living. Higher wages enabled a single-wage-earner household, distinguishing the respectable working class from the lumpenproletariat. The male-breadwinner family aspiration provided a symbolic solidarity between workers, employers, and state officials. Trade unions explicitly used the demand of a "family wage" through the 1890s as a legitimating basis for higher wages. This call resonated with their progressive bourgeois allies precisely because it demonstrated bourgeois family aspirations on the part of the working class.

Coupled with higher male wages, trade unions organized for the exclusion of women from their industry as a means of prevent-ing competition and falling wages. They won a series of successful exclusions in the 1880s and 1890s. Male workers had a rational basis to exclude women's employment: where unions were unable to prevent the spread of women's employment, wages fell dramat-ically due to increased labor supply and women's lower pay. Better employment opportunities for working-class men than women, in turn, made it more rational for working-class families to focus their energies on maximizing wage work for the adult male mem-bers of the household.

Alongside this political advance for higher wages, capitalist competition improved production techniques, driving down the value of consumer goods. Even without wage increases, cheaper commodity products increased buying power, and hence real wages, improving the standard of living of all wage workers. Concurrently, manufacturers gradually shifted production out of the home and consolidated it within factories, ending the putting-out system through which mothers worked for pay in the home. The niche of paid work for mothers disappeared, leading to mothers increasingly engaging in unwaged reproductive labor. Without waged activities that could be done in the home, paid work for most women increasingly took place only before childbirth or as the children aged. This growing division between the factory and the home consolidated a particular gendered, subjective understanding of work, masculinizing wage labor and feminizing unwaged reproductive labor.

In addition, as employers sought to more fully control the work process and eliminate work teams, they significantly reduced the employment of children. A shift away from team-based work increasingly coincided with the mounting political campaign to restrict child labor and children's work hours. As children left the factories, they went into new systems of compulsory public schools, which further indoctrinated them in bourgeois family and sexual ideals. Pushed by socialist organizing, municipal governments built the infrastructure—running water and sewage systems, safe housing, and trollies as mass transit—for these new respectable working-class neighborhoods. These changes dramatically lowered disease and mortality. Transit enabled working-class people to live further from their factories, improving their living conditions by reducing overcrowding. Running water and sewage improved health and allowed workers to adopt more intensive personal hygiene practices, which further distinguished them from the poor. Through better hygiene, working-class people led healthier lives and shared in some of the respectability of the bourgeoisie. Together, these factors converged to enable working-class families to adopt a male-breadwinner form, providing a sexual and gender foundation for an affirmative working-class identity. In family budgets from 1873 to 1914, all layers of the working class in Europe saw a significant rise in the share of family income provided by a single adult male, often stabilizing around 70 to 80 percent. The consolidation of this male-breadwinner norm appears as a U-shaped trough of the economic activity of married women, bottoming out between 1910 and 1920, even without considering the decline of putting-out waged work within the home.[6]

RESPECTABILITY AND THE WORKING-CLASS FAMILY

The respectability afforded to the workers' movement through the male-breadwinner family form had great benefits. Among these benefits, working-class people could claim a previously unavailable respectable dignity by media, elites, and professional and bourgeois classes. Working-class people throughout European and American industrialization—including white workers—were often characterized as biologically subhuman, fundamentally inferior in intelligence and cultural capacity, and utterly unfit to participate in any form of governance. This hostility to working-class people bled into racial subjugation and ideology, as notions of inherent genetic inferiority were weaponized against Black, Asian, Mexican, Jewish, and Irish workers. For the workers' movement, achieving respectability in the eyes of some members of the ruling capitalist class, and dignity in their own self-conception, was a major material achievement. This respectability was a crucial and necessary plank in a broader and ultimately effective struggle across Europe to achieve the right to vote and participate in government, to legalize trade union activity, to decriminalize many elements of working-class life, and to dramatically improve people's standard of living, creating a long-term decline in infant mortality. For many, such respectability was a step in a long-term revolutionary struggle toward full socialism and full emancipation. Today, *respectability* often connotes political conservatism; for many in the workers' movement in the early twentieth century, it was a means to substantial political power and a revolutionary socialist remaking of society, whoever it may also have left behind.

This male-breadwinner family form served as a measure and marker of respectability. Families where mothers continued to work for pay inside or outside the home faced condemnation from their neighbors, and increasingly social exclusion. Male workers, meanwhile, began to link the ability to support their families to a patriarchal sense of pride, accomplishment, and self-respect. Workers pursued this family structure as a way of claiming a moral dimension to their wages, legitimizing pro-worker legislation to bourgeois politicians. Against the functionalism of some Marxist feminist theory, there is little evidence that the male-breadwinner family form was an inevitable outcome of capitalist development, nor that it was engineered and implemented by employers at the end of the nineteenth century. The majority of employers lacked direct control over workers' nonwork hours, choice of family, or domestic arrangements. The working-class family was not engineered by capitalists to serve their interests. Outside of cases of company towns in geographically isolated areas, employers seem to not have struggled for such control. Nor was it a matter of the inevitable expansion of bourgeois family values in working-class life. Key elements of bourgeois families, including inheritance, had little or no relevance for the vast majority of proletarians. This family form was a contingent outcome of class struggle.

Many working-class families were left behind. The bottom tiers of wage workers never achieved a level of income allowing them to survive on a single wage, requiring mothers to continue to pursue informal waged work where they could get it, or balance jobs with child-rearing, suffering the judgment from their better-off neighbors. Workers could favorably contrast their lot to both the lumpenproletariat and colonial subjects. This was a logic of racial heteronormativity, one that also excluded sexual deviants and sex workers from the developing self-conception of the respectable working class. Through the rise of the workers' movement, the family was no longer understood primarily as a bourgeois institution but came to represent and demarcate the distinction between "civilized" white people and "uncivilized" others. The previous social integration of sex workers and proletarian queers with the rest of the class in the mid-nineteenth century disappeared. Sexual deviants increasingly became pariahs excluded from respectable working-class life. The sexual mores of the bourgeois were taken up by socialists and workers broadly, splitting the working class.

CONTRADICTIONS OF THE FAMILY IN
THE SECOND INTERNATIONAL

The workers' movement had a two-sided approach to family politics. The normative pursuit of a male-breadwinner form was in tension with another, contradictory impulse that shaped the movement's struggles over gender: seeing socialist equality as dependent on a shared experience of wage work. This impulse provided an internal basis for asserting the positive abolition of the family through women's employment and collectivizing reproductive labor. The tension between the legitimacy and stability provided by the male-breadwinner family form to the socialist movement, and the equality of universal employment, shaped the debates and struggles over the family regarding the course of the workers' movement.

Regardless of their position on women's employment, socialists of the Second International entirely abandoned the call to abolish the family. Karl Kautsky, the most influential theorist of Europe's largest mass socialist party, the German Social Democratic Party (SPD), explained that while capitalism was undermining the working-class family, everyone could be assured socialists would never politically attack it: "One of the most widespread prejudices against socialism rests upon the notion that it proposes to abolish the family. No socialist has the remotest idea of abolishing the family, that is, legally and forcibly dissolving it. Only the grossest misrepresentation can fasten upon socialism any such intention."[7]

Housewives became the main organizers of working-class neighborhoods and social organizations, without challenging the family form itself. They were integral to building the infrastructure of working-class social life that spread across industrial Europe. The moral legitimacy afforded to this family structure was also a means through which the workers' movement was able to extend its reach beyond the workplace into society as a whole. The working-class nuclear family form and its accompanying stable working-class neighborhoods became a primary mechanism for extending the power of trade unions into social life, constituting the depth of the workers' movement and its identities.

The importance of the family in creating the workers' movement as a mass movement beyond the workplace was evidenced by the vast infrastructure of the SPD. The large numbers of women in the SPD built out its neighborhood infrastructure as the most active volunteer organizers. In turn-of-the-century Germany, the best-selling socialist book was not the *Manifesto* or Kautsky's *Erfurt Program* but August Bebel's *Woman and Socialism*, in which Bebel recounts the long history of gender oppression and foretells a coming socialist future of gender equality. Though he has little to say on the debates about women's work or the family, his vision of women's equality under socialism was popular and compelling. Gender oppression was the dominant concern of the mass base of the largest socialist organization of the Second International, precisely because gender was a main form through which proletarians understood both capitalist oppression and socialist emancipation. Many key leaders of the SPD were women, including socialist intellectuals and leaders like Clara Zetkin and Rosa Luxemburg. Eleanor Marx, daughter of Karl Marx and a socialist leader herself, was well respected in the British section of the International. Though there was substantial disagreement on how the SPD should relate to women's issues, women eagerly pursued the study of women's equality and advocated successfully for the SPD to include an uncompromising women's rights platform.

The problem of women's employment was central to socialist debates. Women's proponents in the Second International argued over whether women's labor-force participation was growing or falling, whether women in industry were detrimental to the cause of the class, whether housewives constituted an important sector for organizing, and whether women's employment was essential to their equality. Rosa Luxemburg, holding down one pole of these debates, centered her claims to women's rights solely based on women's workforce participation rates. Women were political subjects, Luxemburg argued, precisely because they worked. This reflected a major current of women within the Second International who viewed wage work as the sole route to gender equality. Luxemburg saw the rights of proletarian women as fundamentally dependent on their labor market participation: "Today, millions of proletarian women create capitalist profit like men—in factories, workshops, on farms, in home industry, offices, stores. ... And thus, every day and every step of industrial progress adds a new stone to the firm foundation of women's equal political rights."[8] Other socialists saw the achieving of equality through women's labor market participation as too costly, advocating that socialists pursue limits on women's waged work. Clara Zetkin writes against women's employment: "New barriers need to be erected against the exploitation of the proletarian woman. Her rights as wife and mother need to be restored and permanently secured."[9]

The respectability of a housewife-based family was deeply compelling to socialists envisioning a workers' society. The male-breadwinner family, and its accompanying neighborhood, embodied the social respectability on which the SPD based its claims to fitness for rule. Many workers' movement papers celebrated "good socialist wives" who raise "good socialist children."[10] Socialist debates and propaganda regarding women most often highlighted issues faced by housewives, including consumer prices, neighborhood conditions, housing, schooling, power dynamics with their husbands, the allocation of wages within the household, gendered decision-making within worker organizations, and women's suffrage.

RACIAL DIVISION OF THE AMERICAN WORKERS' MOVEMENT

The United States followed a parallel but distinct trajectory in consolidating a working-class family norm during the workers' movement, one interwoven with white supremacy. Chapter 5 discussed two ways that imposing the nuclear family through access to land became a powerful tool of white supremacy: requiring marriage for cotton land tenancy during Jim Crow, and in the distribution of tribal lands to male heads of Native American households through allotment policy. Though excluded from the workers' movement of the late nineteenth and early twentieth centuries, Black proletarians still experienced a narrowing of family forms. While white workers pursued and won this normative family form through greater social power, it was violently imposed on Black and Indigenous people. In both cases, a model of the normative family came to shape working-class life in new ways toward the end of the nineteenth century.

At the end of the century, most Americans worked in agriculture. The Northeast was industrializing rapidly, with a booming manufacturing sector and white workforces largely organized through their European immigrant identities. The Midwest was home to small, white family-operated independent farms that were settled following the genocidal wars against Native American nations. The Southwest, seized from Mexico mid century, saw an influx of white settlers working in mining, growing crops, and raising livestock following the completion of the railroads integrating the region economically with the rest of the United States.[11] The infrastructure of railroads was built by the Chinese and Mexican workers facing violent and brutal subjugation.[12]

The American workers' movement was shaped by these logics of white supremacy. During the nineteenth and early twentieth centuries, cross-class white racial identity obstructed the consolidation of a major labor movement. The settler colonial seizure of land westward offered white workers the opportunity of class mobility and provided a possibility of escape and independence from wage labor. White identity, even for proletarians, was constituted through the real or imagined possibility of property ownership and identification with the country's major landowners. These racialized dynamics of the American workers' movement shaped working-class family forms. For white workers, the workers' movement offered the means to establish patriarchal families based on social status, property ownership, and respectability. For both white family-based farmers and white urban workers, achieving and maintaining conventional family norms was increasingly integral to this respectability. In short, for the American workers' movement of the turn of the twentieth century, whiteness, the male-breadwinner family, and respectability were interwoven.

White Americans through the nineteenth century enjoyed an expanding frontier of conquest and new settlement that allowed and encouraged stable family formation. Many of these family farmers were drawn to the Socialist Party and other leftist populisms but were unable to untangle their class consciousness from a committed defense of property ownership, settler colonialism, and white independence. White unions of the late nineteenth century saw the reproduction and defense of white supremacy as integral to benefiting their membership. The strongest unions of the period were rooted in the all-white skilled trades, well before the later rise of multiracial industrial unionism in the twentieth century. These unions largely shared the gender conservatism of capitalists and independent farmers. Like their European counterparts, these white skilled workers aggressively pursued—and by the end of the nineteenth century, largely obtained—access to a family wage securing a housewife-based family structure. For a time, white workers in both the United States and Europe were able to partially achieve the housewife family form.

This racial stratification of the workers' movement continued into the twentieth century. When an industrial labor movement did finally gain strength in the 1930s, it was unable to secure a foothold in particularly brutal white supremacist regimes of the states of the Southeast and Southwest. These regions today are largely "right to work" states without legal protections for labor union organizing.

Family stability came under pressure during the two world wars. With men on the front lines and women drawn into industrial employment, the gender norms of white America were temporarily upended. The military and war industries were gender segregated and mildly tolerant of homosexuality, and underground and extensive communities of American gays formed for the first time.[13] Americans during World War II experienced a radically new gender order: organized through full proletarianization, the breakup of the family, increased space for homosexuality and women's rights, and massive state control. Newly proletarianized people not yet integrated into a stable heteronormative working-class identity found an unprecedented degree of sexual freedom during the wartime years, coupled with new tyrannies of industrial wage labor and state control. These world wars also provided many African Americans their first access to nonagricultural employment, aiding migration out of the rural South and toward greater political independence. As African Americans left the farms and moved into wage labor from World War I on, they found an uneven reception in the American workers' movement.

Among the demands and successes of the post–World War II civil rights movement, African Americans finally won inclusion in many American trade unions. Anti-racist trade unions attempted to pursue an alternative vision of postwar America, building racially integrated suburban housing around major unionized factories. But white American workers were still not united in their interest in cross-racial solidarity; many were as likely to defend their interests through nativism, xenophobia, and racism as through class solidarity.

ABOLISHING THE FAMILY IN
THE RUSSIAN REVOLUTION

The demand to abolish the family took on a different and new meaning during the workers' movement. While much of the workers' movement abandoned the call to abolish the family, the other tendency toward full proletarianization offered a path to envisioning the overcoming of the working-class nuclear family. Rather than a communist struggle to abolish the bourgeois society, the new form of family abolition called for full proletarianization of women's work through the collectivization of reproductive labor. The previous chapter traced the dominant family form of the workers' movement from the 1880s into the mid-twentieth century. Here I focus on one moment, at the close of World War I: the early years of the Russian Revolution. The Russian Revolution offered the one mass effort to abolish the family firmly within the logic of the workers' movement.

Russia's small industrial working class had not achieved the respectable housewife-based lifestyle of some of their counterparts in Germany and England. Initially the Bolsheviks showed no concern for encouraging such family forms. Instead, Lenin and the leadership of the Bolshevik Party became convinced that the full mobilization of women was crucial to the success and survival of the Russian Revolution. The Bolsheviks implemented a broad and extensive set of pro-women policies, far surpassing those existing elsewhere. The Bolsheviks mandated easy divorce, gender equality in the law, and access to abortion. Informed by progressive sexology, the Bolsheviks also implemented a similarly comprehensive set of pro-gay legislation, including abolishing all anti-sodomy laws, a historically unprecedented move. For a period, postrevolutionary Soviet Russia led the world in women's equality.

Alexandra Kollontai took a leading role in various posts in the early Soviet government, including heading departments of social welfare and women's work. Kollontai offers an immensely compelling and developed vision of family abolition. Kollontai pushed for state institutions to assume responsibility for raising children, feeding the working class, doing laundry, cleaning homes, and all other forms of housework and generational reproduction. Kollontai called for the abolition of the family as an economic unit through collectivizing reproductive labor:

> The communist economy does away with the family. In the period of the dictatorship of the proletariat there is a transition to the single production plan and collective social consumption, and the family loses its significance as an economic unit. The external economic functions of the family disappear, and consumption ceases to be organized on an individual family basis, a network of social kitchens and canteens is established, and the making, mending and washing of clothes and other aspects of housework are integrated into the national economy.[14]

The collectivization of reproductive labor was particularly central as the material mechanism of this abolition. The "workers' state will come to replace the family" even in child-rearing, through the steady expansion of kindergartens, children's colonies, and crèches.[15] Kollontai saw this transformation of reproductive labor as a means to fundamentally change gender and sexual relations in Russia and establish full gender equality: "No more domestic bondage for women. No more inequality within the family. No need for women to fear being left without support and with children to bring up. The woman in communist society no longer depends upon her husband but on her work."[16] Kollontai had her own evolving vision of what sexuality and gender might be like following such a social revolution in domestic life, including deeply egalitarian gender relationships, increasing rights of sexual minorities, and novel forms of organizing intimate relationships and romance. If all reproductive labor is fully collectivized, the family ceases to have any economic function and becomes solely a personal choice.

But Kollontai's vision of women's emancipation was one with a cost integral to the workers' movement's vision of socialist transition: the universalization of wage labor under state authority. Kollontai was explicit that the family had to be abolished precisely because it drained society of the resources that workers should instead devote to labor: "The state does not need the family, because the domestic economy is no longer profitable: the family distracts the worker from more useful and productive labor."[17] Kollontai's vision replaced the family with the factory as the social unity of reproduction, replacing patriarchy with a new tyranny of work and state. In this regard, Kollontai's vision of family abolition reflects the core limits of the workers' movement. Women could escape the family, the drudgery of household chores, and the tyranny of their husbands—but they could only do so by becoming workers, by subjecting themselves to wage labor. This entire process, implied in Kollontai's work, would lead to the massive consolidation of the power in the hands of the state. Where Marx and the communist movement had once offered a powerful critique of the misery of work and the rule of the state, for Kollontai—as for the entirety of the workers' movement—they are the only viable route to equality.

Lenin supported Kollontai's efforts as collectivizing reproduction labor as means of immediate survival. But she was alone among the Bolshevik leadership in aspiring to permanently transform Russian families. With the end of the civil war in 1922, the Bolshevik government withdrew support from efforts to collectivize domestic labor, maintaining only those like crèches that directly enabled women to work in the factories and fields. Kollontai was briefly a leader in the Workers' Opposition opposing the bureaucratization of Bolshevik rule. As Stalin consolidated power, however, she accommodated herself and stopped objecting to his policies. By 1933 Stalin had recriminalized homosexuality, rolled back the legal right to divorce, and introduced pronatalist policies that encouraged nuclear family formation. Kollontai spent her later years in the 1940s living as an ambassador in Sweden apparently loyal to the Stalinist government, not opposing herself to the reimposition of gender inequality and the consolidation of the nuclear family in the Soviet Union.

In the policies of the Bolsheviks, we again we see the core contradiction concerning the family for the workers' movement: the claim to socialist equality and progress through proletarianization is in tension with the claim to legitimacy and stability through the nuclear family. Where the SPD tended toward the latter, the Russian Revolution swung from one pole to the next.

* * *

The workers' movement lasted from the 1880s and 1890s into the 1970s, arguably peaking in power in European social democracy, state socialism in Asia and Eastern Europe, and in the prosperity of white American suburbs. During its period of strength, the housewife-based family form of the workers' movement provided a period of stability to gender and sexual regulation. For white workers this family form was an achievement; for Black workers and Indigenous people it was an imposition. Even Kollontai's efforts to overcome the family remained firmly within the logic of the workers' movement, pursued through full proletarianization, through subjecting all to the tyranny of work. The next chapter turns to the final years of the workers' movement, when a global working-class rebellion sought to fulfill the workers' movement's promises by extending its benefits to those previously excluded. These rebellions of the late 1960s and early 1970s pushed against the limits and constraints of the workers' movement but were unable to escape beyond its logic. Among the limits of the workers' movement that militants refused and sought to overcome, they again sought to abolish the family.

8

Rebellions of the Red Decade

By the end of the 1960s, proletarians globally were in rebellion. Civil wars, street riots, and mass student and worker strikes swept every continent. These rebellions were manifold, pursuing overlapping struggles against imperialism, colonial apartheid, state oppression, gender domination, and capitalism. Following the usage of the phrase in France, I refer to this period of rebellion in the late 1960s and early 1970s as *the Red Decade*. In the United States, the Black freedom struggle successfully toppled the interlocking racial system of legal subordination and violent terror that constituted Jim Crow. The movement continued and escalated through riots, Black Power organizations, militant protest, and institutionalized advocacy. This next phase of Black struggle confronted the conditions of concentrated urban poverty, exclusion from the benefits of the workers' movement, and the state violence of policing and incarceration. By 1970 a new form of rebellion emerged, drawing on the strategies and analysis of the Black freedom struggle, now challenging the gender and sexual regime of the workers' movement. These feminist and queer radicals sought the abolition of the male-breadwinner, heterosexual nuclear family form as a means toward full sexual and gender freedom.

The Red Decade was a unique conjuncture in the history of the workers' movement. Those previously excluded from the benefits of the workers' movement sought to claim its promises for their own: Black Americans demanded access to employment, unions, and welfare benefits; women also fought their way into the labor movement and socialist organizations; queers demanded to be counted as allies in the revolution. The Red Decade was also a radical critique and effort to go beyond the limits of the workers' movement. Rebellions of the period pursued a liberatory politics that also refused the drudgery of work, the racial discipline by welfare departments, the sexual conservatism of the housewife family form, or the stagnant bureaucratization of socialist states. Many radicals rejected altogether the basic coordinates of the workers' movement, seeing in union bureaucracies and socialist states the continuation of oppressive alienation. Yet in important ways, these struggles largely remained within the logic of the workers' movement, unable to forge an entirely novel revolutionary horizon. By 1974 the rebellions of the Red Decade were co-opted or defeated, followed almost immediately—traced in the next chapter—by the beginnings of a multidecade decimation of the workers' movement itself under the pressures of protracted capitalist crisis. During the peak years of the Red Decade, three overlapping rebellions against the gender and sexual conformity of the workers' movement emerged in this era: radical feminism, gay liberation, and Black women's organizing. They revolted against the male-breadwinner family form and the gender and sexual regimes it implied. They rejected the sexual politics of the workers' movement through three principal challenges: to the masculinity embraced by the Left, to the heterosexual nuclear family and the miseries of suburban life, and to the centrality of work itself.

SEX RADICALS

Gays and lesbians exploded into militant visibility at the end of the 1960s, launching radical political organizations that embraced anti-imperialism, socialism, gender transgression, and eroticism. In 1970 gay liberation groups rapidly grew in the major cities of the United States, Great Britain, France, Germany, and Italy. They shared a commitment to the liberating power of erotic joy. Gay revolutionaries like Mario Mieli in Italy, Guy Hocquenghem in France, and David Fernbach in Britain all envisioned eros as a potentially liberating source of human freedom, reflecting a broad sentiment in gay liberationist circles. Eros was repressed and subordinated by the capitalist mode of production, rigidly constrained by heterosexuality and the suburban nuclear family, and was unleashed in the transgressive potential of anal sex. It was erotic solidarity, more than any shared essential identity, that would provide the praxis for a gay communism.

Trans and gender nonconforming people of color, largely lumpenproletarian sex workers, played a leading militant role in the riot at Compton's Cafeteria in San Francisco in 1966, in the Stonewall riots in New York in 1969, and then as a visible presence in the Gay Liberation Front through groups like Street Transvestite Action Revolutionaries (STAR). During a time of political ferment and social toil, Latina and Black trans women played a particularly dramatic and influential role in constituting an insurgent, insurrectionist pole of emerging queer politics. Trans sex workers of color Marsha P. Johnson, Sylvia Ray Rivera, and Miss Major Griffin-Gracy all became legends of the Stonewall Rebellion and fierce opponents to the taming of gay politics through the 1970s. Rivera reflected later on the marginalization and militancy of trans people in the Stonewall Rebellion:

> We were all involved in different struggles, including myself and many other transgender people. But in these struggles, in the Civil Rights movement, in the war movement, in the women's movement, we were still outcasts. The only reason they tolerated the transgender community in some of these movements was because we were gung-ho, we were front liners. We didn't take no shit from nobody. We had nothing to lose.[1]

Among queers in major US cities from the late 1950s on, trans women of color were the most starkly visible members of urban sexual minority social networks, leaving them the most vulnerable to street harassment and violence. They served as the consistent foil representing deviant queerness for police, mainstreaming gays, and gender radicals alike. Trans women of color were—and largely continue to be, today—almost entirely excluded from formal wage labor, instead surviving through street-based sex work and crime. These women likely numbered in the hundreds in many American major cities, but acted as the central figures in a broader underworld of thousands of motley lumpenproletariat queers, including other non-passing gender deviants, homeless queer people, queer people with drug addictions, sex workers, and gay criminals.

Gender and sexual radicals experimented with a range of new approaches to sexual pleasure and family arrangements, including celibacy, free love, exclusive homosexuality, group living, open relationships, banning monogamy, and much else. Similarly, youth rebellions of the late 1960s, even when neither feminist nor queer, advanced a radical commitment to nonregulated sexual pleasure outside the logic of the workers' movement and the society it had helped build. Such sexual and gender experimentation were a feature of some male-dominated Far-Left organizing projects, early lesbian feminist collectives, and gay liberationist groups and their associated queer subcultural scenes. University students fighting the banning of overnight male visitors at a women's dorm, for example, helped spark the May 1968 rebellion in France. Free love, nonmarital casual sex, and birth control were central to the countercultural hippie youth movements of the 1960s, which evidenced a thoroughgoing rejection of alienated society. Militant cadre-based anti-imperialist groups, like the Weatherman and later the George Jackson Brigade, incorporated strong rejections of the monogamous couple form, to mixed success.[2] Militant memoirs and short-lived communes of the era evidence a blossoming discovery of sex as a source of pleasure, freedom, and connection.

The gender and sexual movements of the Red Decade advanced a renewed call to abolish the family. In this demand, they recognized the centrality of the family to the regimes of gender and gender violence. They also challenged the complicity of the historic workers' movement in promoting the ideal of the bourgeois family. Many argued that oppression was built on the conforming sex roles enforced through the nuclear family. Third World Gay Revolution, in their 1970 New York platform, write:

We want the abolition of the institution of the bourgeois nuclear family. We believe that the bourgeois nuclear family perpetuates the false categories of homosexuality and heterosexuality by creating sex roles, sex definitions, and sexual exploitation. The bourgeois nuclear family as the basic unit of capitalism creates oppressive roles. All oppressions originate within the nuclear family structure.[3]

RADICAL FEMINISTS

Among these gender and sexual radicals, all agreed that the heterosexual nuclear family was a place of horror and tyranny. Feminists and women's liberation movements were similarly effectively unified in their absolute opposition to the condition of the housewife as a crux of women's domination. The major distinct currents of feminism varied according to their particular critique of the family form and proposed solution. The most mainstream liberal feminists sought equality in the workforce to enable women to leave bad relationships, and advocated for equality within the household, paralleling the demands of the workers' movement and bourgeois feminists of previous eras. Radical feminists, however, identified the family as the primary instrument of gender socialization, patriarchal tyranny, and gendered violence. They sought a wholesale destruction of the family as a necessary step toward any semblance of true freedom and liberation. Marxist feminists, in contrast to radical feminists, argued exhaustively over the question of the housewife's role in relation to the logic of capitalist accumulation. They differed—in a familiar contradiction of the workers' movement—in either proposing autonomous organizing by housewives or focusing organizing efforts on women in wage work. Despite their divergences, all these disparate feminist tendencies agreed that to be a housewife was both a horrible fate, and also somehow an embodiment of what it meant to be a woman in an oppressive society.

Radical feminists—increasingly distinct from the sex radicals discussed in the previous section—offered a thoroughgoing critique of the tyranny of the family, identifying its qualities of direct domination, violent subjugation, and fundamental alienation. They were the first to recognize how central sexual violence is to gender relations. The nuclear family, they saw, was a system of domestic privacy that protected against scrutiny and struggle, enabling and defending terrors: childhood abuse, intimate partner violence, marital rape, atomized isolation, anti-queer abuse, and coerced gender socialization.[4] The radical feminist and gay liberationist critiques rejected the atomized, isolating, and social conditions of the American suburbs. They were vague in their understanding of what the class basis of the family was, partly because of the success of the workers' movement in modeling its families after the bourgeoisie. The construction of the suburbs had blurred the distinctions among white people between working-class, middle-class, and capitalist family forms.

The widely read feminist classic *The Feminine Mystique* (1963), by Betty Friedan, placed the isolated housewife as a centerpiece of its analysis. Friedan opens her book with a description of suburban life: "The problem lay buried, unspoken, for many years in the minds of American women. It was a strange stirring, a sense of dissatisfaction, a yearning that women suffered in the middle of the twentieth century in the United States. Each suburban wife struggled with it alone."[5] Friedan was a central leader in what became the liberal feminist movement. Her critique of the suburban housewife reflected a widespread and shared sentiment among feminist media and women's rights organizations.

Shulamith Firestone offered the most extensive vision of family abolition by a feminist theorist of the era. Sophie Lewis, in multiple compelling texts, has explored Firestone's bold revolutionary vision, while detailing the ways it is "deeply flawed."[6] Lewis writes of Firestone's *The Dialectic of Sex*:

> Firestone's magnum opus voices scalding refusals of almost every "natural" premise of American society ("almost," because its chapter on race is woefully racist; and because no queer people appear in it). It advances a vision of a future in which children and adults together—having eliminated capitalism, work, and the sex distinction itself—democratically inhabit large, nongenetic households. You see, Shulie deemed the overthrowing of class, work, and markets to be a self-evidently necessary task, barely worth defending. What really interested her was the abolition of culture and nature, no less: starting with patriarchal "love" and its "culture of romance" on the one hand, and pregnancy on the other.[7]

Firestone's vision saw family abolition as a revolutionary horizon, an ethical utopia that would require radically remaking human culture. Radical feminists and queers of the era evoked an abolition of the family in resistant practices and analyses that still resonate today: experimenting with alternative living arrangements and forms of romance, rejecting any aspiration to suburban assimilation, rebelling against capitalist wage labor, refusing constraining sex and gender roles, and seeing interpersonal relationships as thoroughly political. The Third World Women's Alliance called for extended, communal family structures based on gender equality:

> Whereas in a capitalist culture, the institution of the family has been used as an economic and psychological tool, not serving the needs of people, we declare that we will not relate to the private ownership of any person by another. We encourage and support the continued growth of communal households and the idea of the extended family. We encourage alternative forms to the patriarchal family and call for the sharing of all work (including housework and child care) by men and women.[8]

Sometimes these group living arrangements would be apartments turned into informal mutual aid shelters for homeless trans sex workers of color, sometimes deliberate highly disciplined cadre-based group houses with rigorous lesbian feminist dress codes, sometimes rural hippie communes.

BLACK WOMEN RADICALS

Black feminists grappled with the history of the family as a white, normative institution. With mass migration to northern cities from the 1930s on, African Americans both entered segments of the waged blue-collar labor force and were shut out of growing suburban and white-collar employment sectors. Many found themselves in urban "ghettos"—neighborhoods of concentrated poverty, violent racial policing, substandard housing, and uneven access to wage employment. In the mid and late 1960s, as the civil rights movement was succeeding in its dismantling of the legal edifice of Jim Crow through the American South, African American youth in over a hundred and fifty American cities rioted. These uprisings prompted a major reorientation of Black organizations, and the active concern of the federal government.

One response came in the form of a leaked 1965 report by Daniel Patrick Moynihan, written as part of the Johnson administration's "War on Poverty." It argued that the social chaos of Black urban life was the direct result of women-dominated households. "The Negro Family: The Case for National Action," also known as the Moynihan Report, laid out an assessment that continues to guide in various guises much thinking among liberal sociologists, policymakers, and even among gender-conservative Black nationalists. According to the report, high rates of Black unemployment, crime, and other social dysfunction were the result of the excessive preponderance of women-headed households in Black communities, a so-called "Black matriarchy." The report argued that marital and lifestyle choices of Black women, including high rates of wage work and comparatively low rates of marriage, both marginalized Black Americans within a broader society that expected male-headed households and produced a crisis of Black male masculinity and misbehavior of crime, disruptive social protest, and unemployment.[9] Here the exclusion of Black Americans from the characteristic family form of the workers' movement is blamed on Black women, and in contrast that heteronormative, patriarchal family form is seen as the fundamental condition of social order.

Though the male-breadwinner family was not an option for most Black people, Black people's choice to avoid marriage may have contained the desire for sexual freedom. Low marriage rates among Black people may have been a rejection of patriarchal family norms and a call for a different form of family structure.[10] As I argued in chapter 6, Jim Crow mandated marriage as a condition of tenancy; Black people may have been fleeing coerced, state-sanctioned heterosexuality in choosing not to marry. Other, more discussed factors also no doubt contributed to low marriage rates, such as Black men's chronic underemployment due to racist labor market exclusion. During Jim Crow, exclusion from wage labor left Black proletarians out of the workers' movement. With the Great Migration and the dismantling of Jim Crow, Black proletarians entered wage labor, but did not generally have the option—preferable or not—to form male-breadwinner families.

Black feminist theorists challenged the Moynihan Report, pushing beyond the limits of the white family norm. Black women were not willing to sacrifice independence for a desperate, halfway emulation of an impossible respectability, often opting to raise children with friends or female relatives rather than husbands. In "Double Jeopardy: To Be Black and Female," Francis Beale writes:

> It is idle dreaming to think of Black women simply caring for their homes and children like the middle class white model. Most Black women have to work to help house, feed and clothe their families. Black women make up a substantial percentage of the Black working force, and this is true for the poorest Black family as well as the so-called "middle class" family.[11]

Tiffany Lethabo King identifies a family-abolitionist move in a 1970 essay by Kay Lindsay, "The Black Woman as Woman." In it, Lindsay identifies the family as a white institution oppressing Black life: "The family, as a white institution, has been held up to Blacks as a desirable but somehow unattainable goal." Black women must combat and destroy the white family as an institution: "We have an obligation as Black women to project ourselves into the revolution to destroy these institutions which not only oppress Blacks but women as well, for if these institutions continue to flourish, they will be used against us in the continuing battle of mind over body."[12] Black women's radicals recognized in the Moynihan Report the broader regime of racism, misogyny, poverty, and state violence at play in oppressing Black women in US cities. The critique of the Moynihan Report has continued, even well after the rebellions of the 1970s waned. Tiffany Lethabo King, Hortense J. Spillers, Kimberlé Crenshaw, Cathy J. Cohen, Ta-Nehisi Coates, Tressie McMillan Cottom, and others have all used the Moynihan Report as a fulcrum in their arguments challenging the pathologization of Black women and Black kinship.[13]

The Moynihan Report contributed to the efforts of welfare programs to shape Black sexuality. The riots of the mid-1960s significantly bolstered government support for the "War on Poverty," an expansion of the US welfare system to include poor African Americans. Much of the United States' welfare and social security system had been implemented in the 1930s, when major white landowners in the American South still depended on the subordinated labor of Black families. Its various programs were designed to exclude domestic and agricultural workers, the bulk of the African American workforce. These programs were also designed to keep control in white supremacist–dominated local levels of government.[14] Black people were largely shut out of government welfare support in the 1940s and 1950s. In an effort to placate and control the unrest of the 1960s, state and federal governments acceded to the demands of unemployed, single African American women in accessing welfare benefits.

These women, frustrated by the patronizing forms of social control welfare departments they encountered, soon organized in a network of projects that became the National Welfare Rights Organization (NWRO). Composed of mostly African American mothers receiving cash-transfer benefits, through the late 1960s NWRO waged many campaigns to significantly improve access and treatment of welfare recipients, with the ultimate goal of a substantial federal universal basic income. One campaign challenged a welfare program policy that restricted Black sexuality. Welfare departments excluded receipt of benefits for women who had a "man in the house" on whom it was presumed the mother could rely. To enforce this policy, welfare departments conducted "midnight raids," in collaboration with police departments, of late-night inspections to evaluate whether a recipient was cohabitating with a man or was sexually active, and hence ineligible for benefits. NWRO successfully overturned these practices through organizing and litigation, defending the right of proletarian Black people to nonmarital sexual intimacy.

The NWRO was a means of poor African Americans asserting a right not only to sexual pleasure but also against work.[15] Where the Black trade union movement was calling for full employment and jobs programs, these work demands gained little traction among NWRO militants. Many of them had worked throughout their lives and found their jobs unfulfilling and alienated. NWRO materials offered a historical argument that African Americans had built the country across generations of enslaved and subordinated labor, and that they had worked enough. NWRO organized against the exploitation and cruelty of low- and no-wage welfare-to-work jobs programs. Though some in NWRO emphasized that their role as mothers constituted a form of productively contributing to society, others were resistant to such narratives. Instead, they argued for the "right to life" separated from the wage, from work, and from labor market participation. Staging sit-ins and occupations of welfare offices and government buildings, mobilizing in the courts, and encouraging recipients to demand the maximum possible benefits, these militants sought to drive the welfare system into crisis, necessitating a wholesale restructuring that would end the elaborate means-testing, behavioral discipline, and work encouragement of American cash-transfer benefits. NWRO's core campaign of a federal guaranteed annual income or negative income tax was understood by many of its advocates as the means of no longer being forced into chronically dissatisfying work.

This was a radical shift from how welfare had long been understood in the social democratic imagination. Postwar welfare programs in the United States and Europe were largely designed as a supplement to full employment. Elder care, childcare, unemployment insurance, disability insurance, and public healthcare were all designed to complement a lifetime of wage labor. Poverty-relief programs like the program NWRO confronted were structured to minimize competition with labor markets: benefits were usually set well below minimum wage, means-testing sought to exclude the employable, and recipients were encouraged to varying extents to transition into work. In the American South, access to any benefits was restricted based on the seasonal need for agricultural labor. Where and when cash-transfer benefits came close to low-wage employment, this could be justified in circumstances of high unemployment rates and economic crisis. For NWRO and other welfare rights militants of the 1960s, benefits were not only a supplement to wage labor but a means of escape from it.

WAGES FOR HOUSEWORK

Anti-work and family-abolitionist sentiment among working-class women's movements was not limited to the African American welfare rights movement. Wages for Housework was a political international tendency, eventually formalized into the International Wages for Housework Campaign. Wages for Housework offered the most coherent articulation of the misery of unwaged housework being the counterpart to the misery of waged work. Wages for Housework emerged amid the intensity of worker insurrection in Italy in the early 1970s, soon spreading to the United Kingdom and throughout scattered sections of the United States. Mariarosa Dalla Costa's "Women and the Subversion of the Community" located women's oppression as produced through the overall reproduction of the capitalist totality, laying the conceptual groundwork for later social reproduction theory. This offered a major theoretical breakthrough made possible by both the workers' movement itself and the intensity of insurrection against its limits.

Dalla Costa writes that the structure of the family "is the very pillar of the capitalist organization of work,"[16] structuring the divide between waged and unwaged activities: "It has made men wage slaves, then, to the degree that it has succeeded in allocating these services to women in the family, and by the same process controlled the flow of women onto the labor market."[17] With the advent of the housewife-based working-class family, women are relegated to the home, producing the gender division within the working class. Women's struggle must necessarily reject the home, through building alliances with those in reproductive care industries, producing a revolutionary insurgency:

> We must get out of the house; we must reject the home, because we want to unite with other women, to struggle against all situations which presume that women will stay at home, to link ourselves to the struggles of all those who are in ghettos, whether the ghetto is a nursery, a school, a hospital, an old-age home, or asylum. To abandon the home is already a form of struggle.[18]

This struggle against the home is fundamentally not toward wage labor but in rejection of work itself: "Women must completely discover their own possibilities—which are neither mending socks nor becoming captains of ocean-going ships. Better still, we may wish to do these things, but these now cannot be located anywhere but in the history of capital."[19]

Silvia Federici, another central leader and thinker of the Wages for Housework movement, echoes this anti-work dimension:

We can see the revolutionary implications of the demand for wages for housework. It is the demand by which our nature ends and our struggle begins because just to want wages for housework means to refuse that work as the expression of our nature, and therefore to refuse precisely the female role that capital has invented for us.[20]

However counterintuitive it was for many readers, Federici was clear that the demand for wages was intended to enable a refusal of work: "From now on we want money for each moment of it, so that we can refuse some of it and eventually all of it."[21] The Wages for Housework demand was a means of exposing the underlying dynamic of unwaged household labor. Through this anti-work lens, the demand of Wages for Housework may have primarily been a provocation rather than an actual reform policy proposal. Dalla Costa mentions "wages for housework" only in passing and somewhat critically. Silvia Federici's call for wages for housework is argued in an essay "Wages Against Housework." However, no doubt many advocates for Wages for Housework likely understood the demand quite literally.[22]

THE PROMISE OF THE RED DECADE

The visions of Black women radicals, radical feminists, and gay liberationists of the Red Decade go much further in their understanding of gender freedom than previous articulations. Unlike their Marxist predecessors, they recognized the working-class family as a site of personal subjugation, violence, brutality, and alienation. They understood that the self-activity of the class itself, through the direct establishment of alternative kinship and mutual aid relationships, is the primary mechanism for abolishing the family. They began to identify, however tentatively, the relationship between empire, suburban whiteness, the institutionalized workers' movement, and heteronormative patriarchal families. They yearned for home as an expansive, communal site of mutual care, love, erotic pleasure, shared revolutionary struggle, and personal transformation, rather than isolation and control.

In advancing a critique of coercive binary gender expression and normative gender expectations, the Red Decade radicals began to envision the overcoming of narrow gender and sexual identity as the endpoint of the abolition of the family. They saw the struggle to abolish the family as necessitating direct personal transformation in one's expectations and behavior toward others, advancing and deepening the previous socialist critique of male chauvinism as an obstacle to class struggle. In their engagement with economic survival and work, the gender radicals of the 1970s moved toward a rejection of work and a desire to escape from the subjugation of wage labor, rather than solely imagining equality through universal proletarianization. The movements of the Red Decade briefly seemed to be on the cusp of linking the radical, multi-issue critique of the workers' movement to a mass politics of working-class rebellion. Peak struggles of the Red Decade joined the refusal of work with the mass strike, demanded welfare benefits along with a critique of it as a system of social control, and demanded socialist states fulfill their promise of being organs of the working class. These moments, pushing at the limits of social democracy and state socialism, touched an extraordinary emancipatory possibility.

LIMITS AND CONTRADICTIONS OF GENDER REBELLION DURING THE RED DECADE

Despite the immense insights of the uprisings of the Red Decade, their politics is not sufficient for us today. Radical feminists and gay liberationists forged emancipatory visions that can no longer inspire mass gender rebellions in the form of the early 1970s revolts, and rightly came under rigorous criticisms over the coming decades of gender thought and struggle. Many radical feminist and gay liberationist analysis extrapolated their overall understanding of society as a whole from their critique of the atomized heterosexual nuclear family. They identified patriarchy as the fundamental basis of militarism, fascism, colonialism, sexual violence, gender conformity, and private property. Radical feminists located women's oppression as subject to a sex-caste or sex-class system. The imagined women were a coherent social group with a unifying set of easily aggregated interests—just as the industrial proletariat had been envisioned in an earlier era of the workers' movement—subject to a unique form of oppression in the family. This sex-class analysis coherently reflected their own experience of oppression, largely as white women opposed to being entrapped in a suburban family. However, this analysis significantly misunderstands the place of the family within capitalism.

Seeing sex and the family as parallel to other forms of oppression distorts the interrelationship between segments of capitalist society. As discussed earlier, under feudalism the extraction of surplus was a direct, violent process by agents of the state and the aristocracy, resulting in a homology and a direct interlocking between the organization of the state, the economy, and the patriarchal family. Under capitalism, these systems had been partially severed through wage labor; that is to say: direct domination and violence were no longer required to extract surplus value in the production process, so governmental affairs and family dynamics could take on a relative autonomy. Capitalism produced a real separation between the public and private spheres, isolating one form of gender domination within the private walls of the household. The pervasive forms of male domination in government or business, whatever their superficial similarities to gender dynamics of families, took on a fundamentally different character, fracturing patriarchy as a coherent system. Women's oppression under capitalism operated within broader circuits that include interconnecting multiple institutions, including the family, the state, and private enterprise. Extrapolating from their critique of the family and seeing other institutions as homologous ultimately prevented radical feminists from adequately grasping the dynamics of capitalism and the racial state, a point often made by socialist feminists and Black feminists.

Understanding women's oppression through a sex-class analysis led radical feminists to many dead ends. They proved unable to effectively account for or respond to the eruption of debates about class and racial differences between women, as their strategy and vision depended on the eliding of substantial stratifications between women. Trans women, politicizing concurrently with radical feminism and initially active in its ranks, soon became the subject of intense hostility, as the sex-class analysis was revealed to rely on a binary polarization based on biology or early socialization. Radical feminists developed an early hostility to sexual pleasure as inherently mired in patriarchal oppression, leading to an erupting of conflicts between feminists in the 1980s and 1990s known as "the Sex Wars" that continue in debates over pornography, sex work, and kink.

Similarly, gay liberationists were unable to offer a program that sufficiently resonates with us today. Through the 1970s, gay men in some major cities had remarkably open access to frequent erotic pleasure prior to the devastation of AIDS. Though one may be nostalgic for the pleasures and freedoms of this period, few today imagine they offered a path to a free society. The dramatic loosening of sexual mores among queer and straight people alike in the 1970s revealed that sexual repression was not in fact the cohering glue of capitalist domination, as earlier defenders of the power of Eros had argued. Efforts at remaking heterosexuality in the radical youth movements of the period are rightfully remembered as largely unpleasant, with militants striving to "smash monogamy," ensnaring themselves in ever more elaborate forms of misogyny and trauma. Today sexuality pervades popular consumer culture, and it is as much a neoliberal and individualist injunction to enjoy as it is a source of freedom. The idea that the pursuit of eroticism could cohere new, revolutionary solidarities made sense when gay sex was heavily criminalized, but it no longer widely inspires.

This inadequacy of the vision of sexual and gender liberation from the movements of the early 1970s extends to the limits of their vision of abolishing the family. They imagined family abolition as a voluntary activity pursued through deliberate subcultures. They couldn't easily imagine or theorize family abolition becoming generalized as a society-wide restructuring of economic relations. This limit ultimately lay in the persistence of the horizon of the workers' movement. Even as they sought to escape the workers' movement masculinist, narrow focus on wage work, or the limits of the vision of equality to proletarianization, the gender rebels of the period could not envision the abolition of the class relation itself. The workers' movement sought socialist freedom through generalizing the condition of wage labor. Under conditions of wage labor, the family could only be dissolved through the massive expansion of an alternative, nonmarket institution: the state. These youth of the

Red Decade sought to flee wage labor, but they could not envision any other means of collective, communist social reproduction beyond the factory in one form or another. Even as they sought to go beyond the workers' movement, its assumptions continued to have a stranglehold on radical thinking. These movements were the furthest limit of the workers' movement, but they had not yet escaped beyond it.

Much of what was wrong in the existing gender and sexual relations of the New Left became evident to later generations of feminist, queer, and anti-racist thought. The intellectual trends engaging questions of gender and sexual politics of the 1980s and 1990s were mostly academic, under varying names such as post-structuralism, Black feminism, women of color feminism, pro-sex feminism, postcolonial feminism, queer theory, and trans studies. Though much maligned among some leftists today for their varying degrees of idealism, lack of coherent account of the capitalist mode of production, overemphasis on individual experiences, and dis-articulation from mass movements, these intellectual currents in fact produced an extensive, rigorous, and valuable critique of the failures of sex-class theory, revolutionary nationalism, and gay lib-erationism. Multiple movements successfully made major political and theoretical breakthroughs in the politics of gender through close dialogue with the radical academic theories since the Red Decade: AIDS movements in the 1990s drawing from Foucault and queer theory, trans struggles since the turn of the twenty-first century informed by multiple theoretical currents, and militants in Black Lives Matter in the late 2010s identifying as inspired by intersectional Black feminism and Afro-pessimism.

A call to abolish the family in the present cannot just repeat Engels, Kollontai, or Third World Gay Revolution. These historical examples have much to teach us; but we today require a communist feminism able to move beyond the limits of these prior movements against the family. To do so, we must account for the structural transformation of working-class generational reproduction since the 1970s, particularly the decline of the male-breadwinner nuclear family and the fragmentation of gender categories. The next chapter considers this shifting political economy since the Red Decade.

9
Crisis of the Family

"The history of the family," Melissa Cooper writes as the opening line of *Family Values*, "is one of perpetual crisis."[1] Crisis is inherent to the family. As an institution of class society, the family is perpetually destabilized by every period of economic and political transformation. The psychic development of each generation necessarily entails the interweaving of both identification and differentiation against their upbringing. In binding together both care and coercion, the family is necessarily ambivalent, conflicted, and always failing.

Capitalism accelerates and universalizes the inherent crisis of the family. Both capitalism (according to Marx) and the family (according to Freud) are constituted through perpetual crisis built into their basic structure. The dynamics of long-term capitalist development, the demands and uncertainty of reproducing oneself and one's household in the market, and the precarity of proletarian existence all destabilize any given familial arrangement. As a fantasy of white heteronormativity, the nuclear family form can momentarily obscure its myriad contradictions and forms of violence. But the social binds and structures of class society that enable family formation always also rupture their false unity. As Cooper extensively documents, the entire field of acceptable contemporary political discourse is bound together by varying narratives about the crisis of the family and its antidotes.

The crisis of the family has taken a particular form in recent decades. The workers' movement had previously sustained its legitimacy by the partial attainment of the male-breadwinner nuclear family model: households sustained by a single male wage earner, supportive state institutions, a housewife, and the social legitimacy of whiteness and homeownership. Since the 1970s, however, this family norm has become completely unattainable for all but the wealthy. For the sections of the working class that were never able to obtain that norm—Black people, queers, migrants, the poor—the last five decades have seen proliferating catastrophes.

This unraveling of one family norm has enabled some positive gains: the expanding space for queer and trans life, more people able to choose living alone, pockets of celebrating the diversity of actually existing kin relations. But these have come in a period of great costs: stagnant wages, dismantling of welfare states, collapsing public health infrastructures, massive expansion of racist state terror, and the absence of sustained social movements. Together these trends loosened the hold of the family norm while intensifying dependency on the private household.

CLOSING OF THE WORKERS' MOVEMENT

The rebellions of the Red Decade sought to overcome the limits of the workers' movement: to rebel against work, the factory, and the family. Proletarian rebellion of the Red Decade pushed against the limits constituted by the workers' movement toward new visions of communism. Ultimately the positive revolutionary vision of these movements was defeated. By the late 1970s, the uprisings that had been sweeping the world had largely been crushed. Following the defeat of these rebellions, the workers' movement they had sought to overcome also unraveled. Communization theory, introduced in chapter 7, understands the 1970s as the end of the workers' movement. Class struggle has unquestionably continued since, inherent to capitalist society. Many of the institutions of the workers' movement persist, even amid decline and decimation: labor unions, socialist political parties, even a couple of surviving socialist states. But working-class uprisings, even the periodic upsurge of workplace organizing campaigns, are unable to cohere into the kinds of mass stable institutions of the previous era. *Endnotes* writes of efforts to cohere working-class organizations that "these new or revived structures lack staying power, for they are built on the shifting sands of the fully separated society: no matter how much water one pours on them, they refuse to cake up."[2] Here *Endnotes* is noting how workers' identity can no longer overcome the atomization and social fragmentation of capitalist society.

This difficulty of cohering unifying working-class organizations, communization theory argues, is structurally built into the current era of capitalist development. Since the 1970s the global economy has had the ability to produce far more manufactured goods than it is profitable to consume. With the successful reindustrialization of Japan and Germany, followed by BRIC nations (Brazil, Russia, India, China) and East Asia, there is too much competition and capacity to meet the world's demand for manufactured goods. Too many factories and too many nations are competing to provide the products for the world. This overcapacity has led to an overall decline in the average rate of profit, and the deindustrialization of the capitalist core. This global overcapacity in manufacturing is what Marx identifies as the overaccumulation of capital, one side of the "General Law of Capitalist Accumulation."

Partially as a result of this overcapacity and deindustrialization, the world has seen a steady decline of the portion of the working class (and the total number of workers) engaged in the particular form of labor that cohered the workers' movement: industrial manufacturing.[3] Industrial production had provided the workers' movement with its basic model of interdependency, collaboration, the positive possibility of work, and the sense that capitalism could homogenize and unify the working class. The vision of the workers' movement depended on the mass experience of steadily expanding proletarianization into becoming industrial workers. But with the recent decades of deindustrialization across much of Europe and the United States, the slowing of the rapid industrialization of East Asia, and the massive expansion of the informal workforce, the core strategy of the workers' movement has run aground. For the most advanced capitalist nations, expanding employment sectors have largely been in low-wage services, often particularly meaningless tasks that provide little basis for an affirmative working-class identity.

Over the last five decades, the world has also seen the other side of Marx's General Law of Capitalist Accumulation—the creation of surplus people unneeded in capitalist production. The world has seen the growth of a population expelled from the production process. Globally, capitalist development has produced a massive expansion of what Marx (and *Endnotes*) call "surplus populations," people who cannot be effectively incorporated into stable wage labor. The universal proletarianization of the peasantry and the spread of market relations across the world has failed to produce a working class that is able to recognize itself as a unity. Market relations, far from homogenizing or unifying the working class, have fundamentally fragmented working-class life.[4] Together, the global overproduction of manufacturing capacity and expelling surplus populations broke the unity, strength, and coherence of the workers' movement. The workers' movement was undone by the process of capitalist accumulation itself, specifically the simultaneous overproduction of industrial capacity and surplus populations first theorized by Marx.[5]

This framework helps make sense of the shifting politics of family. As discussed in the previous chapter, queers, radical feminists, and Black women of the Red Decade rebelled against the normative white male-breadwinner family of the suburbs, the characteristic family form of the workers' movement. The subsequent decline of the dominance of this family form, however, was not primarily driven by these efforts at mass resistance. Instead, the decline of both the workers' movement and its characteristic family form is a product of capitalist crisis.

Like the broader decline and domestication of rebellions of the Red Decade, those movements previously seeking to overthrow the family turned to a more liberal, reformist political strategy. Feminists, after seeing significant gains in women's equality in the 1970s due to economic changes and legislative victories, faced a political backlash and the persistence of a gender wage gap. The gay liberation movement moderated its energies, shrinking into a narrow rights-based advocacy movement, only renewing a militant phase during the peak of the AIDS epidemic. Welfare rights advocates stopped gaining ground by the end of the 1970s, and soon saw the wholesale dismantling of cash-transfer benefits and social services in a new era of austerity. As the broader wave of struggle collapsed in the mid-1970s, the weakened descendants of these movements increasingly theorized and organized around gender separated from any class politics. When severed from mass economic demands, women's and gay rights movements continue to make other, more limited gains in legal equality.

Yet as radical movements were defeated, key features of the family form they opposed shifted. The effects of the prolonged profitability crisis and defeat of the workers' movement since the mid-1970s ultimately made it impossible for white working-class families to continue to afford to keep an unwaged housewife out of the labor market. The male-breadwinner family form is no longer possible for any but the wealthy. It has lost its social hegemony due to the convergence of several simultaneous trends. In its place, most of the world has seen the dramatic and steady growth of dual-wage-earner households, of people choosing not to partner or marry, of people living alone, and of many accessing reproductive services as a commodity in the market. Together, these dynamics have produced a heterogeneous array of family forms in working-class life.

STAGNATING WAGES, TRANSFORMING FAMILIES

The decline of the male-breadwinner family has been a story of married women going to work. As poor, Black, and migrant women have always worked at high rates, this has largely been a dramatic change in white family dynamics. Women's labor market participation grew gradually with the expansion of white-collar employment from the 1920s on. In the 1950s, during the peak of suburbanization, older women began to work in greater numbers. But with the entry of young married women into work growing through the 1960s and 1970s, the shift became increasingly visible and undeniable to all. For married American women, labor market participation grew steadily from the 30 percent range of the 1960s to leveling off at over 60 percent in the 1990s.[6] Though the persistence of labor market regulations has slowed women's increasing labor market participation in European social democracies, women's employment has still steadily climbed.[7] In the United Kingdom, women's workforce participation grew from 37 percent in 1961 to 53 percent in 1990 and has remained in the mid-50s since. In Germany, the percentage of women in the workforce went from

39 percent in 1970 to 56 percent in 2016,[8] during a period of falling real wages.

Many factors contributed to women's increasing labor market participation, including the increase of feminized jobs in reproductive service labor, white-collar employment, education, and health care; declining fertility; increased availability of part-time work; and women increasingly pursuing employment. In the postwar period, several industries and nations removed "marriage bars," restrictions on married women's employment, including in the Netherlands in 1967 and in Ireland in 1973. The United Kingdom overturned the marriage bar for Home Civil Service in 1946, and for the Foreign Service in 1973. Various marriage bars persisted in the United States until the Civil Rights Act of 1964.[9]

The main driver of women entering the workforce among working-class families was economic necessity. Working-class real wages have stagnated and declined since the 1970s. As a result, maintaining comparable standards of living has required the vast majority of working-class families to send wives into the workforce, supplemented with mounting household debt. Other major shifts in family dynamics have accompanied women's growing workforce participation. People in OECD nations have chosen to marry later, to live together without marrying, to divorce more quickly, and to live as single people. In the United States, divorce rates went from 3.5 per thousand in 1950 to 6.3 per thousand in 1985; in England and Wales, the rates went from 0.9 to 4 per thousand over the same period.[10] In 1950 only 10 percent of European households were composed of a single adult; in 2000 this had grown to 30 percent of households in Great Britain and 40 percent in Sweden, with the lowest figure of the continent being 20 percent in Greece.[11] Higher divorce rates likely enable both men and women to leave bad and unfulfilling relationships, and to pursue better sex and non-traditional family structures, yet they also intensify atomization, isolation, and fragmentation of social life.

Couples today have few children, start having children later and stop earlier. Fertility has declined everywhere; between 1900 and 2000 from 5 children per woman in Germany to 1.3, 3.8 in the United States to 2, 5.8 in India to 3.3, about 6 in Latin America to 2.7.[12] Children are now much more likely to be born outside of marriages. As a percentage of live births, extramarital births have gone from 8 in the United Kingdom in 1960 to 39.5 in 2000, during the same period 5.3 in the United States to 31, 11.6 in the former East Germany to 49.9, and 6.7 to 17.7 in former West Germany.[13] Lower fertility means more of life is spent outside of child-rearing, outside the home, and outside the narrow confines of the nuclear family.

Besides wage stagnation, another element of the prolonged capitalist crisis has contributed to the decline of the male-breadwinner family form, compounding these factors: the commodification of reproductive labor. With declining profit rates in manufacturing and many other sectors, capitalist investment has increasingly sought new opportunities in consumer services. Tasks previously done by unwaged housewives are increasingly done by low-wage service workers employed by for-profit firms. Even many working-class people can drop their clothes off at laundromats and their children at day care centers, grab a meal at a fast-food restaurant, and pay a service to do their housecleaning. The growth of service industry reproductive labor has increased employment demand in feminized sectors, providing more work opportunities to working-class women and queers. Many families have come to depend on what feminist scholars call "global care chains," paid domestic labor by international migrants.[14] By outsourcing reproductive labor to other waged services, people free up time for their more demanding workweeks and reduce their reliance on unwaged labor in the home. This then expands the possibility of employed people choosing to live without a conventional family structure.

CONFLICTED FREEDOMS

Collectively, all these changes have meant an improvement in many people's ability to pursue fulfilling relationships beyond the narrow expectations of family and community. These structural changes driving women into the workforce and destabilizing families have intersected with the gains of the gay and women's rights movements. With the collapse of the workers' movement and its characteristic family norm, much of the world has seen an immense diversification of family forms. These changes largely began in the advanced industrialized world, but similar trends have emerged across the Global South. People today live in a diverse variety of household arrangements.

In recent decades, young women and queer people have radically changed expectations for their sexual and gender lives. Many young people now comfortably embrace a right to nonmarital sex for pleasure and a belief that families can take diverse acceptable forms. Compared to past generations, they are more likely than not to be comfortable with same-sex relationships and gender nonconformity. In recent decades, growing numbers of young people show that a concern for personal well-being most likely guides their sex- and gender-related decisions. All these factors have likely been major contributors in the huge growth in people pursuing gay relationships, gender transitions, and complex nontraditional families. In many ways, these dramatic demographic shifts in how people pursue relationships have been a real, qualitative improvement in people's gender and sexual lives. Youth today come of age in a sexually freer world than that of their grandparents. Amid these economic trends since the 1970s, working-class people today are much more likely to depend on fragmented, extended, and heterogeneous kinship relations beyond the nuclear family in ways that parallel the nineteenth century. Parents of all social classes divorce and remarry at high rates, producing so-called blended families of stepchildren. Same-sex families are increasingly common, with access to wage labor, reduced homophobic sanctions, and increases in social support enabling same-sex couples to integrate with their respective class milieu. Same-sex couples are also more likely to be embedded in heterogeneous, queer networks of dependency that include ex-lovers, step- and half-children, close friends, and other chosen-kin dependencies.

Global migration has been a constant throughout the history of capitalist development, as rural populations are expelled from the countryside and cross continents in search of waged employment. Improvements in transnational communications and travel have enabled migrants to maintain some forms of long-distance care and contact. As a result, migration has been another site of the diversification of kinship and interdependency extending well beyond individual households. Immigrants may send back a substantial portion of their wages to family members in their country of origin. They may benefit from sending such remittances in the long term, hoping to retire in their rural communities with land or housing purchased by their families and later supported by their children. As well, such long-term kin dependency shows deep affective and social commitment to family dependents.

Family life has been radically transformed. The normative family ideal no longer bears much resemblance to anyone's actual lives. In many ways, this has been a huge improvement in human freedom. But these shifts also entail an intensification of another form of unfreedom. The decline of the male-breadwinner working-class family form has shifted the experience of women and queers from dependency on the personal domination of a husband or father to dependency on the impersonal domination of the wage. Just as the male-breadwinner family was enabled by a succession of victories of the workers' movement, prolonged economic crisis and the collapse of the workers' movement has condemned people to material deprivation, market dependency, and alienated work. The new heterogeneous family structures are a symptom of desperation as much as they are of the practice of care, and in this market dependency everyone is subject to new forms of predation. A queer youth freed from a violent relationship with their parents may be subject to the new risks of street-based sex work; young mothers opting not to marry their abusive boyfriends may find themselves working long hours in retail service under managers who sexually harass them. Everyone is forced to find and secure work, competing constantly with other proletarians, and subject to the gender and sexual discipline of employers and the work process. Freedom from the normative patriarchal family may be an improvement for many, but it has not made a free society.

WELFARE AUSTERITY AND THE PRIVATE HOUSEHOLD

In the peak years of the workers' movement after World War II, the working class benefited from substantial and extensive welfare states. In the Soviet bloc and postrevolutionary China, the state provided extensive guarantees in people's material well-being. Western European social democracies enjoyed universal healthcare, affordable housing, and robust public health programs. With the uprisings of the Red Decade, the United States finally extended many of its anti-poverty programs to include Black and brown people. Yet since the 1970s, these welfare systems have all been in steep decline. The near universal character of this decline suggests that it is likely driven by the broader structural changes of global capitalism. With declining global profitability, each country has been forced by economic conditions to shift course. Neoliberalism offered state elites an answer to a pervasive and ongoing crisis: to force the costs of capitalist decline onto the working class.

The collapse of state socialism and the dismantling of welfare states have had far-reaching consequences for families and the private household. Welfare cuts were meant to force people to turn to their families for support. Margaret Thatcher's famous quote embodying the ethos of welfare austerity is worth considering at length:

> I think we have gone through a period when too many children and people have been given to understand "I have a problem, it is the Government's job to cope with it!" or "I have a problem, I will go and get a grant to cope with it!" "I am homeless, the Government must house me!" and so they are casting their problems on society and who is society? There is no such thing! There are individual men and women and there are families and no government can do anything except through people and people look to themselves first.[15]

In the same interview, Thatcher discusses the importance of family, detailing it as a means of socializing children, teaching them how to function as thoughtful and courteous people. Though she defends the need for individuals to get out of abusive families, she emphasizes that marriages should be a lifetime commitment. The interviewer turns to the topic of AIDS, and Thatcher responds by promoting the persistence of the traditional family:

> A nation of free people will only continue to be a great nation if your family life continues and the structure of that nation is a family structure. Now it still is, you know, in spite of every-

thing. It still is. The overwhelming majority of people live in the traditional family. Yes, there will be problems. There always will be and there always have been in life, but the overwhelming majority of people live within the structure of the family and the family continues. ... Most of the problems will be solved within the family structure.[16]

Welfare austerity was a push to increase dependency on the family as a private household. The family, in the imagination of both conservatives and neoliberals, was the proper place for people to turn to for care. Welfare states used to play a central role in providing extensive services to children and new parents, in caring for the elderly, in supporting adults through periods of unemployment or disability. With the cutbacks to welfare support over decades, all those activities were assumed to be taken up by family members. The growing responsibilities of newly privatized care were particularly expected to be borne by feminized family members like mothers, wives, and adult daughters. Welfare austerity went along with state policies attempting to expand marriage and family homeownership. In the United Kingdom, Thatcher privatized council housing, enabling working-class tenants to become homeowners. Like efforts at promoting homeownership in the postwar era, Thatcher hoped this would increase political conservatism and social responsibility.

In the United States, President Clinton implemented the most substantial welfare austerity policy change in 1996 with the dismantling of Aid to Families with Dependent Children, the anti-poverty program that had been a focus of previous welfare rights activists. Clinton was also instrumental in expanding bank credit to Black and low-income families. This enabled an expansion of homeownership and the expanding housing asset bubble of the early 2000s, before its collapse in the 2008 financial crisis. Clinton's welfare reform also claimed to promote marriage among poor African Americans through both the absence of alternative supports and direct marriage incentives. In the United States, welfare austerity unfolded through the racist logics set out in the Moynihan Report, and by later generations of anti-Black analysts. Despite the numerical dominance of white welfare recipients, anti-poverty programs had come to be seen as dominated by greedy, opportunistic Black women. Charles Murray, best known for espousing racist theories on intelligence, also argued that dependency on welfare had destroyed Black family life. Murray claimed that eliminating welfare would ultimately strengthen the Black family, aid people in returning to work, and reduce poverty. This was an influential argument for liberal opponents of welfare, like Clinton.[17] Welfare reform faced relatively little opposition in the United States, benefiting both from widespread anti-Black racism and the hegemony of the Democratic Party over working-class political organizing.

Yet despite these efforts at shoring up and expanding traditional notions of family with welfare austerity, the diversification of actually existing household arrangements continued throughout this period. Welfare austerity did nothing to slow the erosion of marriage or "the traditional family." But it did increase the dependency of proletarians on private households. Welfare austerity has contributed to the overall stagnation and decline of working-class life. The absence of welfare support has made it much more difficult to survive without access to wage labor, or the wage labor of your immediate family members. With most job growth being in very low-wage sectors, this meant households where all adults had to work multiple jobs. If an adult lost their job during the periodic and worsening economic crises of recent decades, they were increasingly likely to have to move back in with their parents, rely on extended family members, or cobble together other nontraditional household arrangements to get by.

Ultimately, welfare reform severely worsened Black poverty.[18] Concurrently, the United States also dramatically expanded its system of mass incarceration, rising from a prison population at just under two hundred thousand in 1972 to over 1.5 million in 2009.[19] Black communities have been particularly devastated by mass incarceration; in 2010 one in three Black American men have felony convictions.[20] Since the Great Migration, Black households had been characterized by unusually low rates of marriage, a prevalence of female-headed families, and structures of mutual aid including extended family members and close friends. The expansion of the US prison system, ongoing police violence, welfare reform, and intensifying Black poverty all further contributed to the fragmentation and destabilization of Black family life. In this climate, Black people continued to form complex kin relationships as strategies of survival, returned to again in the next chapter.

SOLITARY MISERIES

Welfare austerity was concurrent with worsening overall conditions of survival for proletarians. In the difficult circumstances of an overall decline in working-class life, the private household became central to survival. Despite the immense diversification of the ways of organizing households, the role of the private household in proletarian life has intensified. The increasing dependence on the private household has entailed a particular material hardship for those without access to family. Those who fail to cohere a family as household find themselves facing poverty as they age and are less able to work. Amber Hollibaugh has spoken extensively on the isolation and poverty of working-class queer elders.[21] Where working-class heterosexual people are more likely to have children at some point in their lives to help them as they age, queer people are much more likely to find themselves alone in old age. For people who do not partner and form families, aging can mean increasing social isolation as the social world of youth subcultures becomes increasingly inaccessible. Of the many horrors of the coronavirus pandemic was people who once relied on an office, a bar, or a house party for their social connection with others, suddenly finding themselves trapped at home and increasingly alone.

Many people are terrified of ending up single in their old age. The lack of adequate supports outside the family means people have real fears of isolation, disability, and chronic loneliness if they are not able to find and maintain a primary romantic partner. This drives toxic relationships, destructive dating dynamics, and people staying in romantic relationships far longer than they would otherwise. Similarly, the fear of ending up alone without needed care drives some couples to have children when they would not do so otherwise. If the family is the only sustained support people can count on, it drives people to settle for familial relationships that are unfulfilling or even harmful.

Organizing social reproduction in terms of the private family household means society is largely unable and unequipped to care for people who find themselves without families. For all those people who chose not to live in families, our society offers scant alternatives for a decent life. So many have reason to not be in families: those raised by abusers who chose to run away, those who enjoy silence and solitary time, those whose minds and affects make it hard to love or be loved, those unlucky in love or unlucky in their love's death, those who appreciate varied sex with many people, those whose families are too poor or suffering too much to care for them, those just setting out ready to discover the world, those with time-consuming passions, those who are too trauma-tized to open up, and so many more. Everyone needs love and care. Those without families are often left alone, abandoned. A society where social reproduction overwhelmingly happens through families fails all these people. In doing so, it constrains everyone's choices about how to constitute their lives.

PERSISTENT FANTASIES

The housewife-based family form has been undermined by cap-italist development itself. But nuclear families, as contradictory sites of violence and interdependence, still survive. They survive as the intensification of the private household. They also survive in the persistence, or resurrection, of the fantasy of the white, norma-tive family form as the basis of social order.

In the United States, since the 1980s, the Right has had an ongoing and shifting revanchist vision of rolling back the social gains of women, queers, and BIPOC movements. Central to this vision is a return to the family. The changes in family life over recent decades help make sense of this ideological current. White working-class Americans and Europeans have seen a massive realignment of gender and sexual relations compounded by declining economic stability. A housewife and a family wage job used to provide masculine dignity, a place where even a work-ing-class man could demand and enjoy the subjugation of others. The family provided white men, across class, a protected space where they could act out sexual and gender fantasies and have their sexual and affective needs met. It was a refuge from the trials of wage labor. Husbands could be assured that someone else would do the work of reproduction. Proletarian men and women fought for, won, and defended that family form across multiple generations, and now it is no longer available. Some have found a queer feminist politics that holds the promise of a far greater humanity. Others turn to the misogynistic options offered by other embittered white men: fascist organizations, incel discussion boards, self-help misogynistic YouTube channels, the anti-feminist humor of social democratic podcasts, or politicians who celebrate themselves as open rapists and sexual harassers.

The importance of the family as an imagined basis of social order and morality has several manifestations. It is a familiar feature of right-wing, neoconservative politics, and is frequently deployed in religious fundamentalism of all sorts. The patriarchal nuclear family is the ideological bedrock of right-wing religious movements' vision of social order, in their ongoing assaults on the gains of gay rights and women's rights. Religious conservatives share with many social scientists a belief that stable heterosexual couples are the basis for raising moral, socially upstanding children. Even on the left, loyalty to the family marks one's commitment to organizing a normative fantasy of the working class, against the supposed "distractions" of queer, countercultural, and feminist activists. Social science continues to devote reams of research to establishing how nontraditional parenting arrangements, particularly among poor and Black people, are the cause of crime and many other social ills. Mainstream gay activists emphasize the family-like stability and rectitude of their domestic arrangements as a central component of a politics critically termed *homonormative*. All these manifestations—religious conservatives, social scientists, and homonormative gays—share a focus on stable couples as a basis of parenting and a thorough commitment to gender normativity.

The cultural and ideological function of family as a social norm persists today, deployed to largely reactionary ends through a series of diverse political struggles. The outsized role of the family in our contemporary political imaginary is due to the persistence of precisely that which made the male-breadwinner family form once so attractive for the workers' movement: the ideological power of the family as a claim to moral, social, and cultural legitimacy. For those under the direct assault of racist state policies, the language of the family provides a recognizable strategy of self-defense. Even for those who object to the racist or heterosexist norms of traditional family ideals, the family can be extremely compelling as a fantasy of refuge and support. We all yearn for care, for support, for love. We all want a home that feels safe and welcoming. We all want protection from a cruel and difficult world. The form that yearning often takes is the language and fantasy of the family. Given this central role of the family in the popular imagination, what is the meaning of family abolition today?

PART III

Toward the Commune

10

New Alliances, New Kinship

In the first years of the twenty-first century, the US LGBT rights movement faced a juncture. Across much of the country, they had won court ruling or laws protecting people against discrimination based on sexual orientation. Like most US progressive politics, gains were geographically polarized, with few victories in the states that had once been dominated by slavery and Jim Crow. But in several highly populated states, discrimination against gays and lesbians was illegal, and these policies seemed to be spreading. One relatively progressive wing of the movement considered prioritizing political fights to expand anti-discrimination laws to include protections for transgender people. This call overlapped with those who pushed for LGBT organizations to shift to focus on others historically excluded from the gay rights movement: queer and trans people facing poverty, police violence, incarceration, and the violence of state immigration policy. Some pointed to the need for labor unions and generally worker protections to substantively challenge anti-gay employers. Protections against discrimination at work are of little help in a country with "at will" employment— where employers can fire any employee at any time without reason.

These progressive queer voices were drowned out. Instead, by the 2008 presidential election the American gay rights movement had overwhelmingly pivoted its resources to focusing solely on one policy goal: marriage equality. This represented a significant shift in priorities. Marriage was not a significant movement goal in the late 1990s, and few activists had suggested it be central. The following years, however, introduced a number of factors that drove such a pivot. Christian religious conservatives had taken up the issue, preemptively banning gay marriage as a means of galvanizing homophobic constituents. This pushed LGBT activists to take the issue more seriously than they had as a defensive maneuver.

Gay marriage became legal in Massachusetts in 2004, and briefly in California, causing a flurry of high-profile wedding celebrations. But most importantly, gay marriage became the movement's priority because it was the major concern of the movement's wealthiest donors.[1]

Though most LGBTQ people were working class or poor, a small stratum of white gay people had gained a foothold in a handful of high-income professions in the United States, including finance, entertainment, and real estate. They had developed dense social networks and shared values. The used their resources to shape the future of gay organizations. They were generally liberal and disinterested in issues primarily affecting queer and trans people of color or those living in poverty. They were, however, centrally concerned with marriage. Marriage offered significant financial benefits for wealthy couples, including a major reduction in inheritance and income taxes. Gay marriage also took on tremendous psychic importance, precisely because of the symbolic centrality of the family form. Gay marriage signaled the acceptance of gay and lesbian people into the fantasy of the normative family. It meant full acceptance into a mainstream psychic imaginary, one rooted in property and whiteness.

Though most working-class queer people supported marriage equality, it was far from a central priority. As gay marriage was legalized, Black and working-class same-sex couples used marriage ceremonies as a chance to gain recognition from hostile family members. But in general, poor people in the United States marry at much lower rates and enjoy significantly fewer benefits to marriage. Divorce is prohibitively expensive to many, and marriage is usually penalized in disability and welfare support. However, the fantasy of the family based in marriage is a powerful one and is compelling for those Black and working-class people able to access it. As the goal of marriage came to dominate the movement, a vocal opposition articulated a strong critique of gay marriage. Some criticized the history and institution of marriage, including its long roots in misogyny, property ownership, and white supremacy. Others emphasized the need to refuse assimilation, to advocate and defend an alternative mode of queer, anti-normative life.[2] Many critiqued the movement's sole focus on the issue, at the expense of issues like trans rights, queer people in prison, or queer poverty. The gay liberation movement had once championed the overthrow of the private family; now the gay movement that had replaced them consisted of ardent defenders of quite normative family ideals.

In 2006 one particularly compelling critical statement brought together over two hundred fifty LGBTQ activists as signatories. "Beyond Same-Sex Marriage: A New Strategic Vision for All Our Families and Relationships" called for an overhaul of marriage and family public policy.[3] The statement argued that "household and family diversity is already the norm," including the variety of ways people form households and support relationships, such as extended families in migrant households, caregiving relationships for people living with AIDS, close friendships and siblings cohabitating, and alternative parenting arrangements. The statement highlighted the impact of poverty on household formation, and the political right's sophisticated multi-issue strategy to enforce patriarchal marriage relationships. According to the statement, the LGBT movement should support "many avenues through which households, families, partners, and kinship relationships can gain access to the support of a caring civil society." Rather than marriage being the centerpiece of family law, people should have the legal means to state validation and public benefits for the variety of ways people form households. The statement calls on a coalition effort "for creating powerful and vibrant new relationships, coalitions, and alliances across constituencies—communities of color, immigrant communities, LGBT and queer communities, senior citizens, single-parent families, the working poor, and more," pointing to several specific policy struggles.

The "Beyond Same-Sex Marriage" statement reflected many of the principles of an earlier influential essay on queer struggle. In 1997 Cathy J. Cohen authored "Punks, Bulldaggers, and Welfare Queens: The Radical Potential of Queer Politics?" The essay opens by surveying the emergence of queer politics as an effort to link radical activism and academic theory in a refusal of normative and stable identity categories. Cohen identifies the severe limits and failures of this effort. Queer politics, unable to adequately incorporate race, gender, and class, is unable to effectively challenge heteronormativity. She calls for a rethinking of the term *queer*, linking it to intersectional Black feminism and leftist politics. She outlines the long history of racist demonization of Black family life, the role of slavery and racism in shaping Black kinship, and efforts to regulate and discipline Black kinship formation. Central to this analysis is recognizing how racist, normative family politics have attacked heterosexual, poor Black women. In her conclusion, Cohen calls for "radical coalition work," through an "intersectional analysis of who and what the enemy is and where our potential allies can be found," one not "rooted in our shared history or identity, but in our shared marginal relationships to dominant power which normalizes, legitimizes, and privileges." She writes:

> As we stand on the verge of watching those in power disman-
> tle the welfare system through a process of demonizing poor
> and young, primarily poor and young women of color—many of
> whom have existed for their entire lives outside the white, mid-
> dle-class, heterosexual norm—we have to ask if these women do
> not fit into society's categories of marginal, deviant, and "queer."[4]

Cohen points to ACT UP New York's needle exchange and prison organizing as an example of such coalition projects that both destabilize and politicize identity categories. She could also have included her participation in the founding of the Audre Lorde Project, a New York–based organizing effort among LGBTQ people of color. The "punks," "bulldaggers," and "welfare queens" of her title are potential constituencies of this radical coalition vision, all linked together through their marginalization in American family politics.

As Cohen and the "Beyond Same-Sex Marriage" statement demonstrate, the struggle to overcome the family can be a call for radical coalition politics that recognize the interconnections between varied movements. While later chapters of this book will consider the revolutionary horizon of family abolition, this chapter considers the uses of challenging the family as a progressive politics in the absence of a broader revolutionary possibility.

COALITION STRUGGLE BEYOND THE FAMILY

Diverse constituencies have much to gain from a massive overhaul in family law and public policy in regulating private households. Many interconnected groups particularly suffer through the current dominance of the private household and personal dependency as nearly the sole alternative to wage labor. These constituencies and their allies are all currently in struggle, in varying political projects and organizations. A politics moving beyond the family could join the following constituencies together, strengthen their solidarities, and forge new policy agendas reflecting their interlinked concerns:

1. People living with disabilities. Many forms of disabilities make it difficult to reproduce oneself through wage labor. Capitalist society largely defines ability through one's ability to work. Currently, people living with disabilities that prevent them from working are faced with two grim and difficult options: meager social services or depending on one's family. Many people with serious, long-term disabilities remain trapped with their families of origin, leaving them vulnerable to caregiver abuse and violence. If more supports are available beyond the family, people with disabilities could exercise greater autonomy in who they love, how they live, and who they depend on.

2. Trans children and adolescents. More and more children are questioning their genders early in life. When supported and recognized by others, trans children come out. They change their gender presentation and identity in early childhood, elect to avoid the often-devastating experience of gender-discordant puberty, and instead pursue gender-affirming transitioning as it becomes available. But many trans children are born into unwelcoming and unsupportive families. Such families often respond to their children's identities and expressions in ways that can vary from quiet discouragement to murderous abuse. Parents' unilateral and near total control over a child's life offers no alternatives to trans children. The difficulties they face are one example of the broader crisis of violence against children, in-

cluding sexual, physical, and emotional abuse. Reforms that expand care outside the family could enable these children to escape violence and live gender-affirming lives.

3. People in abusive relationships. Intimate partner violence and relationship abuse can take many forms. Feminist activists have long argued that abuse is constituted by multiple linked practices to control and dominate a partner. In heterosexual relationships, women face the vast majority of abuse. Severely abusive relationships can be difficult to leave. Abusers are more likely to have outside jobs, control over financial resources, and control over outside contact. The dominance of the private family as one of the only means of survival for those without wealth or income traps survivors in abusive relationships with few means of escape. To make escaping abuse more readily possible, people need to be confident that leaving their partner will not lead to poverty.

4. People targeted by state violence. Following the long legacy of racist assault on kinship ties between people of color (detailed in Part II of this book), BIPOC families continue to face ongoing state violence. In 2021 Black American men were incarcerated at five times the rates of white men. That same year, one in eighty-one Black adults was incarcerated in a state prison.[5] Every year, US police kill over a thousand men, disproportionately Black men.[6] Moreover, immigration and border enforcement strictly limits who migrants can live with, including for parenting, romantic partnership, and multigenerational households. The practice of US officials of separating detained children and adults at the US-Mexican border briefly gripped headlines under Trump but existed both before and after his administration.[7] State violence, combined with the impact of poverty, has enormous consequences for how people constitute households. It removes partners, parents, and children from their homes and inflicts trauma on everyone who survives it, and on their loved ones and families. People targeted by state violence are far more likely to have unconventional strategies of care and to live outside the normative family ideal. In chapter 2 I outlined Dorothy Roberts's research on the devastating impact of the

family policy system. The end to the family policing system and drastic reworking of the family in public policy could better enable immigrants, BIPOC, and others targeted by state violence to find stability and support in the relationships they choose.

5. People living in poverty. Poverty prevents people from having stable households or family structures, and forces people to adopt unconventional arrangements to make it through life. Poor people are far less likely to marry, less likely to stay with a romantic partner throughout their life, less likely to parent in two-parent arrangements, and less likely to constitute their household exclusively around a two-generation nuclear structure. In research conducted during the implementation of welfare reform, sociologist Katherine Edin interviewed a group of low-income single mothers about their choice not to marry. She found they offered clear, articulate, and fully rational reasons: they identified that marriage could easily undermine control over their own lives, potentially make them poorer, and be a source of violence.[8]

6. Queer adults and others living in nonnormative households. Queers often depend on close friends for support, as they are more likely to be estranged from their families of origin and are less likely to have children themselves. Queer parents often have nonconventional parenting structures, due to both entering into partnerships that involve children from past relationships and deliberate efforts at finding adequate support for raising children. Queer families are sometimes self-consciously chosen, motivated by a progressive, feminist politics that eschews traditional patriarchal families. Queer families are one example of a much broader constellation of nontraditional households that have become widespread.

The overlap between these groups is considerable. This list could be considerably expanded: people living alone, people in old age, anyone struggling with an illness, and so on. Some of these people listed here would primarily benefit from *a means of escape*— positive, affirming, and caring alternatives to their existing households, and the material conditions necessary for supporting themselves outside of their current households. Even when they choose to stay, the means of escape may increase their standing within the household. Others would primarily benefit from an overhaul of public policy, distribution of material resources, and cultural valuation to *embrace and support nontraditional forms of household formation*. Finally, all would benefit from the expansion of forms of care readily available outside the private household. They are all potential constituents in a broad-based political effort to move beyond the family.

PROGRESSIVE ANTI-FAMILY REFORMS

These struggles against and beyond narrow, coercive family forms point us to a broad variety of potential reform projects. Under nonrevolutionary conditions, progressive reform visions can motivate and expand opportunities for struggle, win improvements in people's immediate lives, and lesson the intensity of daily experiences of coercion and violence. Moving a political vision beyond the rhetorical horizon of defending and prioritizing the family draws attention to the potential value of various progressive policies. These are potentially nonreformist reforms, in the sense that their implementation could expand many people's ability to live under chosen circumstances and to be free of immediate violence, thereby allowing them to participate more fully in future social movement activity. Here I outline a few reform visions that could potentially advance a family-abolitionist politics.

Broadly conceived, progressive anti-family reforms are those that expand the capacity of large numbers of people to consensually choose living arrangements, intimate partnerships, and child-rearing practices that work best for them. Such policies lessen the coercion built into family structures by reducing the considerable material and personal costs to opting out of any given family arrangement. They also facilitate and aid people in forming unconventional and nonnormative kinship arrangements. I use the term *progressive anti-family reforms* to distinguish such policy goals from a full family abolitionism that could not occur within capitalist society. Like family abolitionism, anti-family reforms are not opposed to any given chosen-kin relationship, except insofar as a kin arrangement is harmful to those involved. These reforms allow people to form new families as easily as they may choose to leave old ones, and in this sense are sometimes described as pro-family. But conservative and right-wing commentators are onto something when they suggest that expanded unconditional welfare states, for example, erode the basis of the traditional family. When people have substantive and positive alternatives, they are much more likely to leave bad relationships, including fleeing abusive parents or partners. The ability to leave relationships without facing deprivation increases gender and sexual freedom, making it easier for people to pursue sexual desires and gender expressions that their families of origin reject. At the same time, it also provides people the material leverage to be able to call on their families for respect, dignity, and freedom from harm because they have alternatives available. Progressive anti-family reforms expand the ease and availability of such alternatives to dependence on coercive family forms.

The welfare rights movement pursued one such progressive anti-family reform: unconditional, substantially generous cash-transfer benefits, today often termed universal basic income (UBI). UBI has been extensively debated on the left and is increasingly popular in neoliberal and right-wing circles. There are a wide variety of forms UBI could conceivably take. UBI could constitute a progressive anti-family reform only if accessible and generous enough to allow people to comfortably live after leaving bad relationships with parents or spouses, enabling them to move out, achieve economic independence, and then make new choices about who they want in their lives.

Social democratic collective benefits of all sorts have a potential to undermine the coercion of family life: public and social housing, cheap or free mass transit, free universal healthcare, access to quality free food, even free education. These are all potential forms of universal social benefits. Each is a social good that, in some contexts, people access through their family. If you depend on your spouse for health insurance, your parents for housing, or your partner to buy groceries, you are far less likely to leave when things go wrong, or to make radically different choices about how you want to live. Social democratic systems that readily provide social goods increase the range and flexibility of people being able to choose how they want to structure their households.[9] These are progressive anti-family reforms to the extent to which they are easily and widely accessible, generous, not dependent on work, and not dependent on one's family structure and marital status.

Other reforms can particularly aid people in accessing forms of interpersonal care typically provided within the family. Universal free childcare, early childhood education, and public schooling all aid in lessening the labor of raising children. Disabled and elderly people can choose to stay in their homes—or to avoid abusive care providers—if they are able to access adequate state-funded home care support. The US-based National Domestic Workers Association and Caring Across Generations are currently organizing for universal home care for disabled and elderly people. Under such programs, government funds would pay domestic workers living wages to do reproductive services like house cleaning, grocery shopping, food shopping, and aid in personal healthcare and hygiene for elderly and disabled people.

Adolescent social services also have a potential to be progressive, anti-family programs. Queer and trans youth are particularly likely to be thrown out of their homes, or to choose to flee abusive relationships. Poor and BIPOC queer and trans youth often end up homeless, dependent on criminalized hustles, mutual aid networks, and social service programs like queer youth shelters. Expanding the availability of permanent supportive housing for queer young people has the potential to aid children in accessing stable lives outside their families of origin.

Alongside the expansions of state-provided public goods, legal changes in the regulation of families constitute progressive anti-family reforms. Legally married couple relationships are currently given extensive legal and policy benefits in tax codes, property law, healthcare decision-making, parenting and adoption, housing zoning codes, and social supports. Any family arrangements that fall outside the couple-based nuclear family structure face various forms of penalties and restrictions. These vary by nation and by regional laws and policies. The multiple movements pushing against and beyond the narrow family form have much to gain in a massive overhaul of family law to eliminate the considerable disparities between normative and nonnormative household arrangements.

These various anti-family reforms have particular power for improving the well-being of queer and trans youth, women in abusive relationships, and disabled and elder proletarians. They can benefit Black and migrant proletarians more likely to choose unconventional household structures. They have the potential to expand gender and sexual freedom for all working-class people. Those committed to gender and sexual liberation should pursue working-class-led struggles to win and implement such progressive anti-family reforms.

Just as this book was being edited in September 2022, Cuba passed a comprehensive reform to its national family code. Incorporating months of thousands of neighborhood-based discussions, the national referendum legalized same-sex marriage and adoption, redefined parenthood as responsibility rather than custody over children, banned corporal punishment, expanded rights to self-determination for elderly and disabled people, and extended labor rights to all who care for children. In its opening statement of principles, the code defines *family* as relationships based on dignity, and principles of "equality and non-discrimination, plurality, individual and shared responsibility, solidarity, the seeking of happiness." A flurry of Twitter commentators linked the new family code to family abolition critique. Cuba's family code is a powerful example of the kinds of reforms that could support nontraditional household formation and undo the normative valorization of some family forms at the expense of other care relations.

CHOSEN FAMILY

In addition to demanding major reforms to bolster life outside of the private household and nuclear family, millions of people are attempting to forge immediate alternatives to normative family life right now. These are efforts to constitute households that differ in varying and often self-conscious ways from oppressive family ideals, and the isolation of the private nuclear household. These efforts draw from diverse political traditions, including many covered in chapter 8: feminism, gay liberation, Black liberation, anarchism, and trans radicalism. Efforts to build alternatives to the nuclear family are most ardently pursued by those excluded from family life, often due to racialized poverty. These are often called *chosen family*.

As detailed in previous chapters, since the Great Migration, working-class Black Americans have formed households that horrified white observers. Generations of Black people were raised by female-headed households, saw adult women working outside the home, and formed households without stable and present fathers. This was driven by the structural conditions of racial capitalism, including chronic underemployment, poverty, and mass incarceration. It also reflected a commitment to a degree of sexual freedom and choice by Black women. Under these conditions, Black women have turned to extended family and complex kin relationships for support in parenting and surviving poverty.[10] Black feminist theory, drawing on Black women's care practices, has offered powerful theorizing of mutual care, kin-making, and love. Alexis Pauline Gumbs has developed the concept of *mothering* as radical practice and theory of care. In her dissertation "We Can Learn to Mother Ourselves"[11] and in her coedited volume *Revolutionary Mothering*,[12] Gumbs traces a revolutionary orientation to care and nurturing in Black lesbian and Black queer movements. Drawing on Spillers, she distinguishes between *motherhood* as a white, patriarchal status, and *mothering*, "natural work, that survival dance."[13] Gumbs detailed efforts by Black lesbians in the late 1970s and 1980s to radically rethink mothering: At a 1979 National Third World Lesbian and Gay Conference, Audre Lorde announced "All children of lesbians are ours,"[14] suggesting a collective vision of responsibility and mothering. A participant at that conference wrote "All third world lesbians share in the responsibility for the care of nurturing of the children of individual lesbians of color."[15] In a 1979 lesbian periodical, a multiracial couple Mary Peña and Barbara Carey offered their vision of lesbian parenting, refusing the concept that children are property of their parents:

THEY WILL NOT BELONG TO THE PATRIARCHY
THEY WILL NOT BELONG TO US EITHER
THEY WILL BELONG ONLY TO THEMSELVES.[16]

Working-class queer and trans people also have a broad history of efforts to establish alternative households and care arrangements. Many queer and trans people are estranged from their families of origin. As detailed in chapter 9, they are less likely to have kids or extended family to rely on in old age. AIDS wreaked mass death and chronic disability for generations of gay men. In response to these conditions, queer and trans people have self-consciously formed mutual support relationships as chosen family.[17] Many young queer people deliberately have sought out group houses as a form of intentional supportive community.

Poor Black and Latinx LGBTQ people constituted one of the most lasting and developed practices of chosen family in the ballroom scene. Ballroom brings together thousands of people through periodic competitive dance events. Participants join *houses* that function as central support networks of mutual aid. House members establish formal relationships of support and guidance with each other named for biological kin relations—an elder trans woman has House Mother as a formal title; a house member has Sisters, Brothers, Nieces, and Nephews, along with other members of the house. The ballroom scene has been instrumental for large numbers of young Black and Latina trans women to be able to secure adequate support and resources to transition.[18]

Chosen family of Black, queer, and proletarian life has been a strategy of survival and resistance in the conditions of capitalism. Radically alternative household forms, in addition to being consciously chosen, are often formed in the face of poverty. It takes wealth or stable access to wage labor to form a nuclear family. Those excluded from such property relationships turn to other strategies to survive. All of these alternative, resistant families can be powerful expressions of yearning toward human freedom and articulations of family abolitionism in the present. They can all offer the chosen, mutually supportive care fundamental to a free society. These potentially healing and radical families are all worth, in many contexts, defending and expanding. Chosen family are moments of family abolition, expressions of the desire to move beyond a normative family form. Efforts to pursue chosen family have been a primary form through which proletarian people have cared for each other, have moved toward freedom, and have glimpsed the possibility of collective emancipation.

LIMITS OF REFORMING THE PRIVATE HOUSEHOLD

Both progressive anti-family reforms and chosen family face considerable limitations in a capitalist society. People can and do fight for the anti-family reforms detailed above through the language of embracing family diversity, defending chosen family, or expanding the meaning of family. These are rhetorical devices that still exclude the immense diversity of potential chosen living arrangements, kinship ties, care relations, and strategies of social reproduction. Chosen family and family diversity, while worth defending, do not include the myriad ways in which people may choose to relate to each other. Leftists and social democrats exclusively focusing on defending the family betray the working class in its full rich diversity. Further, any expansions to social benefits face considerable obstacles. As outlined in the previous chapter, global capitalism has faced a protracted economic downturn since the 1970s, resulting in a transnational organized ruling-class offensive to displace the costs of this crisis onto the working class. Broadly termed *neoliberalism*, this offensive has included substantial rollback of welfare state programs won in the post–World War II era. In this context, it has proved extremely difficult for working-class and poor movements to win an expansion or preservation of welfare benefits. The handful of examples of nations that have expanded welfare provision during this time have largely depended on oil revenues or other commodity boom exports, not a strategy available everywhere. Social democracy might be enjoying a popular revival in the Anglophone world, but it has achieved few major policy victories.

Welfare programs can only offer progressive anti-family reforms when they are structured in ways that do not enforce and regulate family forms. Welfare states have long structured access to benefits in ways that attempt to coerce people into conventional family structures and punish those who live otherwise. These policies were tied not only to conventional heterosexism, misogyny, eugenics, xenophobia, and anti-Black racism, but also to the particular limitations of welfare provision in a capitalist society. Funding welfare benefits under capitalism depended on the steady expansion of profitable industries, full employment, and social policies that discouraged workers from opting out of the labor force. States found substantial welfare programs affordable only so long as the bulk of the working class were in heterosexual households with a wage worker. While the struggles of the 1960s and 1970s tried to move beyond the heterosexual and racist logic of social democracy, it was never clear if this was achievable under capitalism. If anything, it has since become even more unlikely and difficult.

Within the constraints of capitalist states separated from direct mass working-class control, welfare programs were rarely sympathetic to their recipients. Often, poverty-relief programs are deeply dehumanizing. Need-based welfare programs were often deliberately following cruel and abusive policies, involved elaborate impersonal and discouraging bureaucracies, and were generally resented by all involved. Nancy Fraser has argued that neoliberalism's attack on social democracy, state programs, and welfare benefits gained ground in part because it seized on and co-opted the anti-state sentiments of social movements of the 1960s and 1970s.[19] Winning welfare programs again will have to contend with the grim fact that almost no one remembers them particularly fondly. The true radical democratization of anti-family reforms will ultimately require overcoming the capitalist state.

Chosen families, too, encounter significant limits. They can quickly run into many of the oppressive logics of the family. Some of the contradictions and harms of the family are inherent to functioning in capitalist society. These logics shape and distort the shared freedom dreams of chosen family. As they combine dependency and care like the family does, they are also potential spaces of personal coercion and violence. All chosen families today are lived under capitalist conditions, constrained and torqued by the brutality of wage labor and racial capitalism. So long as members of households have to navigate labor markets or state programs in order to survive, the forces of racial capitalism put damaging pressure on the internal relationships between household members. Extended networks of caring friendships often break down in the face of inevitable economic crisis. In queer countercultures, for example, the common occurrences of people relocating for work or even having a child can rapidly rend long-standing networks of care. People's lives are profoundly bisected by class and racial stratifications, and aspirations of mutual care rarely can survive intact in the face of crises of severe chaotic drug use, prolonged unemployment, incarceration, or mental illness. Capitalism and the conditions of working-class life destabilize the broader communities and social networks that chosen family may rely on.

Other critics, including Sophie Lewis and Ariel Ajeno, have pointed to the exclusive character of chosen family. Conventional families have the pretense of unconditionality—you are welcome because you are family: no one has to choose you. But needing to be chosen requires the active sympathy of others. This allows for considerable coercion, evaluation, and status competition. If chosen family becomes necessary for material survival, survival becomes bound up with status and the opinions of others. What happens to those who are not chosen?

NEW CARE, NEW KINSHIP

Whatever their limitations, chosen family and progressive anti-family reforms have powerful potentials. The family serves as an institution that organizes multiple forms of personal domination, property, and social legitimacy. Because the family links multiple forms of oppression, it excludes or oppresses diverse and varied constituencies. Coalition struggle, in joining multiple constituencies, must go beyond just a transactional exchange of calculated self-interest. Instead, collective action can also forge new bonds of care and solidarity. In collective action, people can learn to fight alongside each other, learn to trust each other, learn to value a positive form of interdependence. Like chosen family, these can become new chosen relationships of care. This shared solidarity, this camaraderie, is a powerful basis of love. AIDS militants and Black feminists are two overlapping movements that have contested and expanded notions of family through the experience of struggle itself, and with it forged new ideas of the meaning of love and care.

The language of kin and kin-making, though not without problems, has inspired many radical critics of the family. Struggling together is a form of making new kin. This making kin through collective struggle is a naming of the positive quality of solidarity and love that many people search for in families. Making kin, or becoming kin, is a powerful and rich theoretical concept. Theorists have used kin-making to explore heterogeneity in care formations cross-culturally, emphasized nonnuclear family arrangements, traced solidarity between human and nonhuman life, and linked multiple radical conceptual tendencies.[20] Across multiple currents of writing, kin-making is a means of negotiating difference, of bridging radically differing experiences beyond a logic of affinity based on sameness. Becoming kin goes beyond the communities of affinity that often constitute chosen family. It can be an ethical, spiritual, and political practice of opening onto the transformative possibility of connection to with others. In our highly segregated and divided world, I argue that such radical forms of kinship are most possible through shared collective struggle. Mass movements have the potential to forge solidarity across difference as a necessary strategy of survival and care.

As one example of making kin in struggle: In New York City, queer youth of color facing police harassment in the gentrifying piers of Greenwich Village, organized through an organization called FIERCE. FIERCE has fought curfews on the piers, opposed police harassment, and sought to expand the political power of queer youth of color. Many members of FIERCE have spent time homeless and have relied on their chosen family for support. Many come from poor Black and Latinx families of origin that have borne the brunt of NYC's deindustrialization, welfare austerity, and mass incarceration. FIERCE is substantively multiracial, bridging multiple BIPOC communities, as well as substantively gender diverse. At the end of many of their protests, FIERCE members together recite a chant three times, at increasing volume. It is a quote by Black revolutionary Assata Shakur that embodies this spirit of revolutionary love as a form of solidarity:

IT IS OUR DUTY TO FIGHT FOR OUR FREEDOM.
IT IS OUR DUTY TO WIN.

WE MUST LOVE EACH OTHER AND PROTECT EACH
OTHER.
WE HAVE NOTHING TO LOSE BUT OUR CHAINS.[21]

To fulfill the vision of revolutionary mothering, of chosen family, of progressive anti-family reforms, we need to go beyond class society. Discussions of chosen family do offer something essential to a revolutionary project: a recognition of the power of love and solidarity through collective action. This capacity for solidarity is essential in the coming chapters, as we move toward imagining revolutionary horizons beyond the family.

11

Communist Social Reproduction

Over the last decade, the call to abolish the family has reemerged. Black feminists, trans communists, and other radical thinkers have written powerfully on the limits and violence of the family, as well as the need for its overcoming. After the decline of the Red Decade, some feminists maintained their critiques of the family through the late 1970s and early 1980s. But from the late 1980s into the twenty-first century, family abolition nearly completely disappeared as a current of explicit thought. Now it has appeared again in radical research.

Why has family-abolitionist thought emerged now, in the twenty-first century? The protracted capitalist crises since the 1970s have effectively destroyed the basis of the housewife-based family ideal, as detailed in chapter 9. Through the 1980s and 1990s, the steady erosion of this family form was attributed to various specific social groups: gays and lesbians, the sexual choices of Black women, women pursuing professional independence, or a turning away from Christian doctrine. Meanwhile, through the 1990s and 2000s the protracted stagnation of the rate of profit was obscured by multiple asset and commodity bubbles. Those households who saw the growth in the value of their mortgaged homes or retirement accounts could avoid recognizing the broad erosion in working-class life. The 2008 world financial crisis shattered the illusion of widespread affluence and brought together in popular understanding the crisis of social reproduction, the erosion of traditional family forms, and broader macroeconomic forces of stagnant wages and wealth inequality. This recognition that the changing dynamics of family forms had deeper origins than individual or countercultural choice has been accelerated by the effects of COVID-19. People are attempting to understand the deep links between the family, capitalist social reproduction, and multiple overlapping crises. Recognizing that the present crisis of the family is unsustainable, many also do not wish we could or should return to some prior era of imagined family stability. Recent radical currents of thinking—such as queer and trans radicalism, social reproduction theory, Black feminism—have helped many to make sense of this conjuncture. Contemporary family abolitionists are speaking to this widespread need for something radically new in how we organize our domestic lives.

Family abolition's reemergence was marked with the 2015 essay "Kinderkommunismus: A Feminist Analysis of the 21st-Century Family and a Communist Proposal for its Abolition." In it, trans communists J. J. Gleeson and K. D. Griffiths offer one of the first explicitly family-abolitionist texts of the current era.[1] Following an account of the transformation and persistence of the family as "a loose, flexible, yet socially binding institution," they offer a critique of the insufficiency of "queer rejectionism"—individual and counterculture anti-assimilationist refusal of mainstream culture as the central axis of radical queer politics. They follow this with a theorization of the family in capitalism and the meaning and potential of its abolition. They go on to propose "the anti-dyadic crèche" as a speculative form of the "counter-familial institution" to meet the social needs for generational reproduction. The universal crèche would be a voluntary institution to raise children for their first two decades, consolidating all childcare programs, schools, and universities to actively break down existing forms of stratification and social division. Skilled providers would form intimate long-term relationships with infants in these collective institutions, followed by a full program of development and skill training to adulthood.

In a 2018 article, Madeline Lane-McKinley grapples with the concept and practice of childhood. Their work offered an early explicit formulation of *care* as the social good provided by families that may be broadened in family abolition. They write of such shared practices of collective interdependence: "How does the revolutionary horizon of the end of 'the family' as a unit of private property mobilize us toward a fuller, less exploitive vision of care? This longing for collective caretaking must be hand-in-hand with any discourse against the family—otherwise doomed to logics of self-management and autonomy."[2] Lane-McKinley richly traces the figure of the child in popular discourse, both idealized as innocent and utterly subordinated. They argue that we must abolish "the border between child and adult," and issue a revolutionary call to "re-think the adult-child relationship as one of mutual care and learning," based on comradeship. That same year, Tiffany Lethabo King reviewed the rich tradition of family critique among Black radical theorists, engaging Kay Lindsay, Hortense Spillers, and the fiction writer Sapphire.[3] King offers a powerful linking of Afro-pessimist critiques of the human as a category constituted in opposition to the slave and the logic of the white family. She points to "the violent ways that the family emerges as a category of violent forms of humanism. I consider the possible abolition of the family (and Black family) because I fear that the institution crowds out the dynamic and emerging ways that Black people reimagine and invent new modes of relation."[4] In King's account, even queer, Black, alternative family forms can reinforce "liberal humanist epistemes and economies of intelligibility"[5] integral to anti-Blackness. She concludes by pointing toward a revolutionary possibility in Black "life outside of the current categories that blunt efforts to re-craft what it means to be human. There are other ways to name each other as our relations."[6]

Kathi Weeks wrote a 2021 article in *Feminist Theory* explicitly in support of family abolition. She extensively explores the family in three facets: as "a privatised system of social reproduction, the couple form, and bio-genetic-centred kinship,"[7] focusing as I do here primarily on the family as a privatized system of care. She draws extensively from feminist theorists of the 1970s and 1980s. She emphasizes the need for "a systematic critique and wholesale alternative to the family,"[8] and abolitionism as a protracted process with necessary intermediate reforms.

The most prominent family-abolitionist theorist of the recent era is Sophie Lewis. Lewis's 2019 book on the politics of gestational surrogacy—evocatively titled *Full Surrogacy Now: Feminism Against Family*—successfully catapulted family abolition as a major topic of debate in leftist circles. It raised the ire of social democrats, captured the imagination of other trans communists, and evocatively spoke to a range of feminist, queer, and radical readers. Lewis went on to do a series of interviews, short articles, and public appearances on the topic.[9] Lewis's most extensive treatment of the topic is offered in their 2022 book *Abolish the Family: A Manifesto for Care and Liberation*, published while the present text was in production. Lewis's argument is extensive, paralleling my own here.[10] Lewis provides a powerful engagement with the many personal fears, anxieties, and critiques evoked by demands to abolish the family. The text ranges broadly across history, providing a succinct but remarkable summation of two hundred years of family-abolitionist thought. Lewis engages deliberately with the racial tensions of family abolition politics and highlights the Black radical legacies of abolition. Lewis also provides an extensive listing of recent writing on family abolition, a reading list worth pursuing in depth.[11] *Abolish the Family* movingly concludes by calling for "comrades against kinship":

> *Being together as people* and ending the separation of *people*—this is a future that can be imagined, even if it cannot be fully desired yet, at least, not by us. I don't know how to desire it fully, but I can't wait to see what comes after the family. I also know I probably won't see whatever it is. Still, I hope it happens, and I hope it is a glorious and abundant nothing.[12]

For Lewis, as the family is an organized form of scarcity, the nothingness that is put in its place is an abundant freedom.

In contrast to the academic queer theorists of the 1980s and 1990s, several of these authors—Griffiths, Gleeson, Lewis, and Lane-McKinley—are all concerned with the revolutionary project of communism. King similarly takes a broader and revolutionary political view through an Afro-pessimist critique that points beyond the limits of the social and psychic category of the human. These works emphasize family abolition as conceivable only within major and fundamental social transformation, rather than an individual or countercultural lifestyle. Each of these authors attempt to account, in varying ways, for the fragmentation of gender relations through the political and economic transformations of the family since the 1970s. They each seek out some means of restructuring the activity of generational reproduction that enables a nearly inconceivable horizon of human freedom. They also all speak both from and to the current conjuncture, as four decades of capitalist crisis and eroding working-class reproduction are no longer possible to ignore.

The remainder of this chapter theorizes the qualities of family abolition to be a basis of a free, communist society. The following chapter then uses this framework to identify emergent efforts to go beyond the family in popular mass protest movements, finally turning in chapter 13 toward imagining a potential form of the future commune. Together, these three chapters are an effort to theorize revolutionary family abolition beyond racial capitalism.

STRATEGY, RHETORIC, AND REVOLUTIONARY MOMENTS

Opponents of family abolition are numerous. On the right are those who (possibly accurately) argue that family abolitionists are seeking to destroy the basis of the patriarchal heterosexual family and civilization itself. The entire political center is unified around a romantic embrace of families and defends a vast range of social policies on the basis that they strengthen or aid families. Many serious Black, Native, and Latinx activists have expressed skepticism about anti-family politics, given the necessity of the family as a support system for many BIPOC and the long-standing white supremacist state attack on BIPOC families.[13] Perhaps the most vocal opponents of family abolition come from the social democratic left.[14] Among their many objections, social democratic opponents to family abolition argue that the phrase and its adherents alienate the majority of the working class. This raises questions about rhetoric, strategy, and revolutionary thought. In the course of concrete organizing around housing, workplace issues, or state violence, it is a widespread truism that one should not present a political line likely to immediately alienate one's potential supporters. From the perspective of those trying to build majoritarian politics, family abolition seems needlessly provocative.

Family abolition, admittedly, is not a slogan likely to inspire mass enthusiasm in the current political climate. It invokes a politics fraught with misunderstanding and anxiety, including among many of the constituencies that may have the most to gain in overcoming the family form. Progressive anti-family reforms may be easier to win if rhetorically presented as strengthening rather than undermining families. I support those engaged in concrete struggle wishing to forge political coalitions capable of exerting leverage and winning substantive reform demands. If raising family abolition is going to undermine a concrete progressive campaign, avoiding doing so is logical and reasonable. But it is a mistake to restrict the political vision of collective emancipation exclusively to nonthreatening slogans. A free society is enormously difficult to conceive. Capitalism depends on a shared, mass resignation that reflects the actual conditions of powerlessness common in working-class life. From the dehumanizing drudgery of wage labor to the opportunistic machinations of electoral reform campaigns, actual practical experience under capitalist society leads to a truncated pragmatism. Under such conditions, there are real limitations to actions that necessarily condition one's thinking and imagination.

It is only during periods of mass unrest that it becomes possible to glimpse revolutionary possibilities. This is dramatically evident in the recent emergence of abolition as a widespread and shared revolutionary horizon. Discussed briefly in chapter 3, since the 1970s, police and prison abolition has gained a passionate following of committed organizers, rooted in struggles by current and former prisoners, Black critical theorists, and other varying radical leftists. Despite the robustness and persistence of this organizing, however, prison or police abolition remained to most to be entirely inconceivable. It was only with the 2020 uprising following the murder of George Floyd, as millions of people marched against police brutality and tens of thousands rioted, that police abolition briefly came into mainstream focus. Suddenly mass discussions about a society beyond policing swept through social media, street protests, and proliferating essays and books. Teenagers burning down a police station in Minneapolis made police abolition a national topic, with a bill passing in Minneapolis City Council. Unfortunately, the uprisings of 2020 did not manage to constitute an immediate revolutionary threat to the state or property. As the riots died down, police abolitionism faded from mainstream attention but left a lasting impression on those radicalized by the rebellion.

Revolutionary ideas can only take on mass appeal during revolutionary moments. The rest of the time, they can only gain traction among marginal and disaffected sections of society. But even when unrecognized, they speak to persistent and deep-set social contradictions, widespread dissatisfaction, and social problems with no obvious pragmatic solutions. Developing and maintaining revolutionary ideas between the revolutions, as I and other contemporary family abolitionists are attempting to do, is a necessary task.

UTOPIANISM AND PROVOCATION

Much excellent writing on family abolition skillfully sidesteps the question of what is to come. All these family abolitionists discussed previously offer powerful critiques of the family form, argue persuasively and explicitly for the need to abolish the family, and point to present refusals of the family. Some, like Madeline Lane-McKinley, Sophie Lewis, and Tiffany Lethabo King, are wisely leaving it to the future to find new ways of life. This move is sound and defensible. In this and the following chapters, I join with Griffiths and Gleeson in doing something much trickier: imagining the revolutionary future.

In *The Origin of the Family, Private Property and the State*, Engels argues that the lovers of a future communist society will have little use for the judgments of those of us living in the capitalist present: "Once such people appear, they will not care a damn about what we today think they should do. They will establish their own practice and their own public opinion, conforming therewith, on the practice of each individual—and that's the end of it."[15] Marx and Engels offer an extensive critique of what they termed *utopian socialism.*[16] Utopian socialists like Fourier, Robert Owen, and Saint-Simon grossly err in their understanding of social transformation. According to Engels, they imagine that a compelling vision of a just society could convince the elites to cede land, power, and the means of production to new deliberate efforts at social planning. For Marx and Engels, utopians fail to grasp that socialist revolution would never come about through deliberate, peaceful planning. It could only occur through the revolutionary eruption enabled by the inner contradictions of capitalist society. Capitalism produces the proletariat, a class robbed of any means of survival besides the cruelty of wage labor. These proletarians are driven by capitalist dynamics to periodic bouts of class struggle and rebellion, possessed with the unique revolutionary potential to overthrow class society altogether. This class would benefit from a thoroughgoing grasp of the nature of capitalism—offered by *Capital* and other scientific works on the capitalist mode of production—and the tools of practical organizing. In the assessments of Marx and Engels, utopian visions are unnecessary because the future could only emerge through the dynamics of struggle itself.

In response to a critical review of *Capital, Volume 1*, Marx references the utopian social theorist August Comte: "Thus the Paris *Revue Positiviste* reproaches me in that, on the one hand, I treat economics metaphysically, and on the other hand—imagine!—confine myself to the mere critical analysis of actual facts, instead of writing receipts (Comtist ones?) for the cook-shops of the future."[17] This phrase "writing receipts for the cook-shops of the future" became the general condemnation by generations of Marxist activists for any discussion of a postrevolutionary society.

Indeed, utopian visioning has shown little purchase in creating a new society. Utopian socialists depended on the colonial dispossession of the settler frontier to secure the land necessary for their experiments. This includes Robert Owen's New Harmony in Indiana and twenty-eight Fourierist communes across the United States in the 1840s. To this list I would add the Israeli Kibbutz movement, where socialist values depended on settler colonialism and state-backed genocidal dispossession to secure necessary resources. Without any intention to overthrow capitalist society by violently seizing land and the means of production, utopian socialists relied on the endorsement of racial capitalism available through settler colonialism. Not surprisingly, Fourier and most utopian socialists were uncritical of European colonialism and white supremacy. They also failed to instill any lasting change.

Communization theorists like Théorie Communiste have their own critique of proposals for the future society, but one that extends to include most Marxists. They critique the effort to imagine the future society through extrapolating the current experiences of working-class activity. They call this *programmatism*, defining it "as a theory and practice of class struggle in which the proletariat finds, in its drive toward liberation, the fundamental elements of a future social organisation which become the *programme to be realized*."[18] The very notion that socialism would be a worker's society, based on the domination of the factory and the wage, illustrates the problems and limits of programmatism.

Is discussing scenarios of family abolition in a revolutionary future committing utopianism's error? Marx and Engels are absolutely correct that any future revolutionary society will be made only by those who build it. They will likely care very little about what we have to say now. The revolution, as Engels aptly puts it, cannot be "worked out in advance."[19] But unlike many Marxists and communization theorists, I see speculative visioning as a helpful component to ongoing struggles. When revolutionary moments do emerge, every participant becomes an agent of history. At such moments, people draw on their imaginations, their inchoate hopes, their deep-felt yearnings, all to practically meet the challenge of the moment. At revolutionary moments, people take up ideas circulating in the world, evaluate whether they serve the moment, debate them with comrades, try them out, see how they work, and then come up with new ones. As new waves of struggles swell in future years, people will seize on and radically remake ideas they find at hand that speak to new emergent possibilities. At revolutionary moments, everyone is called on to be a utopian planner.

Even in nonrevolutionary moments, utopian, visioning impulses can play a powerful role in fleshing out the implications of present-day movement values and practices. Speculative fiction offers people a chance to think through what freedom means to us. Far too often, radicals today internalize the anti-utopian realism of the capitalist present. Instead, the speculative impulse to imagine something better could support and invigorate day-to-day struggle. Revolutionary Black feminists like Alexis Pauline Gumbs, adrienne maree brown, and Walidah Imarisha have brought speculative imagining into movement work, with powerful and rich effects.[20] Gleeson and Griffiths's "Kinderkommunismus" was so powerful in inaugurating the current period of family-abolitionist writing by bravely attempting to imagine the future.

Family abolition names and attempts to describe a necessary dimension of overcoming class society, the way a broader revolutionary transformation may reshape our personal lives. It is not a program nor a plan to be implemented nor a slogan to be rallied around. It is a way of naming and thinking about what a free society could mean in how we raise children, how we survive, how we love, and how we age. Family abolition is a provocation. It is not meant to enrage, though no doubt it unfortunately will. It is a call on every one of us to imagine, to debate, to think about what social forms could foster lives worth living.

NOT THE STATE, NOT THE WAGE, NOT THE FAMILY

Visions of family abolition are all necessarily responses to the problem of social reproduction. Who cooks our food? How do we end up living with a particular group of people? Who does a newborn learn to recognize first? Who will change our diapers if we are lucky enough to live to very old age? Today, those questions are answered through three primary organizing institutions: commodity exchange in the capitalist market, state-provided services, and personal relationships of dependency that typically take the form of the family. To briefly summarize the relevant sections of chapters 1 and 2: The family serves as the main institution that mediates proletarian dependency on the wage. For many proletarians unable to work, including infants, small children, people who are disabled, and elderly people, the main means of securing resources are from personal, familial relationships of dependence on a wage laborer. In our society, love and care are bound within the dependency and obligation of the family, and with them much of the labor of social reproduction. The family therefore takes a contradictory form in our world: both the means of love in the midst of a harsh and dangerous world and a space of private dependency with little protection from the risk of internal abuse and violence. For those unable to live well under the family's gender regime, the gamble of who your family happens to be is a matter of life and death.

This schema is helpful for parsing and evaluating different political frameworks for relating to the family. Conservative and liberal defenses of the family emphasize it as a refuge from the horrors of the market, as caring for those unable to work, and nurturing the next generation. Both defenses share something in common: an understanding of the family as an adjunct to the capitalist labor market. Some rely on the family as a bulwark against the cruelty of state violence, or at least as a solace when this violence is unstoppable. On the other hand, people from an abusive household may celebrate the opportunity to move out, get a job, and be able to choose to live alone. These people are embracing the impersonal domination of the market as a preferable alternative to the direct personal domination they experienced in their families.

Ideas about family abolition can be mapped and understood through how they rely, in turn, on increasing dependency on wage labor or the state. Griffiths and Gleeson are comrades and friends of mine who have done a tremendous amount to create the very possibility of discussing family abolition today. However, I also argue that their vision may suggest a massive expansion of the state.[21] Kollontai, for all her brilliance, was describing a vision of family abolition based on the near universalization of wage labor and the expansion of state management of social provision. The socialist state takes the place of the individual family, becoming a new universal family. Many Marxist feminists of the 1970s and early 1980s hint toward a withering away of the family through an expansion of services provided by a social democratic or socialist state. No doubt the state as initially imagined and pursued by Kollontai and other socialist family abolitionists is a vastly less evil state than those produced by the capitalist world. The progressive anti-family reforms detailed in the previous chapter could all be pursued by social democratic or socialist states and would be worth defending. Here I call for a vision of family abolition, however, that refuses the consolidation of authority into the hands of even a benevolent state.

This book has touched on multiple critiques of the state. Marx and Engels identify the state as one component of the bourgeois society, alongside the market, the church, and the family—all institutions that must be abolished. The setter colonial state eagerly pursued genocidal campaigns against Indigenous life, including supporting the boarding school system initially started by the Catholic Church. Newly urbanized sex workers and queers of the nineteenth century faced the state as a force of policing, social control, and violence. The rebellions of the Red Decade fought against the disciplining regimes of even social democratic and socialist states. These historical moments imply a theoretical critique of the state with wider implications. The modern state was forged as a capitalist social institution, serving the general reproduction of capital in tension with the competing interests of various sectors of capital. Even socialist efforts to use the state form have repeatedly reinforced wage labor, racial and national domination, and bureaucratic social control. Socialist states have largely maintained, rather than undermined, the dictatorship of capital. Revolutionary nationalist efforts to use the state form against its racist and colonial history have also led to consistent dead ends. Such postcolonial revolutionary states produced new elites, oriented to the world market for survival, and crushed working-class insurgency.

Here the state is understood as an institution that rules over social life yet is separated from the direct relationships between people. States emerged with private property and class rule, and took their present forms with the dominance of capitalism. A socialist state that maintains this separation from the social body as a whole would still be an instrument of class rule, and historically served as such once the mass democratic insurgency of working-class rebellion was replaced by a stable state form. States necessarily require the compulsion to work—wage labor, slavery, or a similar instrument of impersonal domination—to manage the activity of people removed from its decision-making.

Classless societies will require vast systems of administration, collective decision-making, and social planning. To replace the market and the price form, social administration may require a far greater portion of human activity than does the modern state. Yet in a stateless, communist society, this administration would be undertaken by popular mass organs enlisting the majority of the population, a part of the fabric of day-to-day life, and directly integrated with production and distribution. Such mass organs of collective decision-making and administration have emerged during peak periods of rebellions historically, in the forms of soviets, workers' councils, and popular assemblies. I distinguish such forms of communist administration from states, and argue they have a different relationship to the society as a whole.

This abstract rejection of the state and wage labor as instruments of class rule becomes much clearer and concrete in imagining a state-mandated form of family abolition, using this definition of the state. Imagine a society where all people giving birth are immediately visited by a state agent, perhaps their own physician. This state agent removes that newborn into another bounded institution separated geographically, socially, and administratively from the birthing parent, managed by a decision-making entity with no direct ties to the social world the birthing parent inhabits. This is done regardless of the decision-making, intent, or consent of the birthing parent or those in immediate relationship to them. Claims that this separate institution would not be racist or oppressive would do little to reassure. It does not require a romantic idealization of the mother-child bond to recognize that the experience of conception and gestation can often lead to an emotional tie, and that universally severing this tie could be a form of injustice. Such practices, throughout human history, have been the basis of genocide, class rule, and oppression. It does not require nefarious intent nor malfeasance by the administering state agency to make this scenario abhorrent to most, especially racial and national groups who have faced the brutal oppression of CPS, the family policing system, or forced boarding schools. One could either imagine a benevolent socialist state that is adjunctive to the family—voluntary universal childcare, for example—or an altogether different social institution that replaces both. But a scenario of the socialist state literally and directly replacing the family is rightfully terrifying to many.

Similarly, dissolving the family into wage-based market relationships is also inimical to freedom. The last fifty years have seen the market and wage labor replace the family for many people's day-to-day social reproduction. Many people in major cities no longer rely on family members to cook their food, do their laundry, clean their homes, or care for their children for the majority of their waking hours. Such a dissolution under capitalist conditions is hardly something to celebrate. Whatever gains this has offered in allowing for a diversification of family forms have been more than offset by intensifying class inequality, the low wages in service industries, the overall erosion of the working-class standard of living, and the misery of direct domination in the workplace.

To be a basis of human freedom and collective emancipation, family abolition must concurrently be the overcoming of capitalist society, including the state and wage labor. The remainder of this book attempts to imagine an overcoming of the family that does not replace it with the other institutions of capitalist society. What if your food was made by neither a restaurant worker nor a family member? What if children belonged to neither their parents nor a state-administered crèche? What if disabled or elderly people could rely on a form of universal care that wasn't administered by a separated social institution? In other words: how could human life be reproduced without the family, the state, and the wage? This is the question of communist social reproduction.

QUALITIES OF COMMUNIST SOCIAL REPRODUCTION

Communism, as understood in this book, is a classless society, founded on the revolutionary abolition of capitalist social relations and institutions. *Communist social reproduction* names the generalized practices necessary to directly meet human needs without the mediation and domination of capitalist relations. Here I theorize a few of the general qualities of communist social reproduction. As a general maxim, I use Marx's succinct description: "From each according to his abilities, to each according to his needs!"[22] This maxim provides the basic coordinates for extrapolating the qualities of communist social reproduction. I organize these points under the following three component words of this concept: communist, social, and reproduction.

Communist

1. *Classless society.* Capitalist society interconnects multiple institutions and forms. Some, like wage labor, commodity exchange, the state, and debt markets, preexisted capitalism in previous

class society but only became experiences for the majority of people with the dominance of capitalist social relations. Others, like the family, religious institutions, slavery, and xenophobia, were forged by previous class societies but have been dramatically and deeply remade in capitalism. Communism would be the abolition of all capitalist social institutions—both those invented by capitalism and those remade from previous eras of class society. Communism would be a society based on human freedom, where large numbers of people work to undo and remake institutions, dismantling the social basis for domination.

2. *Abolition.* Communist social reproduction is the abolition of capitalist social relations. This necessarily entails the abolition of private property, wage labor, the state, the family, borders, prisons, and police. In a communist society, a positive potential of each of these social institutions would be preserved while their present form is destroyed. From wage labor would be preserved purposeful, interdependent human activity; from family, relations of care; from prisons and police, a commitment toward shared safety and well-being. The positive aspects of their social roles would be incorporated into new, freer social institutions that may be completely unrecognizable compared to their previous form. To constitute communism at all, the structural basis for white supremacy, nationalism, settler colonialism, and xenophobia would necessarily be destroyed.

3. *Unconditional access to the means of survival.* In capitalist society, the means of life are conditional. They require the ability to work for wages, or the support of a family member, or the approval of a state policy. The scarcity of the means of survival coerces people to work, producing the value on which capitalist society depends. Various authoritarian collectivist futures may dispense with capitalist value production but still restrict access to make the means of survival based on kin relations, fidelity, or identity. To be a basis for human freedom, communist social relations must provide "to each according to their need"—the basic necessities of life to all, without condition. A free society must offer other motivations to engage in possibly unpleasant but socially necessary tasks, without primarily depending on

restricting access to the means of life. Unlike some visions of socialism that rely on the compulsion of wage labor, communist social reproduction severs the relationship between work and survival. It offers to all a right to life, including to people with serious disabilities, people who deal with drug addictions, and social outcasts.

4. *Collective goods, not private property.* Communist social reproduction would be based on overcoming private property. Rather than the private management of production and distribution, the material conditions of society would be collectively managed. Human life depends on interdependence and interconnection. Sometimes these are direct face-to-face relationships, sometimes they are dependencies that extend across the world in supply chains. Under communist social reproduction, these interdependencies would involve the shared decision-making of everyone involved.

Social

1. *Beyond public and private.* Central to the abuse and violence possible in families is producing a private domain of control and authority separated from outside engagement. The privacy afforded to normative families shields them from observers and intervention. Children are treated as the property of their parents. All these features of privacy make horrific abuse possible. Those who are terrorized within families are often not seen by others. When others do recognize they are being harmed, there are few means of intervention beyond the often racist and violent investigation of state authorities. Breaking down the distinction between the private and the public is integral to challenging abuse that can take place within families. People need to be able to share with others what is happening, to be seen and recognized far beyond the narrow boundaries of a private home, to be cared for and helped by those outside. Communist social reproduction would necessarily create multiple and varied practices of people engaging in each other's domestic lives and being able to collectively come to the aid of people facing abuse.

2. *Beyond segregation and homogeneity.* The isolation of the family not only enables abuse; it also cuts people off from a broader social world. Capitalism, despite bringing together large numbers of diverse people in major cities, produces an enormous amount of segregation and division. The family, along with neighborhoods, schools, and social networks, functions as an institution of segregation and homogenization. Communist social reproduction would include exposing children to a rich diversity of cultures, languages, and experiences of the world. This affirms the human need for connection to others and enables greater human development.

3. *Shared joy, shared pleasure.* More and more people in our world are deeply isolated. Collective experiences are often restricted to the workplace, businesses selling experiences, or highly policed and regulated public spaces. The family, where we are expected to experience the most intimate forms of belonging and togetherness, works to isolate us from the outside world. Family life is often reduced to passively consuming media in isolation from one another. Communist social reproduction at its best would include proliferating and widely varied shared spaces—public but transformed beyond the public/private distinction. These shared spaces could offer the means for deliberative decision-making about managing society, for sexual and erotic pleasure, for cultural and artistic creation and consumption, for a wide range of collective activities meeting diverse human desires.

Reproduction

1. *Facilitate human flourishing.* All people have rich capacities for creative, intellectual, and spiritual lives. But fully developing ourselves requires space, time, and the support of others. Capitalism, in producing mass poverty for large numbers of people and requiring most others to devote themselves to working for others, denies people the possibility of discovering their own potentials. Even those with considerable leisure time or disposable resources are often so taken with the self-absorption characteristic of whiteness and class privilege that they remain

deeply stunted. Because surplus resources are currently amassed through the exploitation and violence of racial capitalism, those consuming them require a constant denial and disavowal that spiritually and psychically distorts human growth. Communist social reproduction would provide the social minimum of the means of survival, but also the conditions for learning, growing, thinking, developing, and discovering one's capacity.

2. *Appropriate love and care.* Along with material needs, people also require the love and care of others. Humans deprived of necessary care get stuck, unable to develop and mature. At each stage of life, this interpersonal care takes varied forms: infants need extensive attention, physical help, and the close love and protection of a small number of focused adults. Adolescents need some measure of both autonomy and boundaries, recognition from peers, and exposure to a variety of modes of life. Adults need rich collaborative relationships, and some measure of erotic joy and romantic connection. People in old age and people with disabilities or illnesses at all ages may need considerable physical help in meeting daily tasks. When possible, communist social reproduction should include social forms that affirm and facilitate age-appropriate love and care, as the family is imagined to provide now.

3. *Autonomy and dependency.* Every person depends on others, and every person needs some developmentally appropriate level of autonomy. Families might meet basic dependency needs while unequally distributing autonomy. Some people, like infants, need only very bounded and limited forms of autonomy; others, like adults, do best when they have considerable agency in making their decisions about who to live with, who to love, and how to spend their time. Some people find joy in raising children or being available to care for others but are hesitant to do so because parenting and caretaking can involve ceding so much autonomy in one's life. Communist social reproduction would both meet dependency needs and enable varied but substantial levels of autonomy and consent in life decision-making.

GENDER FREEDOM AND COMMUNIST REPRODUCTION

This framework of communist social reproduction guides the remainder of the book as I attempt to theorize family abolition. To flesh out and illustrate the qualities of communist social reproduction, in this section I will focus on one example that is particularly close to my own political commitments and life experience: the life conditions faced by transgender and gender nonconforming people.[23]

Under capitalism, gender and sexual freedom is severely constrained. First, it is constrained by the family. Many trans people first question their genders in childhood. At that stage, it is a gamble how one's parents respond. Within their family, children are subject to the arbitrary bigotry and domination of their parents, isolated in atomized housing units. They face high rates of violence, abuse, and medical neglect. The history of CPS suggests state intervention likely only aggravates this harm. The coercive force of the family does not end in childhood, however. Children of wealth are bound for life by the promise of inheritance and property; children of proletarians by needing periodic financial support and aid during bouts of unemployment and disability. The family can constrain gender-affirming transition long after children stop living in a family home.

When old enough, proletarian children can leave home and achieve a measure of independence, but only through becoming bound to dependency on wage labor. Work itself is an elaborate regime of gender and sexual discipline on the lives of all proletarians, including enforced dress codes, the gendering of the labor process itself, affective labor in the service industry, workplace sexual violence, and the arbitrary bigotries of employers. Not surprisingly, gender nonconforming and trans people face very high rates of workplace discrimination and are usually quite poor. According to a 2015 study of over twenty-seven thousand trans-identifying people, 29 percent lived in poverty, twice the national rate.[24] A NYC-based match-pair study found 42 percent net discrimination against trans job applicants.[25] In a society where capitalism and wage labor dominate our lives, gender freedom is impossible. In some cases, proletarians can instead rely on the state for their survival outside of the family or wage labor, through welfare cash-transfer benefits, state-provided housing and health care, or prisons. These institutions, however, have long served to reinforce and constrain gender and sexual expression. Welfare programs are usually designed to force recipients into narrow gender and sexual roles. Accessing benefits depends on being able to present oneself as being among the deserving, respectable poor. State institutions impose the collective shared bigotries of the ruling class and its professional adjuncts onto the lives of the poor. Because the state depends on the functioning of the market economy, it faces strict limits on the extent to which it can promote human freedom. State agencies, in short, have never been good allies to trans people.

Gender freedom therefore relies on the widespread accessibility of a means of survival and reproduction that does not rely on the family, wage labor, or the state. Until transphobia within the hearts and minds of everyone is eradicated—a nearly inconceivable goal—coming out as trans is likely to have some impact on one's romantic and kinship ties. In the unfreedom of the private family form, this in turn impacts one's standard of living and material well-being. A free society would require the separation of material survival from the bigotry of parents, potential romantic partners, state bureaucrats, or employers. Sometimes intervention in child-rearing is necessary to identify and stop abuse and gender coercion. Such institutions would need to provide children with multiple avenues of escape when necessary. Yet the well-being of trans people relies not only on freedom from coercion but also the positive presence of supportive care. This includes the care of mutual love and support; care of the positive labor of raising children and looking after the ill; care of erotic connection and pleasure; care of accessing gender-affirming medical treatment; care of aiding each other in fulfilling the vast possibilities of our humanity—all the forms of care that are the basis for a life worth living, including through our gender. Care in our capitalist society is a commodified, subjugating, and alienated act, but in it we can see the kernel of a non-alienating interdependence and love. Positive freedoms are enabled by the foundation of universal material support. They also depend on a queer, feminist, anti-ableist, and anti-racist cultural transformation centering love and supporting our mutual self-development. Building revolutionary caring institutions must adequately meet these basic needs.

These caring institutions must provide the generational reproduction of a free society, offering a much greater degree of openness, dynamism, transparency, and interdependence with broader social units than the present private family form. Such institutions could free both children and their parents from bonds of coercive obligation, dependence, and isolation, without unnecessarily separating loving parents and children. Further, such institutions would necessarily provide substantial care in the growth of children, including addressing their developmental and emotional needs; challenging coercive gender imposition; exposing children as they grow to a nonatomized, heterogeneous, nonsegregated, and nonstratified human cultural and social variation; and ultimately to best support the full human development of all caregivers and children. Trans freedom depends on overcoming the private family and establishing communist social reproduction.

* * *

Communist social reproduction is a theorization of the basic coordinates of a free society. It articulates both freedom from coercion and the positive presence of care necessary for the flourishing of human potential. No utopian plan will ever guide mass revolutionary struggle. But envisioning alternative futures and revolutionary values can enrich our lives, our struggles, and our freedom dreams. This book, in attempting to theorize family abolition, is an invitation for everyone to imagine how social reproduction, intimacy, and care could work in a free society. Beyond the private family, beyond the racial state, beyond capitalist wage labor, we can collectively imagine a society of shared care and dignity. But how do we get there? Beyond the reform-oriented coalitions proposed in chapter 10, what political moments point toward the revolutionary overcoming of the family? The next chapter speculates on one such possible route to the revolutionary overcoming of the family.

12

Around the People's Kitchen

Back to the streets of the Oaxaca commune. Women and men are living on the barricades. They cook, they fuck, they gossip on the radio, they hand out looted groceries, they study politics, and they argue strategy. On the barricades, women are moving past the narrow confines of the private household, the conjugal heterosexual marriage, the patriarchal family. There, women live collective and interdependent lives based on direct relationships and direct negotiation. Similar moments reappear across many struggles.

I offer here a few examples from my own life of social reproduction transformed during collective protest. As a teenager growing up in Oregon in the early 1990s, I remember driving between bakeries, collecting donated bread. We would haul it and other bulk donated groceries into the forests of the Cascade Mountains, feeding protesters living in a road blockade into the forests surrounding Warner Creek. There we would sit around a wood stove and argue about exactly what sort of anarchism we found most compelling. The next day I would head back to town, running by the Federal Building to drop off juice for a protester on an extended hunger strike in a tent outside.

In 1998 and 1999 a coalition of radical white environmentalists and members of the Mendota Mdewakanton nation joined in a two-year urban land occupation to stop the rerouting of a highway through South Minneapolis. I joined the protests as a college student. Protesters first lived in houses from which most residents had been evicted, and then moved to tents after a massive police raid of the occupation. The life of the camp was the heart of many months of constant marches, lockdowns, and arrests. One friend was arrested shoplifting nearly a thousand dollars' worth of supplies from a sporting goods store, stolen for the camp. Unlike many rural environmental and Indigenous protests, the camp was in the middle of a major American city. The occupation built extensive coalitions—with Black ministers who were protesting the demolition of public housing and with Minneapolis' large urban Indigenous neighborhoods that had once birthed the militant protest organization the American Indian Movement. At the camp, protesters reproduced their lives, eating together, singing together, sleeping together, praying together. Collective singing was particularly important to the life of the camp.

In 1999 I lived for a time in London. A few friends I met at an Earth First! conference invited me to a queer chocolate potluck not far from my dorm. The gathering was at 121, a squatted social center in Brixton that had lasted seventeen years. Now it was in its final months before eviction, and our regular potlucks were darkened with barricaded windows. A woman I was lucky enough to briefly date built me a bicycle from scrap at an info shop called 56a in Elephant and Castle. I made it up to the Faslane Peace Camp, a permanent protest site near one of the United Kingdom's nuclear arsenals in Scotland. Multiple generations of anti-nuclear protesters lived at the camp, coordinating thousands of blockades and protests. I heard many stories of the 1990s occupations to stop the construction of the M11 highway in East London. Local residents, squatters, radical environmentalists, and anarchists joined together during months of fighting with police.

Then I went traveling on the continent, seeing the squatted social centers of the autonomous movement. I danced to a Russian ska band at a massive squatted warehouse in Rome. In Milan I had a vegan Easter feast in the yard of a former boys' boarding school turned punk squat before retiring to the evening activity of watching recorded video footage of riots. At a permaculture farm outside of Barcelona, I helped bake bread that was distributed to the many squats surviving in the city. In Geneva I served chai to hundreds of Indians protesting the International Monetary Fund. The Indian activists complained about the tea's poor quality and their European hosts' racism, while drinking it around campfires burning on overturned car hoods. In Madrid I listened to a woman making coffee for a migrant solidarity kitchen explain to me why she wouldn't visit a neighboring squat because they hadn't properly dealt with a sexual assault.

Later in 1999 I arrived in Seattle with a contingent of Minneapolis militants. We found ourselves at the warehouse of the Direct Action Network, the hub of the massive blockades that successfully shutdown the first day of meetings of the World Trade Organization (WTO). There I volunteered for childcare, for dishwashing, for sweeping up, and for banner- and sign-making. I would also sit in on the spokes councils, where affinity groups split up the map area surrounding the WTO meetings like a giant pie and argued about their degree of solidarity with the property-destruction-oriented black bloc that I and many present were planning to join. The social reproduction of that warehouse enabled the phenomenal success of the barricades, freeing up blocks of Seattle streets where rioters and protesters roamed freely without police intervention.

Just over a decade later, I found myself a frequent visitor to Occupy Wall Street in Zuccotti Park. Protesters slept in tents, ate from a communal kitchen, borrowed books at a library, held an excessive number of bad drum circles, argued endlessly, and organized at least daily marches to the stock exchange. The Occupy movement, beginning with Occupy Wall Street, spread across North America in hundreds of full-time urban camps protesting wealth inequality. The movement paralleled mass urban occupations across Europe and the Arab world, constituting the movement of the squares. Collective decision-making, sleeping alongside each other, communal eating, shared study, and social connection were all interwoven in the life of the square protests.

Of the many other occupations in my lifetime that I never had the chance to visit, one has been particularly studied for its extensive and sophisticated systems of social reproduction: the No DAPL protests. Over ten thousand protesters, led by members of the Standing Rock Nation, encamped for months in 2016 to stop the construction of the Dakota Access Pipeline, and the further threats against fresh water, the climate, and Indigenous survival. Activists would lock down construction equipment and barricade roads during the day. The life of the camp sustained the protests—a massive cooking and eating operation,[1] collective discussion, sleeping accommodations in tents, political education for children through Defenders of the Water School,[2] conflict resolution—all the elements of domestic life, remade collectively in the reproduction of protest. Extended blockades by the Wet'suwet'en against gas pipelines in unceded territory in western Canada continue into the present.[3]

In all these examples, social reproduction was transformed in the collective activity of protest. In the previous chapter, I outlined the qualities of social reproduction in a communist society that would be necessary dimensions to family abolition. How people feed and care for each other amid mass protests, this chapter argues, suggests possible routes through which it may be possible to overcome the family and create the basis for new forms of care.

INSURGENT SOCIAL REPRODUCTION

These camps are all examples of *insurgent social reproduction*— the meeting of direct daily needs in the midst of extended mass protest. During periods of prolonged protest, people constitute self-organized collective forms of social reproduction. When large numbers of people directly confront the state and capital from a shared location for multiple days, they often develop practices for collectively reproducing their basic needs. These include strategies for procuring food, cooking, and shared eating; for organizing sleeping arrangements in proximity to each other; for sharing child-rearing responsibilities; and for aiding disabled comrades. Under capitalism, many of these tasks of daily life are typically done within the private household or through buying service commodities. At protest encampments, these become collective actions subject to democratic coordination. All these practices are the shared work of care.

In the book *Protest Camps*, the authors survey the functioning of over fifty direct-action camps globally, including the Oaxaca commune, protests in Thailand, and the movement of the squares from New York City to Egypt. They extensively document how people form new infrastructures, make collective decisions, produce media and communications, and negotiate their complex relationships with the outside world. They write of the integral role of social reproduction in the life of protest camps:

Care work and re-creational infrastructures are often strongly gendered and rendered 'private'; they are often made or kept invisible from the centre of a social movement's politics. As exposed and vulnerable places of politics, protest camps make visible reproductive labor and the infrastructures in which this labor takes place. The social and biological becomes political.[4]

Insurgent social reproduction can also help enable diverse participation. Though protest camps can sometimes become unwelcoming to some, they often depend on a steady influx of new participants. Freely available food and sleeping space, along with inclusive social activities, can make it easier for a range of people to show up at the camp and become involved. Many groups both share reasons to object to current state and corporate policies, and are without access to stable means of social reproduction: unemployed people, homeless people, migrants, people with serious mental illnesses, young queer people running away from their families of origin, and others. If a protest camp is able to effectively meet people's needs and accommodate their involvement, they all have a great deal to potentially offer in political insight and strategic capacity.

When protest camps do not encourage diverse participation, it can severely hamper their work. Occupy protests involved considerable conflict between well-housed activists who were there for solely and self-consciously political motives, and unhoused activists who came with fewer alternatives or supports. This distinction was often highly racialized. The full participation of unhoused people would have required a significant cultural change, and much greater collective supports, within the Occupy movement. But it could also have deepened the militancy, political depth, and scale of the protests. Similarly, people living with known drug addictions are often excluded from protest camps for multiple and somewhat justified reasons. Yet incorporating harm reduction and other care practices could similarly enable and support these individuals' involvement.

Examples of insurgent social reproduction are moments of family abolition. Of course, families may show up together and live at a protest camp; small children are brought by parents or other caregivers, for example. But in participating in the collective life of the protest, they stop functioning primarily as a private household. From protest canteens to childcare areas, protest encampments replace the private household and private family with something else. Protests can be moments of overcoming the private household in action and creating new strategies and practices of collective survival. Beyond the protest camp, insurgent social reproduction can also be found in guerrilla armies, national liberation struggles, barricades, riots, strikes, among refugees, at homeless encampments, and elsewhere where people rebel together. In all cases, collective acts of social reproduction can challenge and transform family relations. In "The Algerian Family," Frantz Fanon described how the Algerian anti-colonial struggle against French occupation remade familial relations. Patriarchal fathers had to accommodate themselves to the leadership of their adult children in the revolutionary struggle, upending strict family hierarchy and enabling new forms of solidarity between family members.[5]

All aspects of family life can be contested and remade in the course of insurgent social reproduction. They collectivize reproductive labor that might otherwise be done by feminized family members in isolation. They create new shared forms of intimacy and friendship beyond the boundaries of conjugal marriage and parents who believe they own their children. Insurgent social reproduction opens new avenues for contesting gender and sexual relations, through which people may challenge the norms and expectations demanded of them within the family. They create new shared spaces of collective joy and solidarity, directly challenging the atomized household structure of the nuclear family. Though people can still choose to form or maintain familial bonds while living at a protest site, the practices of protest life undermine both the coercive pressures and economic compulsion typical of families.

COMMUNES UNDER RACIAL CAPITALISM

These examples of protest camps are not preplanned utopian communities or isolated deliberate living arrangements; they are lives remade in the midst of direct struggle against state violence and capitalist dispossession. Yet insurgent social reproduction shares some qualities with collective living arrangements like communes or group houses. In both settings, people form multiple complex relationships with each other. They collectivize reproductive labor, share some resources, and have some group governance and decision-making process. They also share in the collective life of entertainment, cultural production, and socializing.

Twentieth-century communes include back-to-the-land collective farming communities in the 1960s and 1970s, group houses of hippies and punks, queer families living together, and utopian planned communities. Such arrangements are legitimate strategies for trying to live less alienated lives in the atomizing conditions of the market. Such practices are an admirable part of radical traditions, but as they operate within capitalist conditions, their limits are severe. This section parallels some of the critiques of chosen family explored in chapter 10. There are important differences that distinguish communes from protest camps and insurgent social reproduction broadly. Because group houses and communes are generally legal arrangements within a market society, they require the stability of property ownership and income flows similar to private families. Collectively owned property requires the approval of courts and state regulators. Communes in a capitalist society are forced into the shared poverty of economic self-sufficiency and isolation to depend on significant contributions from wage labor or inherited wealth. Group houses may function similarly to private households, dependent on the inherited wealth of one member, the steady income of another, and the tangle of dependency and care that holds people together. Though perhaps less oppressive than many nuclear families, they are subject to all the same forces of pressure from capitalist labor markets and the state, producing many of the same internal contradictions. The pressures of state policies, poverty, class differences among residents, or lack of mental healthcare inevitably exacerbate interpersonal conflict and often lead to the collapse of such deliberate communities. Like in society at large, within deliberate communal living arrangements, only considerable class privilege offers long-term stability.

I grew up in a region of the United States that was home to many back-to-the-land hippie communes in the 1970s. Their shared utopian impulse masked deep class divisions that later became more evident. Those commune residents who had family wealth eventually capitalized on these developing social networks in order to start and run my hometown's many businesses that produced and sold goods like tofu, juice, sprouts, yogurt, or artisanal crafts. Many of these small business owners came to oppose their employees' unionizing, used their authority to sexually harass employees, and joined with other regional capitalists in supporting regressive policies. Those hippies without the invisible support of family wealth often ended up in prison, dead from overdose, or living in poverty. The intent to create radical community could not overcome the determining role of class and family in shaping life outcomes while embedded within racial capitalism.

Further, many proponents of such planned communities mistakenly imagine that their very existence will inspire their gradual spreading in the shell of a capitalist society, providing the means of living some form of anti-state communism in the present. Such thinking has produced the blossoming of isolated countercultures, but nothing suggests it could ever offer an exit from the rule of capital and the capitalist state. The structural conditions of proletarianization, market dependency, and state violence make such a vision of a revolutionary transition impossible without generalized insurrection, and leave such communities inherently unstable, inaccessible, and isolated.

Protest camps have no pretensions to avoiding instability. Instead, they embrace a degree of tension with the surrounding world. Because they do not rely on ownership, steady jobs, or state approval, they are unable to consistently reproduce themselves within the restrictive terms of capitalist society. For food or supplies they rely on either theft or a gift economy of donations from local businesses and individuals. They are generally illegal in various ways, in direct combat with state forces, courts, and police. They require an enormous quantity of uncompensated collective volunteer hours, often from people who depend on the camp for their material survival while organizing.

This antagonistic relationship with the surrounding economy and state can also allow these camps the possibility of resisting many of the internal contradictions inherent to the private household. Within the protest camp, little is owned by an individual or private family. Even if some activists have greater access to donors or wealth, this rarely significantly alters the material conditions of living together at camp. A protester's material survival does not typically depend on maintaining relationships with any single individual who has disproportionate access to resources. Living at a camp is still conditional but depends on a broader range of relationships to multiple people engaged in shared governance and collective process. If a protester hasn't been thrown out of the camp by multiple other people, they are likely to be able to eat at the canteen, find a tent to sleep in, a workshop to sit in on, and a few others to connect with. Protesters may move in and out of the camp in a relatively fluid way, visiting for brief periods or staying for months. Though a number of these factors may differ in a strictly hierarchal guerrilla camp, insurgent social reproduction broadly shifts the basis of survival from individual and familial resources to shared practices.

SEXUAL ASSAULT AT THE PROTEST CAMP

Insurgent social reproduction does not automatically solve the problems of interpersonal harm, however. Protest camps often include much of the violence, bigotry, and oppression widespread in families and in racial capitalism more generally. At the Blackjewel Miners' Blockade in Harlan County, Kentucky, queer and trans working-class anarchists both played an integral role in establishing the protest camp, and later were driven out by a Nazi trucker.[6] The Occupy movement was gripped by frequent struggles over racism and white chauvinism. The direct-action forest-defense camps of my youth often struggled over homophobia, trans inclusion, and gender relationships. In *Protest Camps*, the authors find many examples of interpersonal harm committed by movement participants. Violence at camps often reflects broader social contexts like poverty, male domination, racism, and coercive sexual cultures. In addition, protest camps have their own specific aspects, like frequent casual hook-ups, that can provide opportunities for abuse.

Women often face sexual assault at protest camps. They may be harmed by romantic partners with whom they are sharing tents or sleeping accommodations, or movement leaders who use their status to pursue sexual relationships with vulnerable women. In other cases, strangers or movement opponents come into a camp specifically to sexually assault women. The authors of *Protest Camps* detail some of the extensive struggles around on-site sexual assaults at Occupy camps, identifying in them a tension between the biopolitical issue of camp reproduction and the intended emancipatory politics of protest camps.[7] Sexual assaults at Occupy protests were dealt with in various harmful ways, including by discouraging women from going to police and by attempted cover-ups within the movement. Struggling against powerful outside antagonists can put pressure on survivors to hide their experiences to protect the reputation of protesters.

These are grim realities that are not easily overcome. There is no known social form that eliminates the risks of sexual assault. For those committed to erotic joy and sexual pleasure as an important part of political life, it is necessary to also confront the inescapable possibility of sexual harm. However, the collective life of the camp provides an opportunity to struggle over sexual violence that is unavailable to most within a private family, the wage, or the state. Survivors at protest camps, even when unsupported by hostile leaders, are in a much better position to find allies and caring support in the midst of a large camp than when assaulted by a family member or lover at home. If a woman is raped by her husband, there are few means of redress that do not rob her of her home or put her in jeopardy of losing her children. At a protest camp, those committing sexual assaults may be expelled, beaten, handed over to police, or forced to undergo an extended accountability process. Some camps, like Standing Rock, expelled and banished those committing sexual assault.[8] None are easy or perfect solutions, but they are made possible by the shared life of insurgent social reproduction.

All the protest camps I encountered would have benefited from a major internal reckoning around gender relations and sexual violence. They required major and deep cultural changes in the relations between movement participants. But unlike the private space of the family, insurgent social reproduction provides many collective opportunities for attempting to undertake exactly such a struggle. Under normal family conditions, children are typically entirely powerless to fight their parents, and abusive partners have means of making resistance nearly impossible. But in a camp the question of how to respond to harm is one that can be debated and acted on together. Similarly, when gender roles are reproduced at protest camps that parallel the private family, the shared collective space provides some possibility these roles could be contested and struggled over. There is the potential—if not frequently the reality—of forging radically better, abolitionist, and feminist responses to violence.

The limits and potentials of insurgent social reproduction in addressing sexual and gender violence suggest the possible political terrain of a post-family future. Insurgent social reproduction, in pointing us beyond the limits of capitalism and the family, suggests a different mode of organizing domestic life. Post-capitalist, post-family alternative forms will absolutely still be potential sites of interpersonal harm, including sexual violence and intimate partner abuse. But more collective, alternative, and politicized forms have the possibility to become sites of collective redress, accountability, and effective response. The shared life of insurgent social reproduction can ultimately provide unique and powerful spaces of healing. What comes after the revolutionary overcoming of the family will not be perfect, but it can open new opportunities for struggle and transformation.

COMMUNIZATION

Insurgent social reproduction is the closest we come in the present to seeing how our domestic lives may function in a communist society. The elements of insurgent social reproduction point toward the kinds of social forms that could replace the family, and the particular types of struggles that could lead to that overcoming. In recognizing a possible link between protest camps and the revolutionary commune, I draw from communization theory.

No one knows with any certainty how the revolutionary break with capitalism may come about. Marx and Engels initially polemically propose the inevitability of mass immiseration and homogenization to unite the working class; but by the time Marx wrote *Capital*, he already had identified the mechanisms of capitalist society that could forestall mass immiseration. Kautsky and the Second International counted on the eventual universal proletarianization, an outcome prevented by the persistence of semi-peasant land relations into the late twentieth century, and the continuous proliferation of a middle strata of small property ownership.[9] Leninism identified the consolidation of a revolutionary party of disciplined cadre, embedded in mass working-class autonomous institutions, as key to overthrowing the capitalist state. This party would then institute a period of proletariat dictatorship and begin a gradual socialist transition to communism. This strategy was successful in advancing capitalist development in the rural countryside across Eastern Europe and Asia but got no closer to establishing a classless society.[10] Other anarchist, council communists, and insurrectionist tendencies have all floundered in demonstrating any lasting capacity for working-class power. The Black Radical Tradition and Indigenous sovereignty movements have powerful reflections on freedom, but when envisioning a strategy to explicitly overthrow capitalism, they often draw directly from Marxism. In short, if our goal is communism, none of us know how to get there.

Looking to insurgent social reproduction for examples of family abolition points us to another, more obscure political tradition: communization. Earlier, I engaged communization theory in outlining the thesis of the workers' movement (chapter 7), the current protracted crisis of surplus populations and capitalist overproduction (chapter 9), and the critique of programmatism (chapter 12). Here, I engage communization in terms of its theory of revolution. Communization theory offers a unique theorization of revolutionary transition. Communization theorists draw from the left communist critique of state socialism and couple it with the anti-work critique of Situationism and the rebellions of the Red Decade. Unlike many other revolutionary traditions, communization does not offer a program to rally around, nor a specific guide for revolutionaries. It is instead an effort to theorize "the specific revolutionary undoing of the relations of property constitutive of the capitalist class relation."[11] Communization theory is an effort to conceptualize the necessary features of communist social relations.

Communization reclaims Marx's argument that the proletariat must abolish all class relations, rejecting the notion of a workers' society and many of the core principles of the workers' movement. *Endnotes* writes, "Such an overcoming must necessarily be the direct self-abolition of the working class, since anything short of this leaves capital with its obliging partner."[12] Communization theory broadly refuses the idea of a gradual socialist tradition, arguing that the persistence of wage labor and the state necessarily maintain capitalist social relationships. In maintaining the working class, "the transitional period places the real revolution on a receding horizon, meanwhile perpetuating that which it is supposed to overcome."[13] Communization is the destruction of all mediating institutions of capitalism, and the direct activity of people in meeting the practical questions of survival in a revolutionary situation.

Communization is the global generalizing of communist measures, of the immediate appropriation of the means of production for collective human need. Leon de Mattis writes:

> Communising measures will not be taken by any organ, any form of representation of anyone, or any mediating structure. They will be taken by all those who, at a precise moment, take the initiative to search for a solution, adequate in their eyes, to a problem of the struggle. And the problems of the struggle are also problems of life: how to eat, where to stay, how to share with everybody else, how to fight against capital, etc.[14]

Like insurgent social reproduction, communization sees the revolution as consisting of the direct tasks of reproducing, maintaining, and expanding direct anti-capitalist and anti-state struggle.

Despite disagreeing with or remaining agnostic about many elements of communization theory, I argue that it provides exciting and promising avenues for thought. The notion of communist social reproduction proposed in the previous chapter is informed by communization theory. Communization also helps theorize communist social reproduction as emerging from the generalization of insurgent social reproduction, of which protest camps are one example. Communization theory can point toward a vision of family abolition that does not rely on any top-down institutional policies, but the mass bottom-up transformation of society in the midst of a revolutionary struggle.

Within communization theory, there is a split in how to understand the role of prefigurative, autonomous protest. Tiqqun and the associated Invisible Committee, among the most influential communization theorists in France and the Anglophone world, emphasize prefigurative autonomous institutions (such as currently existing communes, land projects, and protest camps). Other communization tendencies—those I draw from, like *Endnotes*, Théorie Communist, and Leon de Mattis—see communization as only possible in the midst of generalized rebellion driven by large-scale class struggle that manages to destroy the basis of capitalism. The latter rarely suggest outright what exactly communization would look like, implying that such envisioning would be a form of programmatism or imposition of a platform. It is rarely stated, but generally assumed, that it would take the specific form of a global insurrection.

Here and in the next chapter, I abandon the prohibition on speculation by many communization theorists by imagining a possible form of communization that overcomes the private family. Using communization theory, insurgent social reproduction, and a lot of imagining, this scenario offers a speculative vision of family abolition.

In protracted riots and rebellions, people may fight the police, loot stores, and convene in ad hoc assemblies to discuss what to do next. Rioters gather in each other's kitchens to cook looted food, form medic teams to treat injuries from fighting police, or check up on each other for safety and care. In an imagined communization scenario, these insurrections are able to survive the retaliation of the state and the forces of capital.[15] Forms of insurgent social reproduction take root, becoming the basis for day-to-day survival. Protest kitchens do not just feed a few hundred protesters but are expanded out into coordinated canteens spread throughout neighborhoods to feed millions. Medical care is not just a tent in the corner of an occupied square, but teams providing free medical care to entire movements, neighborhoods, and cities in insurrection. The rebellion at this phase is characterized primarily by widespread looting, occupations, combat with state-loyal forces, and collective forms of consumption like protest kitchens and medical centers.

Such an insurrection, if militarily successful against the forces of reaction, could potentially abolish capitalist social relations, including wage labor, prisons, police, and the state. Human life, however, depends on collective reproduction, on the positive activity of people to support each other's well-being. To survive, the rebellion would have to seize, transform, and restart the infrastructure of production and mass services, only now to meet direct human needs rather than commodity exchange. Occupied hospitals put their medical technologies to use in providing direct, free medical care. Occupied factories restart manufacturing, making noncommodity free goods necessary for collective survival, to equip the ongoing insurrection. Occupied farms begin to grow and distribute food to the urban canteens. Insurrection can only survive through establishing large-scale communist production.

The collective Angry Workers imagines such a potential communizing revolutionary process in the United Kingdom, focusing on the essential industries that must be taken over for an insurrection to persist, in a pamphlet aptly titled "Insurrection and Production."[16] The authors correctly assess that the survival of any insurrection must quickly confront how to produce basic necessities. They carefully map which industries (like finance) would be swiftly eliminated and their skilled workforce redistributed, where the food may come from if the United Kingdom were to be temporarily cut off from global supply chains, and which sectors of skilled workers may be essential to restart communist production. Their pamphlet suggests a research program and investigation appropriate in other regions as well.

To thrive, communism would have to quickly become global. Establishing communist production in a few regions may be temporarily possible. But to endure, these struggles would have to expand worldwide. The history of twentieth-century socialist states makes clear how isolation amid a capitalist economy and capitalist nations can help distort and destroy revolutionary possibility. Waves of insurrection historically have often been international, cutting across dozens of countries: the period between 1916 and 1920, the Red Decade, the wave of riots and mass protests around 2018 through 2020. If communization was successful in one place, it would likely be attempted elsewhere.[17] During mass communization, what would happen to social reproduction and the institution of the family? The insurgent social reproduction of the protest kitchen gives us hints, if we imagine, as I try to do in the next chapter, its logic generalized throughout society.

13

Communes to Come

Imagine the world on the cusp of communist revolution, a communization of collective life. The factories, farms, and hospitals have been seized by workers councils, operating them directly for human need without commodity exchange. They distribute the goods necessary to keep the struggle going, all free and given to those who can use them: food, clothing, weapons, medical care, radios, and eventually cell phones, computers, and mass entertainment. The communist movement encompasses the majority of the population, counting in its ranks necessary skilled workers like nurses, computer engineers, trauma therapists, and combat strategists. Due to extreme luck or decades of prior crisis, the forces of capital and reaction are weak and retreating. The territory under the control of the popular insurgency is growing, coming to encompass continents. What happens to domestic life? In the course of the struggle, gradually the logic of insurgent social reproduction provides the nucleus for generalized communist reproduction, embodying the qualities extrapolated in chapter 11. Rather than arising from the implementation of a plan, new social forms could arise spontaneously out of insurrection. As masses of proletarians directly confront state, capital, and oppression in their personal lives, they will need to turn to strategies of collective survival beyond the family.

Like the women of Oaxaca called off the barricades to return to serving their husbands, reassertion of the family at this moment could shatter the emerging world of communism. The obligatory nuclear family and wage labor would operate as direct obstacles to such shared survival, freedom, and the persistence of the insurrection. Isolated households lack the means of materially reproducing themselves without access to either land or the market and market-based systems of distribution like supermarkets and box stores as well as their associated supply chains. Patriarchy, coercive heterosexuality, and imposed gender roles within the family all constrict the scope of human imagination and participation in struggle. If the nuclear family is not radically challenged, its counterrevolutionary logics of property, misogyny, heteronormativity, and domination remain untouched.

In the course of our imagined revolutionary struggle, insurgent social reproduction has deepened and expanded. People may initially appropriate large buildings as centers of social reproduction, with collective canteens, shelter, childcare centers, medical care, and halls for democratic assemblies. Protest canteens in every neighborhood distribute food; occupied clinics care for the sick; childcare sections of protest camps have become crèches during the day while their parents fight fascists on the front lines or dedicate their time to producing the basic needs for shared survival. The struggle has come to include sophisticated practices of support and care for the most marginalized groups, including those struggling with drug addictions, people with serious disabilities and chronic illnesses, newborns, or the elderly. Their lives are unconditionally valued at the very least, and whatever contributions they can make—*from each according to their ability*—is appreciated.

The protest kitchen, the tent encampment, the childcare center, and the medic tent together help replace the family at protest sites, without constituting a new state form separated from the collective social body. Taking their essential logic and generalizing it, imagining it encompassing society, may take a new form: collective living arrangements encompassing hundreds of people, constituted directly in the midst of struggle. The Angry Workers collective envisions the formation of such collective domestic units that would manage shared collective food production and consumption, alongside the communization of production. They write:

> The uprising and takeover of essential industries has to go hand in hand with the formation of domestic units comprising 200 to 250 people: communal spaces (former hotels, schools, office blocks, etc.) as central points for distribution, domestic work and local decision-making. The quick formation of such domestic units is as important as the takeover of the essential industries.

Mainly in order to break the isolation of domestic work and gender hierarchies, but also to create a counter-dynamic to the centralisation in the essential industries: a decentralisation of certain social tasks and decision making.[1]

Such collective units of domestic life constitute the emergence of the commune. This is not the commune as it exists under capitalism or settler colonialism; it is made possible only in the midst of mass communization. It is through the form of the revolutionary commune that communist social reproduction becomes possible, embedded in the broader expansion of communist society. Just as the communal kitchen has arisen in past insurgencies, the commune as the prevalent mode of social reproduction could arise under a wider condition of communization. There could be a spontaneous, general tendency toward the formation of the commune as a primary unit of domestic life. Communes are answers to the essential question that will arise in a revolutionary process: *How can we take care of each other?*

FUNCTIONING OF THE COMMUNE

As an insurrection unfolds and engulfs larger parts of society, collectivizing domestic, social reproductive labor through the commune offers a strategy of survival and community. Canteens become far more effective ways to organize obtaining, preparing, and distributing food than through stores and private families. Childcare, medical care, aging care—all could be semi-collectivized into these new residential institutions. Communal, shared, and collectivized units of consumption could act on the basic tasks of survival and be a forum for direct decision-making. They could effectively replace the private household as the basic unit of social reproduction. These communes could consolidate within them collective reproductive services, including childcare and education; collective laundry, apartment cleaning, and canteen food cooking and serving; repair and maintenance of household goods; mental health and regular medical care; and group entertainment activities. Collectivizing many forms of consumption would reduce the social resources and carbon consumption necessary for providing abundance to all. Advanced, high-skill services requiring substantial facilities could be organized regionally, such as surgical care or specialized education. As the new society stabilizes, it could expand full digital access to global networks of communication and collaboration. Communes could be encouraged to form a variety of networking relationships across other communities.

To survive as the basis of freedom, the commune must be a part of a broader and successful effort to destroy the coercive mechanisms of the racial state, to seize the means of production and collective survival, and to defeat the class enemies of the revolutionary struggle. Establishing such free communities must be a part of an expanding, universalizing, and revolutionizing process that also develops fully communist modes of production and circulation of material goods. These communes would not be self-sufficient agricultural communities or isolated units struggling to survive in a market society. A communist transition would take time and would unfold unevenly in different places. But to survive, it must continue to expand, and ultimately destroy the means of reinstating the domination of the state or the market anywhere. These communes would be integrated with a communist production system expanding to a global reach, depending on the highest level of technology compatible with human decency and ecological sustainability. Interdependence in production would require practices of shared deliberation, decision-making, and coordination bridging across many communes.

Both during the insurrection and following, communes of between two and five hundred could encompass several suburban blocks around a large building, like a former school or hospital. Those centralized buildings could become the site of the canteens, the meeting halls, the laundries, and the crèches. Individuals and family units could still continue to live in stand-alone homes or sections of houses but could participate in the shared life of the commune in spaces within convenient walking distance. In major cities, a commune might cover a couple of blocks dense with apartment buildings.

The communes must work around an internal commitment to fostering a culture of mutual respect across lines of difference. Though individuals can harbor whatever beliefs they choose, their relations with others would be subject to public challenge and political struggle, including with children. People within the commune could challenge examples of abuse and harm they see in each other. Even disliked or harmful people must be able to find a home in a commune. This raises the question that is common in discussions of police and prison abolition: what happens to those who commit serious harm? Many forms of crime may disappear in a classless society, but interpersonal violence like sexual assault is likely to persist. Without the intervention of a state and against the practice of banishment as a matter of principle, communes would need to develop well-resourced internal practices to address harm. Many current efforts at transformative and restorative justice, for example, could be implemented with much greater resources and shared support than currently available. These could include long-term monitoring of individuals through the constant rotating presence of friends both to prevent them from further harming others and to support their rehabilitation.[2]

Revolutionary communes should include people who cannot work, including those disabled through physical conditions, age, mental illness, or drug addiction. Harm reduction, mental health support, and addiction recovery resources would all be central concerns of those initially setting up the communes. The communist society will take many generations to heal from the traumas of capitalism and war. Collective and just life needs deliberate practices to welcome complexities of human biological variation in the forms we now define as disability, neurodiversity, and mental illness. The reproductive labor of these communes would include means of managing and supporting those going through particularly difficult times.

DANGERS TO THE COMMUNE

The commune would face many threats. Those family householders most resistant to self-abolition—white property owners, abusive patriarchs, homophobes, and others most invested in the normative family—would need to be challenged through feminist, queer, and communist struggle both within their families and in the broader society. The more loving and chosen the family, the more amenable it may be to abolishing itself by joining a large, well-functioning commune.

As the insurrection secures more stable, large-scale material conditions, the countertendency toward the reassertion of the family could reemerge. If these communes failed to become the generalized form of social reproduction, and the nuclear family again became the main unit of consumption, society would see the return of the capitalist family's current logic of conservatism, whiteness, property ownership, and self-isolation. The return of the family would contribute to counterrevolution, the reassertion of the state, and the failure of communism. Those seeking to reestablish the private family and private-property-based life would become a force of counterrevolution. Reestablishing the private household as the basic unit of social reproduction would depend on a successful counterrevolution and the reestablishing of class society. The private household cannot function without class society. The communist reproduction of material life must resist dependency on obligatory family relations and participation in wage labor.

Other threats to the life of the commune would have to be tackled internally and in their relationship to the broader world. Chosen families and group houses are often very selective in who they allow to participate. If imagined as the basis for society as whole, this logic is deeply counter to the basic ethics of communism: *to each according to their need*. The commune must be welcoming to all, refusing both evaluation and homogenization. The commune must not be an institution based on shared affinity or similarity. Instead, it must overcome the distinction between the particular and universal, the specific community and general human needs. There is much yet to be discovered in terms of what social practices or forms may make this possible.

To avoid becoming centers of survivalism, ethno-nationalism, white chauvinism, or gender fascism, such communes must also resist tendencies toward religious and social homogeneity. Many would be tempted to form homogenous communities centered on shared values or religious practices. But these would potentially reproduce many of the harms of racial capitalism, now recast in a collectivist form. If a religious or cultural sect wants to live on their own on a self-subsistent basis, it may make sense for that to be tolerated by the surrounding networks of production and communal life to avoid reproducing the imperialist violence of a white liberalism that seeks to "save" anyone against their will.[3] But access to outside goods could be conditioned on also allowing outside contact for all residents, giving women, queers, or others experiencing oppression a chance to encounter and choose the outside world. The free circulation and migration of people between communes could be an essential contribution to such heterogeneity. Individual adults would not be permanently bound to their community and could choose to relocate at will, enjoying a similar assurance of material well-being in any other similar commune.

Within the commune, residents would need to find ways of making shared decisions that do not consolidate a new form of class rule controlling and manipulating their governance. Direct-democratic governance and internal struggle would be essential for these communes to avoid internal class stratifications. Though some tasks could be delegated to elected bodies, the essential decisions of the community must be made through group assembly, deliberation in extended conversation, and weighing the concerns of all affected. Where world production would have to be organized through other internet-based and networked mechanisms, decisions immediate to daily life could be made by each commune's assembly. A few hundred people is about the maximum size of an in-person assembly where everyone is able to directly take part in decision-making and have occasional opportunities to speak to the entire group.

Similarly, communes becoming competitive with each other, with grossly unequal standards of living, could be a return of capitalist social relations. Among the many unresolved questions in imagining communism is preventing stratification between communes. What practices could assure the universality of *to each according to their need*, without the impersonal domination of a state removed from, and governing over, the social body? The lack of property, wage labor, and markets would limit communes' capacity to dominate others, but communes may try to consolidate some forms of private production toward their own consumption internally. How could society prevent some communes from coming to enjoy significantly better living standards than others? Or negotiate conflicts over resources between communes? Or dismantle the existing distribution of geographic inequality, uneven development, and racial stratification that organizes capitalist space?

Those who imagine socialism as impersonal services delivered through a state managing a market economy have intelligible and ready answers: they can outline policies that deliberately counterweigh against inequality through bureaucratically investing in underdeveloped areas, taxing wealthier areas, and promoting policies of desegregation, even making forms of reparations. But with decision-making dispersed throughout the society as a whole, and the communes functioning as a primary site of consumption, we would require new and currently unknown practices to mitigate against potential inequality in consumption between communes and assure a basic material well-being for all. The commune as imagined here is an effort to theorize a basis of communist social reproduction; its practical form can only be discovered in shared collective struggle. It is not a plan or program to be implemented, but a speculative imagining to encourage and facilitate others to imagine throughout our struggles.

FOURIER AND THE COMMUNE

This vision of the commune shares some elements, but not others, with various accounts of family abolition. It joins with Marx and Engels in calling for the abolition of private property and bourgeois society. Unlike them, it also suggests a radical remaking of working-class domestic life. Like Kollontai, it collectivizes reproductive labor and drastically reduces the labor done within the family unit. Contrasting Kollontai, the commune of communization does not require or enable the central dominance of the state or the expansion of wage labor. Like the radical group houses of the 1970s, decision-making is shared and democratic; unlike them, the commune as imagined here brings together hundreds of unchosen, heterogeneous people. Joining with Black feminist and queer critiques of the family norm, this vision completely dispenses with the state regulation and fostering of the private, property-owning, respectable household.

Surveying the historical record of family-abolitionist visions, the communes imagined in this chapter most closely resembles the proposals of Charles Fourier. Fourier's phalanxes are spaces of shared production, consumption, and social life. Like the phalanx, these revolutionary communes depend on overcoming market society, commodity production, and private property. They are both radical alternatives to the private bourgeois family. They both offer to residents the possibility of a more enriching psychic and social life. The estimate of Angry Workers' estimate of around two hundred people per commune is perhaps preferable to Fourier's sixteen hundred. The shared kitchen would create a natural initial size, given the logistics of cooking for substantial groups.

Fourier offers a conceptual antidote to the problem of equality between communes. In committing both to the social form of the commune and the guarantee of a social minimum, he engages the problem of equality without a centralized state ruling over society. The need to resist homogenization and include diverse populations within each commune parallels Fourier's vision of the phalanx thriving through a harmony of every possible personality type. Like these communes, Fourier is not advocating for a community of affinity based on evaluating people's worthiness, but instead a universal social form available to all.

Fourier also points us to another dimension of the commune: it includes multiple forms of collective pleasure and joy. The commune could become the center for new forms of communist sociality, art, expression, community, sex, and love. These communes could be the center of a new communist sociality, both challenging and transforming oppressive practices of interpersonal subjugation, stratification, and alienation. As well as supporting shared survival and ongoing rebellion, the new institutions of the commune could come to offer new forms of joy and belonging. The commune could provide a basis for cross-generational friendship. Just as some protest kitchens today offer many opportunities for making cross-generational contacts, connecting with new people, or feeling like a part of something larger than oneself, the canteen and the commune offer people a chance at richer social lives. Today, if you want to have a long-term and close relationship with a person of a different generation, the family is one of your few opportunities for doing so. The shared life of the commune, in contrast, provides ample space for rich and diverse relationships. For example, the structure of the commune could make it relatively easy to play a very active role in nurturing and supporting a young person, without the massive life-changing commitment required of parents under capitalism. Being able to easily form diverse relationships could help break down the multiple forms of segregation inherent to class society. Over time, this could open up space for new, transformative modes of identification and relating that could transcend some identity categories.

The isolation of the private family opens onto collective entertainment and culture making. The divisions that typically organize cultural production—professional producers versus passive consumers—could be broken down within the commune. From songs sung during the evenings to regular DJs at commune dance parties to high-production, large-scale entertainment involving multiple communes, making culture could also become a part of domestic life. Many protest camps and group houses include forms of collective entertainment. Equipped with the resources afforded by controlling the means of production, these forms of collective entertainment could include every existing scale of music, film, immersive experiences, visual art, theater, and more.

As people encounter a free society, the numbers of people identifying with nonnormative sexuality could grow. While Fourier treats standards of attractiveness and ugliness as transhistorical, such standards are instead very likely to transform and broaden. Queer culture, queer leadership, and queer movements are an essential resource to communist struggles pursuing richer forms of human freedom, as are movements against other narrow sexual standards, like against fat-phobia and ableism. Combined with the collective character of the commune, such queer tendencies could unfold into new dynamics valuing consensual, positive, and healthy sexual relations.

Sex and sexual pleasure could become collective concerns, both challenging sexual coercion and abuse and supporting people in finding paths toward sexual fulfillment. Unlike Fourier, I recognize that full sexual satisfaction and perfect harmony is likely not possible, given psychoanalytic insights about human development.

But the commune provides the opportunity to transform sexual practice and eroticism into something that could be collectively considered as a human need, a source of well-being, and a field of ethical care. This might occasionally take the form of Fourier's imagined mass planned orgies. But more often it would look like helping people in their sexual health and sexual satisfaction by having long, supportive conversations and incorporating sexuality into mental and physical health education. Polyamorous relationships could be more common. A social acknowledgment that good sex is a source of human well-being could help undo heteronormative misogyny.

To resist the threat of a reassertion of the patriarchal family as a counterrevolutionary force, ongoing struggles around gender and sexuality within the commune would be essential. Like Fourier, I imagine self-interest coupled to transformed consciousness would be integral to maintaining the collective commitment to the commune. Women and feminized partners could refuse the reimposition of the family, having witnessed the reduced domestic labor of the collective commune and the opportunities the commune affords to contesting sexist relationship dynamics. Queer and trans people could recognize in the commune the means of resisting the abuse and domination of the family for themselves and future queer and trans children. Those who have experienced the insurrectionary commune could recognize in it the material basis for a freer gender and sexual order, and choose to defend and expand its reach. All those who come to realize what is at stake in winning communism could join queers, trans people, feminists, and radical women of color in resisting the return of the family, and instead fight for the family's full replacement with the commune.

CHILDREN OF THE COMMUNE

The commune could provide the material basis for family abolition. As the communes begin to offer material stability and supportive community, many less-normative families may choose to self-abolish, joining communes and dissolving their economic and social insularity into the broader community. In a revolutionary process, the many constituencies that have much to gain from overcoming the family may be the first to see the benefits of the commune: queer chosen family, women-headed families of color impacted by migration and mass incarceration, families living in poverty, and those surviving through other nonheteronormative working-class kinship relations. Once living within the commune, individuals could continue to maintain familial bonds with each other. They could choose to romantically partner, choose to raise children, choose to be involved in the care of the very old or very young. But these relationships would not function as private households, would not be regulated by a racist state as a domestic norm, and would not provide the basis of property ownership or power. Instead, they would be social relations within the broader world of the commune. In this sense, family abolition is not the destruction of kinship ties that currently serve as protection against white supremacy, poverty, and state violence. It is instead the expansion of that protection into broader communities of struggle. It is a commitment to care for all, an answer to the plea for love.

Within the commune, kinship ties could persist in many forms but would be integrated with a broader, interdependent community. Individuals could opt into an arrangement of coparenting with one or more adults, creating family-like arrangements for the purposes of raising children. Research into psychological development suggest that children do benefit from the consistent attention of a small number of adults early in life.[4] This challenges some historical family-abolitionist currents that have mistakenly seen mother-infant bonds as inherently oppressive and in need of complete prohibition. Among the heterogeneous arrangements of close relationships within a commune, people may choose to raise children they gestate or with whom they have a biological relationship; or they may choose other arrangements; or they, their child, or those immediately in their life may change those arrangements as a child ages. Similarly, a few may choose to form lifelong relationships with their biological family or choose to partner romantically for the long term with one other person and incorporate child-rearing as a practice.

Yet these close parenting or familial units would not serve as an economic unit in any sense. They would not organize material consumption nor social reproduction. Instead, they would only act as a voluntary and personal arrangement to be entered into within a broader economic unit, within the ready availability of multiple alternatives for anyone to opt out. If a child found their living situation intolerable, there would be many other adults interdependent with them and in social proximity who could observe the situation, intervene collectively if needed, and offer easily accessible alternative housing arrangements, including other families the child could join, or crèches specializing in such tasks. Children could pass through multiple households and living arrangements as they grow up—including time in children-centered group housing—always being within a building or walk of the original group of adults who they may identify as their parents. These alternatives allow parents to pass in and out of a child's life over time, while assured their children's material and social needs will be met by others. Commune members would share a general commitment to providing adequate care for each other, but the particular forms this takes in relationships could be negotiated and changed according to varying capacities and needs. When children come of age, as Fourier imagined, they could set out to travel across continents exploring the richness of the world, maintaining digital remote contact with their friends and many forms of familial relations.

Gradually, new forms of architecture, design, and construction would reflect the needs for both a combination of heterogeneous private living space for individuals and small chosen clusters, and shared space for reproductive labor and consumption. In the design of new physical spaces for communes, people could have sufficient private and personal space for themselves and their self-chosen kin. But many things now done in the private home could be far better done in shared space: canteens could replace most kitchens and dining rooms; crèches could replace children's individual playrooms; shared entertainment rooms could serve as places to watch television or hang out in groups; personal studies could instead be shared libraries and coworking areas; home maintenance and cleaning equipment could be available in common space; vehicles, when necessary, could be similarly shared. The commune of a few hundred is small enough that all these things could be close at hand and easily accessible at any hour, but reduces the need for individualized consumption and isolated living space to a reasonable minimum. In most cases, private space could be limited to clusters of comfortable bedrooms for those opting to live in family-like arrangements grouped around a single shared room easily accessible to the commune as a whole.

The commune could come to prioritize gender discovery, exploration, and expression for every person. New gender modalities could be integrated with child-rearing, with games and social spaces, with entertainment, and with medical care. Gender liberation is an essential feature of creating a new basis for communist human well-being. In the communization of society and the abolition of the family, gender would undergo massive transformations to no longer serve as a basis for the division of labor, interpersonal domination, or sexual violence. Instead, gender could become what is already prefigured in trans experience: gender as a form of expressing subtle personal truth, the beauty and richness of human expression, and the wielding of aesthetics toward personal fulfillment. The commune could provide all the qualities of communist social reproduction, enabling full gender freedom for the first time since the rise of class society. If queers, trans people, and their allies are successful in establishing a general culture in support of gender expression, the material conditions of the commune enable its full flourishing. Unlike the private nuclear family that can successfully prevent the intervention of queer cultural change, the commune could enable collective struggles around gender and sexual freedom to come to full fruition.

A child coming out as trans could quickly find allies and supporters. If their parents happen to be bigots, the surrounding neighbors are integrated enough in their daily life to quickly identify and intervene in child abuse. Interventions against such abuse, rather than permanently severing contact between parents and children by removing children altogether, could instead enable them to continue to relate to each other regularly in collectively shared spaces, but with many means available to stop abuse or violence. The shared culture of the commune could support the child's free gender expression. Completely accessible medical technologies could make age-appropriate transitioning relatively easy. As they grow, adolescents could be supported in pursuing age-appropriate romances and sexual pleasure, while also being protected against predatory childhood sexual assault. The commune, unlike the family, makes it possible for such affirming experiences to become universally available.

*   *   *

The communes as imagined here are a speculative vision of family abolition, derived from what I identified as qualities of communist social reproduction, coupled to analyzing forms of existing mass protest. It offers one hypothetical way in which care could be organized to overcome the private family, destroy private households, and support human flourishing. As a possible social form, it allows for people to continue to establish and maintain familial relationships. But within the commune, these relationships could be less coercive than the present-day family, and no longer the basis for anyone's material well-being, class position, or social power. What you have would no longer be based on who you love. Family abolition as proposed here is not taking anyone's children away, nor a further atomization by the market, nor an expansion of state power. Family abolition here is our capacity for care and love becoming the basis for radical new social forms, made universal in the overthrow of class society. Through the revolutionary commune, we can take care of each other.

This imagined commune is not meant as a blueprint or program to be actualized. I see little benefit to attempt to create such institutions in the present of racial capitalism, beyond the existing and limited experiments with alternative living already underway. If needed, people will form such communes through the course of the revolutionary struggle itself. If we are lucky, perhaps someday some of us will be among those in such a revolutionary moment, facing alongside others the immediate questions of how to keep the rebellion going, how to care for each other as the struggle unfolds. Speculations now may or may not be of any use at such moments. But they can aid us in the present—by helping to clarify our values, explain our aspirations, and grapple with complex social questions about our shared political desires. Our movements would benefit from more such speculation that identifies both the qualities of a free society we want to see and potential social forms for their realization.

Conclusion
Toward Beloved Community

This book has focused on the material dynamics of social reproduction, including how families depend on the support of state
policy, access to property and stable wages, and their particular
role in reproducing capitalist society. Using a materialist analysis, I
have sought to trace the transformation of the family—and hence
the arguments of its critics—concurrent with the changes in capitalist development. Central to the reproduction of capitalist society
are the labor activities of human care. Though care has appeared
throughout this book, here I summarize those arguments again
inflected through this concept.

Care are those activities that directly help us reproduce our
physical health and development, our psychic well-being, and our
capacity for rich relationships and pleasures. Care is a material
relationship, a set of forms of labor. It is a form of labor, performed
as a relation between people, that offers a use value necessary for
living tolerable lives. For many, it takes the particular forms of
personal dependency within the family. Care in the family may
be a mother changing an infant's diaper; a romantic couple having
decent sex; a person cooking and serving food to everyone in a
private household; conversations about emotional challenges; or
helping a disabled aging parent get in and out of bed. Increasingly, care also takes the form of a commodity exchange, a service
you buy on the market or for which state services pay. Care on the
market may take the form of the laundromat where a young professional drops off their clothes; a fast-food restaurant where an
overworked wage laborer picks up dinner; a meeting with a weekly
therapist; hiring a sex worker for a night; or a home care atten-
dant, paid for by health insurance or a government program, who
comes and changes sheets. Care is not necessarily good or done
with kindness.

There is no firm conceptual line separating care labor from other forms of labor, because all forms of labor in society are interdependent on each other. Care is, in this sense, an aspect of the use value of the labor relation. Often it is most simply identified with gender: care labor are those forms of labor associated with women and feminized people. Like the gendered division of labor, its exact parameters are historically contingent and malleable. Like social reproduction, it cannot be fully extracted or defined apart from the totality of capitalist social relations. Under capitalism, care is alienated. Access to the care in a family requires submitting to state policies, cultural norms, and the direct domination of another person. Access to care in the market requires finding a capitalist employer who wants to exploit your labor, or having access to resources produced through other people's work. These material conditions compound other forms of oppression that can unfold within care relations. They foster racial domination, misogyny, sexual violence, and childhood abuse. These capitalist social relations allow homophobia, transphobia, racial prejudice, and anti-queer bias to easily circulate as a basis of distributing harm and poverty. These material conditions of racial capitalism enable intensified forms of racial stratification, supporting some families while condemning others to legal kinlessness and violent separation. Yet all these forms of care contain an element of use value, in the form of directly meeting human needs. Care, in a nonalienated form, is helping each person or group heal from psychological and physical harms. It is providing people with the resources, education, love, and support to be able to explore all their capacities for intellectual, creative, and physical action. People need diverse forms of care, based on their varying bodies, neurocognitive organization, and passions. Nonalienated care are those activities that help us flourish as full human beings.

Family abolition, throughout this book, is understood as a material process of struggle, concurrent with overcoming capitalist society. Family abolition is the creation of the material conditions for full human flourishing, and for minimizing and redressing harm. It is a commitment to making nonalienated care available to all. It means unlocking care from its restriction to the private family and transforming it into something that is collectively and democratically shared. Family abolition is the dimension of care specific to a classless society. *Family abolition is the communization of care.*

Attending to the use values of care points us to another dimension of a free society, beyond the immediate material conditions that have been the focus of this book. Care is an affective relationship. In caring for others, and in being cared for, we can experience the possibility of love. Some socialists, informed by a liberal philosophical tradition, emphasize that socialism would be those material conditions where your material well-being does not depend on anyone liking you, or you liking anyone else. To an extent, this is obviously true. Communism could only be meaningful if the material conditions of survival were universal, and unconditionally available to all. Even the most loathsome, violent, and harmful person still needs a place to sleep under humane conditions. But in a different sense, this model of socialism completely misses an essential element of a just society: that we have the chance to grow to love each other, to grow to be loved, to express and act on that love in rich consensual ways, to use that love to fulfill and enrich our lives. A free society is one built on mutual care. Care, in its unalienated form, is not just the labor of meeting human needs; it is an affect of communism. Care, under communism, is the facilitation and support of full human flourishing. Love, care—these are words heavy with the meanings that they carry in our alienated, capitalist society. They also point us to an often-neglected question: What might it be like to experience a free, communist society?

MARTIN LUTHER KING JR.'S BELOVED COMMUNITY

Marxist theory has largely neglected the affects and experiences of communism. Concurrently with rejecting a utopian visioning impulse and a general neglect of the psychology of human relationships, Marxists have written quite little about the emotional life of a free society. Communist theory could be enriched by turning to other theoretical and political traditions.

The most vibrant theorization of affect into contemporary struggle has come from feminism, queer liberation, and Black struggles. Feminism has extensively theorized affects of care and the right to refuse care labor. Queer liberation has brought to the fore the power of erotic joy and sexual pleasure as an essential condition of human freedom. Black struggles have repeatedly emphasized the basis and capacity in Black love, Black joy, and embracing the pleasure of Black life. Black theory sees beyond the alienation of racial capitalism built into the circulation of Black arts and identifies in them the capacity for rich Black love. Religious traditions also have a great deal to offer in theorizing the affective experience of communism. The concept of *Bodhicitta*, in Mahayana Buddhism, includes a universal love for all sentient beings, inseparably connected to seeing through the common delusions of conceptual thinking. Many religious faiths have some element of universal love; a just society is imagined as one where this universal love is able to flourish. Malcolm X was drawn to the Muslim concept of *Ummah*, the universal solidarity of the global Muslim community that transcends all differences of nation, class, and race. Christianity, too, is saturated with notions of love.

Martin Luther King Jr. offered a powerful link between the collective solidarity of Black struggle and the progressive elements of Christian theology.[1] As a socialist, anti-imperialist, and devoted religious man, King saw the need to remake global society on the basis of shared solidarity and love. He came to see nonviolence as a tactic embodying this emancipatory promise of love, but he also expressed some sympathy and solidarity with those engaged in forms of violent struggle. Though I do not share King's profound commitment to nonviolence, I see in his thinking a powerful way of theorizing the effects of communism. Nonviolence, even if limited as a tactic, is a powerful principle for thinking through what it means to care for each other. King was a powerful political figure for a number of specific reasons: the unique conjunctural political conditions of the Jim Crow South in the 1950s that made nonviolent protest strategically effective; the importance of the Black Southern church as one of the few community institutions autonomous from white control; and his compelling oration and profound charisma. To be clear, the African American civil rights movement was driven as a mass struggle of millions of working-class Black people that has been unfairly recast by racist nostalgia as the act of a few extraordinary leaders. But despite the flawed historiography that valorizes King to explain a much broader movement, he was indeed an extraordinary figure.

Among King's most compelling formulations was *beloved community*. The concept appears multiple times throughout his writing and speeches. King often emphasized that the beloved community was the endpoint of nonviolence. Through nonviolence, the rend of segregation and oppression could be overcome, and people could finally have the chance to recognize each other as fully human. These points are evident across several speeches and writings between 1957 and 1960. In three different speeches in 1957 and 1959, King uses minor variations of the following: "The way of violence leads to bitterness in the survivors and brutality in the destroyers. But, the way of non-violence leads to redemption and the creation of the beloved community."[2] In 1960, during an interview for *US News & World Report*, King elaborates this distinction:

> If we ever succumb to the temptation of using violence in our struggle, unborn generations will be the recipients of the long and desolate night of bitterness—and our aim is not to defeat or to humiliate the white man, but to win his friendship and understanding. One of the ways we seek to do this is through this nonviolent protest, thereby arousing the dozing conscience of the white community and hoping to ultimately achieve the beloved community and the type of brotherhood that is necessary for us to survive in a meaningful manner.[3]

Beloved community is a deliberate intention, a guiding principle that informs nonviolent action. For nonviolence, "the intent is always to create the beloved community."[4] Its immediate form is reconciliation: "There is another element that must be present in our struggle that then makes our resistance and nonviolence truly meaningful. That element is reconciliation."[5]

Earlier, I called family abolition a *horizon*, a way of theorizing about a postrevolutionary free society. Throughout these comments, King is emphasizing that the practice of nonviolence offers its own revolutionary horizon, that of beloved community. Though later Black thinkers and activists came to emphasize the beloved community forged in the midst of struggle, for King during these years it is an endpoint, a goal, a distant horizon: "Our ultimate end must be the creation of the beloved community."[6] What is this beloved community, on the other side of a nonviolent transformation of the world? In another 1960 speech, King elaborates that it includes a universal respect for human dignity and the value of human life: "The end which we seek is the creation of the beloved community. The end which we seek to create is a society in which all men will be able to live together as brothers and respect the dignity and worth of all human personality."[7] In a personal letter in 1960, beloved community is similarly equated to universal brotherhood, to be approached incrementally: "May the days ahead bring us nearer to the 'beloved' community and a society where the brotherhood of man is a reality."[8]

This concept of the beloved community has been powerfully taken up by subsequent generations of Black theorists. In bell hooks's 1995 book *Killing Rage*, she concludes with a moving chapter entitled "Beloved Community: A World Without Racism," repeating the evocation of the beloved community as a horizon of massive social change. Like King, she links beloved community to the possibility of interracial respect. She emphasizes that beloved community is only possible not through a renunciation of difference but by embracing and valuing difference. Beloved community is one "bound by a shared belief in the transformative power of love."[9] Our experiences of love and support in the present can be a reminder that beloved community is possible.[10] In a 2012 discussion with George Brosi, bell hooks emphasizes beloved community as entailing learning from the oppressed: King "had a profound awareness that the people involved in oppressive institutions will not change from the logics and practices of domination without engagement with those who are striving for a better way."[11] hooks links this to restorative justice and community-based strategies to resolve conflict. Community is an essential dimension of human interdependence, counter to liberal individualism.

Deborah N. Archer, in a recent Martin Luther King Jr. Keynote Lecture, explains her understanding of Dr. King's vision, one where "everyone could live lives of joy and dignity because everyone was invested in the well-being and dignity of their fellow human being."[12] She contrasts it with multiple forms of ongoing white supremacist state policy. The concept of the beloved community has also been put to use to discuss queer Black joy, such as in Jafari Sinclaire Allen's article on Black queer dance club culture.[13]

Joshua F. J. Inwood provides a detailed theorization of King's beloved community. Love is not sentimental but is based on Christian notions of redemption, close to the Greek word *Agape*, which King defined as "a willingness to go to any length to restore community."[14] As King's thought developed, justice was increasingly bound up with an international struggle against colonialism, and for massive global wealth redistribution, requiring the eradication of "racism, materialism, and militarism."[15] King expressed a conditional sympathy for Karl Marx, the Black Power movement, armed revolt, and the growing anti-colonial struggles of the Global South. Dr. King, Inwood concludes, "radicalizes the concept of community" in ways that are directly counter to today's neoliberalism.[16]

King primarily understood alienation as a separation, as a severing of humanity from itself. Beloved community is the coming back together, the rejoining that is our shared birthright. Less clear in his writing is another fundamental dimension of the alienation that constitutes racial capitalism: subjugation. King certainly recognized subjugation as a major dimension of white supremacy and dedicated his life to overthrowing the institutions that incarnated this subjugation. Capitalism not only separates us from each other in the violence of market exchange; it also constitutes a power that rules over human life and subjugates us all. King's beloved community must be the overcoming of separation, and the overthrowing of this subjugating power. While joining with the yearning toward recognition of shared humanity that motivated King's commitment to nonviolence, I see violence as often necessary to ultimately overcome domination and oppression. Marx and the Marxist tradition offer a crucial critique of this subjugation.

GEMEINWESEN

Community is a concept laden with meanings under capitalism today. For neoliberal commentators, communities are expected to replace the welfare state, to keep the family strong, to collaborate with policing efforts, to enable a vibrant civil society. For many in marginalized social groups, community is the fantasy that we could belong somewhere, that the people we see at parties, protests, or gatherings are people who may love us, may care for us, may be our chosen family. For many activists, community is the primary driver of collective action, the site and fulcrum of alternative practices of accountability, the space of learning and creative expression. We are all yearning for beloved community, and sometimes we pretend we have found it.

Yet just as neoliberalism has come to centrally rely on and deploy ideas of community, the forces of racial capitalism constantly tear communities apart.[17] Constrained by labor markets, people move away from friends and family in search of decent jobs. As people age, many activists tend to isolate increasingly within their family units, unable to maintain active engagement with the shared spaces of community life. Racial violence directly assaults community: urban redevelopment bulldozing neighborhoods, ICE raiding workplaces and conducting mass deportations, mass incarceration removing thousands of poor men of color from their neighborhoods, constant police harassment and the threat of police violence driving out young people of color from public socializing. People may rely on what they call community for help with rent or a place to sleep, but ultimately people feel abandoned by their communities as often as they feel helped. Communities evaporate; within any given circle, people who care about each other are unlikely to live in proximity for more than a few years at time. Communities are always precarious.

Communities fail to live up to our aspirations for them because they do not control the means of production. Capitalists and capitalist states have the monopoly on everything we need to survive. People may love those they consider their community, but the priority must be finding a way to sell their capacity to work. The demands of employers and labor markets dominate people's lives. Without having the resources to actually provide for people, what we call communities are subject to constant instability. Miranda Joseph critiques notions of community as deployed by nonprofits. She argues that community takes the place of widespread and collective aspirations to be free of capitalist violence, the dominance of property and wealth, and universal coercion—in short, *community* is a word in the place of our desire for communism.[18]

Marx uses the word *Gemeinwesen*, often translated as *community*, but can also be translated as *the communal being*. It appears in Marx as the community that collective revolts move toward. Gemeinwesen includes both the universal shared nature of humanity, including our capacity for creative action, and the possibility of a collective form adequate to this capacity, the commune. Gemeinwesen, as understood by Marx, is not the community of precapitalist collectivities of feudal or preagricultural societies. Instead, it reflects the full diversity of human expression possible in modernity, while overcoming the alienation of capitalist society. Gemeinwesen is only possible through the mass collective action of the working class. Marx writes:

> A social revolution takes the standpoint of the *whole* because— even if it were to occur in only *one* factory district—it represents man's protest against a dehumanized life, because it starts out from the *standpoint* of a *separate real individual*, because the *community* [Gemeinwesen], against whose separation from himself the individual reacts, is man's *true* community, *human being*.[19]

Like King, Marx understood social revolution as overcoming our separation from our basic shared humanity. Marx also grasped alienation as a force that rules over human life. Under capitalism, the product of labor is separated from the laborer. It becomes the private property of the capitalist, who directly subjugates and dominates the laborer. The more the laborer works, the more she creates the basis for her own subjugation. Marx also understood that this dominating force takes on an impersonal, universal quality. Through the generalization of market dependency, the abstract forces of the market dominate the whole of human activity. Capitalists and laborers come to rely on the capricious and irrational violence of market competition, on what Marx understood as the global regulating regime of value. Social revolution is simultaneously the destruction of the domination of value and all the capitalist social relations that accompany it.

Jacques Camatte dove into Gemeinwesen as the goal of the revolutionary movement. A French Marxist in the 1950s and 1960s, Camatte was a student of Italian left communist Amadeo Bordiga. In the 1970s and 1980s, Camatte came to move away from Marxism into currents of primitivism and anti-civilization thinking. In his 1977 essay "Marx and *Gemeinwesen*," Camatte is still a close reader of Marx.[20] Camatte identifies Gemeinwesen as the community of human beings that can never be found in actually existing community under capitalism, because capitalism fundamentally alienates humanity from its being. Gemeinwesen is the potential of humanity, the collective dimension of our individual capacities. Camatte writes:

> To get out of this world one has to acquire a body tending towards a community, and thus to not lock oneself into an individual phenomenon, but to rediscover the dimension of *Gemeinwesen*. It is here that we find the fundamental theme of Marx's philosophical works: to explain the relationship between the individual and society and how to abolish their antagonism. More than a social being, man is a being who has the dimension of the *Gemeinwesen*, that is to say that every human being carries in herself, subjectivated, the *Gemeinwesen*.[21]

For Camatte, Gemeinwesen is the common thread connecting humanity. It is the unity in diversity possible through the self-realization of each individual. Gemeinwesen is the "common thread, common substance," the community possible only through a mutual "knowledge-recognition of all others, their acceptance in their diversity. ... With an accession to the community, human beings will have finally found their world."[22] Camatte and Marx's notion of Gemeinwesen and King's account of beloved community share fundamental qualities. They are both potentials to be realized through mass struggle. They are both inherent to our shared humanity, expressions of basic goodness, an acceptance of diversity and difference, an achievement to be realized. They are both means of overcoming the opposition between individual freedom and collective well-being. King increasingly came to recognize that beloved community was fundamentally incompatible with capitalism, empire, and materialism. He was discovering that beloved community could only be realized through the overcoming of class society.

Like Marx and Camatte, Dr. King was not using the word *community* in the sense widely deployed today, of some assumed group sharing an identity, experience, or geographic locale. Nor was he romantically pointing to the tightly knit, dense social networks that the civil rights movement depended on, nor the sedentary life of many rural agricultural workers. King was also not appealing to sentimentality, to our day-to-day experience of emotions. For King, the beloved community was the spiritual, interpersonal, affective dimension of a free society, one that is the sought-after goal of justice struggle. Beloved community is the experience of communism. Beloved community is the abolition of the family.

RED LOVE

Family abolition is the horizon of collective love. We place vast hopes and desires in the family: for care, for sex, for consistency over time, for unconditional support, for material aid, for entertainment, for providing stability in daily life. At these, the family is generally a catastrophic failure and often an alienated disappointment. Our available alternatives are rarely any better. These positive human needs can only be fulfilled in the overcoming of the family and all the institutions of capitalist society. It is only through our collective emancipation that we can forge the relationships of love and care that we all yearn for, that we all desperately need.

Among the many apt connotations of the concept of *horizon*, we cannot see what lies beyond it. The commune as offered here is just one tentative speculation. The beloved community must go beyond our current conceptions of care, beyond how we recognize ourselves, and beyond how we conceive of our relation to each other. If the slave is the necessary counterpart to the human, as Afro-pessimist theory has claimed, the collective emancipation of beloved community must go beyond our conceptions of the human and humanity. Red love is a collective potential between us all yet to be discovered. It lies beyond the end of the world. To fully know the content of a classless society could only be prophecy, beyond the limits and tasks of theory. But however unknowable it may be, it is a promise that we can glimpse and yearn for, a promise we can fight for, a promise we can live for. Freed from the rigid social roles of heteronormative gender and sexual identity, the domination and material constraints of capitalism, the cruel genocidal logic of whiteness and white supremacy, and remade in the intensity of revolutionary struggle, the potential of red love, of communized care, can be finally freed onto the world. The abolition of the family must be the positive creation of a society of generalized human care and queer love. Family abolition and communist social relations are the realization of the beloved community. A society based on communist social reproduction would be the chance to genuinely care for each other, to be cared for, and for that care to extend through the vast global fabric of our interdependence. In a free society beyond capitalism and beyond the family, we can finally know what it means to love and be loved.

Notes

INTRODUCTION

1. The following analysis of social reproduction on the barricades of the Oaxaca Commune is entirely indebted to Barucha Peller, "Self-Reproduction and the Oaxaca Commune," *ROAR* 1 (2016): 70–77. Other writing on the Oaxaca Commune also informs this account: Gerardo Rénique, "The Uprising in Oaxaca," *Socialism and Democracy* 21, no. 2 (2007): 57–61; Lynn Stephen, "'We Are Brown, We Are Short, We Are Fat. ... We Are the Face of Oaxaca': Women Leaders in the Oaxaca Rebellion," *Socialism and Democracy* 21, no. 2 (2007): 97–112; Marco Estrada Saavedra, "The Popular Assembly of the Peoples of Oaxaca (APPO)," in *Oxford Research Encyclopedia of Latin American History* (Oxford: Oxford University Press, 2020).
2. Peller, "Self-Reproduction and the Oaxaca Commune," 72.
3. Ibid., 72.
4. Quoted in Ibid., 74.

CHAPTER 1

1. Stephanie E. Jones-Rogers, *They Were Her Property: White Women as Slave Owners in the American South* (New Haven, CT: Yale University Press, 2019).
2. David Brooks, "The Nuclear Family Was a Mistake," *The Atlantic*, March 2020.
3. See, for example, the excellent book by Dean Spade, *Mutual Aid* (New York: Verso, 2020).
4. See Michèle Barrett, *Women's Oppression Today: Problems in Marxist Feminist Analysis* (New York: Verso, 1981).
5. Melinda Cooper, *Family Values: Between Neoliberalism and the New Social Conservatism* (Princeton, NJ: Princeton University Press, 2017).
6. Michèle Barrett and Mary McIntosh, *The Anti-Social Family* (New York: Verso, 1982).
7. Kathi Weeks, "Abolition of the Family: The Most Infamous Feminist Proposal," *Feminist Theory*, 2021; Sophie Lewis, *Full Surrogacy Now: Feminism Against Family* (New York: Verso, 2019).
8. Patricia Hill Collins, "It's All in the Family: Intersections of Gender, Race, and Nation," *Hypatia* 13, no. 3 (1998): 62–82.

9. "Wages for housework" is discussed in more depth in chapter 8. See also Louise Toupin, *Wages for Housework: A History of an International Feminist Movement, 1972–77* (London: Pluto, 2018).

CHAPTER 2

1. Lauren Aratani, "'Invasion' and 'Fake News': El Paso Manifesto Echoes Trump Language." *The Guardian*, August 5, 2019, https://www.theguardian.com/us-news/2019/aug/05/el-paso-shooting-suspect-trump-language-manifesto.

2. Renaud Camus, *The Great Replacement* (Translated by /pol/'s /RWTS/, published online), 10. See https://dokumen.pub/the-great-replacement-part-i-9791091681032.html.

3. Ibid., 31.

4. See, for example, Paul Gilroy, "It's a Family Affair: Black Culture and the Trope of Kinship," *Small Acts* (London: Serpent's Tail, 1993); Patricia Hill Collins, "It's All in the Family: Intersections of Gender, Race, and Nation," *Hypatia* 13, no. 3 (1998): 62–82; Anne McClintock, "Family Feuds: Gender, Nationalism and the Family," *Feminist Review* 44, no. 1 (1993): 61–80; Sophie Bjork–James, "White Sexual Politics: The Patriarchal Family in White Nationalism and the Religious Right," *Transforming Anthropology* 28, no. 1 (2020): 58–73.

5. Patricia Hill Collins, "It's All in the Family: Intersections of Gender, Race, and Nation," *Hypatia* 13, no. 3 (1998): 62–82; Hortense Spillers, "Mama's Baby, Papa's Maybe: An American Grammar Book," in *Black, White and in Color: Essays on American Literature and Culture* (Chicago: Chicago University Press, 2003), 203–29; Tiffany Lethabo King, "Black 'Feminisms' and Pessimism: Abolishing Moynihan's Negro Family," *Theory & Event* 21, no. 1 (2018): 68–87, 75.

6. Dorothy Roberts, "Abolish Family Policing, Too," *Dissent* (Summer 2021). See also Dorothy Roberts, *Torn Apart: How the Child Welfare System Destroys Black Families—and How Abolition Can Build a Safer World* (New York: Basic Books, 2022).

7. The isolation and self-interest inherent to the private household is central to the critique offered in Michèle Barrett and Mary McIntosh, *The Anti-Social Family* (New York: Verso, 1982).

8. Center for Disease Control, "Preventing Child Abuse & Neglect," 2022. https://www.cdc.gov/violenceprevention/pdf/can/CAN-factsheet_2022.pdf.

9. Emily Petrosky et al., "Racial and Ethnic Differences in Homicides of Adult Women and the Role of Intimate Partner Violence—United States, 2003–2014," *Morbidity and Mortality Weekly Report* 66, no. 28 (2017): 741–46.

10. M. C. Black et al., "The National Intimate Partner and Sexual Violence Survey (NISVS): 2010 Summary Report," Atlanta, GA: National Center for Injury Prevention and Control, Centers for Disease Control and Prevention, 2011.
11. United Nations Office on Drugs and Crime, "Killings of Women and Girls by their Intimate Partner or Other Family Members: Global Estimates 2020," 2021.
12. Walter S. DeKeseredy, "Male Peer Support and Women Abuse: The Current State of Knowledge," *Sociological Focus*, 23, no. 2 (1990): 129–39.
13. Walter S. DeKeseredy, Molly Dragiewicz, and Martin D. Schwarz, *Abusive Endings: Separation and Divorce Violence against Women* (Berkeley: University of California Press, 2017).
14. Sampson Lee Blair, "The Division of Household Labor," in *Handbook of Marriage and the Family*, eds. G. W. Peterson and K. R. Bush (New York: Springer, 2013), 613–35.

CHAPTER 3

1. Larry Buchanan, Quoctrung Bus, and Jugal K. Patel, "Black Lives Matter May Be the Largest Movement in U.S. History," *New York Times*, July 3, 2020.
2. Maria Sacchetti, "Curfews Follow Days of Looking and Demonstrations," *Washington Post*, June 1, 2020.
3. National Guard, "National Guard Response to Civil Unrest," Press Release, June 8, 2020, http://www.nationalguard.mil/Resources/Press-Releases/Article/2213005/national-guard-response-to-civil-unrest/.
4. Meg Kelly and Elyse Samuels, "Who Caused the Violence at Protests? It Wasn't Antifa." *Washington Post*, June 22, 2020.
5. The Associated Press, "George Floyd Transcript: Read It in Full Here," *Twin Cities Pioneer Press*, July 9, 2020.
6. Manny Fernandez and Audra D. S. Burch, "George Floyd, From 'I Want to Touch the World' to 'I Can't Breathe,'" *New York Times*, April 20, 2021.
7. Toluse Olorunnipa and Griff Witte, "Born with Two Strikes," *Washington Post*, October 8, 2020.
8. Ibid.
9. Alexis Pauline Gumbs, "We Can Learn to Mother Ourselves: The Queer Survival of Black Feminism 1968–1996" (Doctoral dissertation, Duke University, 2010).
10. Sophie Lewis, *Abolish the Family: A Manifesto for Care and Liberation* (New York: Verso, 2022), 21. See a longer discussion of *Abolish the Family* in chapter 11.
11. Susan Buck-Morss, *Hegel, Haiti, and Universal History* (Pittsburgh: University of Pittsburgh, 2009).

12. Wilson Sherin, "Working for Abolition Means Abolishing Work," *Spectre*, no. 5 (Spring 2022).

CHAPTER 4

1. Karl Marx, "Thesis on Feuerbach," in *Marx Engels Collected Works*, vol. 5 (London: Lawrence & Wishart, 1845), 7. All citations to works by Karl Marx or Friedrich Engels from the *Marx Engels Collected Works*, hereafter *MECW*. Years listed are for original publication dates.
2. Ibid., 8.
3. Marx and Engels, *The Manifesto of the Communist Party* (*MECW*, vol. 6, 1848), 501.
4. Engels, *The Condition of the Working Class in England* (*MECW*, vol. 4, 1845), 332.
5. Ibid., 405.
6. Ibid., 396.
7. Wally Seccombe, *Weathering the Storm: Working-Class Families from the Industrial Revolution to the Fertility Decline* (New York: Verso, 1993), 74.
8. Claudia Goldin, *Understanding the Gender Gap: An Economic History of American Women* (New York: Oxford, 1990), 48–49.
9. Marx and Engels, *The Manifesto of the Communist Party*, 501.
10. Marx, *The Eighteenth Brumaire of Louis Bonaparte* (*MECW*, vol. 11, 1851), 149.
11. Ibid., 61.
12. Engels, *The Peasant War in Germany* (*MECW*, vol. 10, 1850), 415.
13. Ibid., 407.
14. Ibid., 408.
15. Marx and Engels, *The Manifesto of the Communist Party*, 501.
16. Ibid., 501.
17. Engels, *The Conditions of the Working Class in England*, 181; italics in original.
18. Ibid., 179.
19. Marx and Engels, *The Manifesto of the Communist Party* (*MECW*, vol. 6, 1848), 502.
20. Marx & Engels, *The Manifesto of the Communist Party*, 501.
21. Marx, *The German Ideology* (*MECW*, vol. 5, 1867), 49.
22. Marx, *Economic-Philosophic Manuscripts of 1844* (*MECW*, vol. 3, 1844), 297. In the excerpt presented here, I substitute *MECW*'s translation of *Aufhebung* "positive transcendence" with "abolition."
23. For the context of these debates, see Richard Weikart, "Marx, Engels and the Abolition of the Family," *History of European Ideas* 18, no. 5 (1994): 657–72.
24. Marx and Engels, *The Manifesto of the Communist Party* (*MECW*, vol. 6, 1848), 505.

25. Engels, *The Origin of the Family*, 188.
26. Ibid., 189.
27. Ibid., 183.
28. Ibid., 188.
29. For a fuller account of homophobia in Engels and Marx, see http://www.columbia.edu/~lnp3/mydocs/sex_gender/engels_homophobia.htm.
30. Letter, Engels to Marx (*MECW*, vol. 43, 1869), 295. *Guerre aux cons, paix aus trous-de-cul* could be translated as "War to the cunts, peace to the assholes."
31. Fourier, quoted by Marx and Engels, *The Holy Family* (*MECW*, vol. 4, 1845), 196.

CHAPTER 5

1. Quoted in Laurel Clark Shire, *The Threshold of Manifest Destiny: Gender and National Expansion in Florida* (Philadelphia: University of Pennsylvania Press, 2016), 144.
2. Sarah Carter, *The Importance of Being Monogamous: Marriage and Nation Building in Western Canada to 1915* (Edmonton: University of Alberta Press, 2008), 22.
3. Richard Phillips, "Settler Colonialism and the Nuclear Family," *Canadian Geographer* 53, no. 2 (2009): 239–53.
4. Carter, *The Importance of Being Monogamous*, 78.
5. Ibid., 75.
6. Stephanie E. Jones-Rogers, *They Were Her Property: White Women as Slave Owners in the American South* (New Haven, CT: Yale University Press, 2019).
7. See, for example, Glenda Elizabeth Gilmore, *Gender and Jim Crow: Women and the Politics of White Supremacy, 1896–1920* (Chapel Hill: University of North Carolina Press, 1996) and Sarah Haley, *No Mercy Here: Gender, Punishment, and the Making of Jim Crow Modernity* (Chapel Hill: University of North Carolina Press, 2016).
8. Ian Austen, "'Horrible History': Mass Grave of Indigenous Children Reported in Canada," *New York Times*, May 28, 2021.
9. Ian Mosby and Erin Millions, "Canada's Residential Schools Were a Horror," *Scientific American*, August 1, 2021, https://www.scientific american.com/article/canadas-residential-schools-were-a-horror/.
10. US Congress, "An Act Making Provision for the Civilization of the Indian Tribes Adjoining the Frontier Settlements," 3 Stat, 516, March 3, 1819.
11. Quoted in David Wallace Adams, *Education for Extinction: American Indians and the Boarding School Experience, 1875–1928* (Lawrence: University of Kansas Press, 1995), 178.
12. Denise K. Lajimodiere, "American Indian Boarding Schools in the United States: A Brief History and their Current Life," in *Indigenous*

Peoples' Access to Justice, Including Truth and Reconciliation Processes, eds. Wilton Littlechild and Elsa Stamatopoulou (New York: Institute for the Study of Human Rights, Columbia University, 2015), 255–61.

13. Lajimodiere, "American Indian Boarding Schools," 259.
14. Margaret Robinson. "Two-Spirit Identity in a Time of Gender Fluidity," *Journal of Homosexuality* 67, no. 12 (2019): 1675–90.
15. Max Mejía, "Mexican Pink," in *Different Rainbows*, ed. Peter Drucker (Chicago: Gay Men's Press, 2000), 43–55.
16. Carter, *The Importance of Being Monogamous*, 104.
17. Quoted in David Graeber and David Hedgerow, *The Dawn of Everything: A New History of Humanity* (New York: Farrar, Straus and Giroux, 2021).
18. Carter, *The Importance of Being Monogamous*, 104.
19. Antonia I. Casteñeda, "Gendering the History of Alta California, 1769–1848: Gender, Sexuality and the Family," *California History* 76, no. 2/3 (1997): 230–259, 230.
20. Ibid., 235.
21. Ibid., 235.
22. John Grenier, *The First Ways of War: American Warming on the Frontier* (New York: Cambridge University Press, 2012), 144.
23. Roxanne Dunbar-Ortiz, *An Indigenous Peoples' History of the United States* (Boston: Beacon Press, 2014).
24. Ryan Paradis, "The Sixties Scoop: A Literary Review Prepared by the Manitoba Association of Friendship Centers" (Winnipeg: Manitoba Association of Friendship Centers, 2015).
25. Quoted in David B. MacDonald, *The Sleeping Giant Awakens: Genocide, Indian Residential Schools, and the Challenge of Conciliation* (Toronto: University of Toronto Press, 2019), 98, and Margaret D. Jacobs, *A Generation Removed: The Fostering and Adoption of Indigenous Children in the Postwar World* (Lincoln: University of Nebraska Press), 7.
26. Angela Davis, "Reflections on the Black Woman's Role in the Community of Slaves," *The Massachusetts Review* 13, no. 1/2 (1972): 83.
27. W. E. B. Du Bois, *Black Reconstruction in America, 1860–1880* (New York: Vintage [1935] 1992), 11.
28. Davis, "Reflections on Black Women's Role," 88.
29. Saidiya Hartman, *Scenes of Subjection: Terror, Slavery, and Self-Making in Nineteenth-Century America* (New York: Oxford, 1997), 98.
30. Hortense Spillers, "Mama's Baby, Papa's Maybe: An American Grammar Book," in *Black, White and in Color: Essays on American Literature and Culture* (Chicago: Chicago University Press, 2003), 203–229, 218; emphasis in original.
31. I return to these debates and their political context in chapter 8.
32. This argument is quite counter to widely held conceptions of Black life during Jim Crow, including those held by many mid-twentieth-century Black theorists. The central role of sharecropping policy in enforcing

Black marriage is substantiated by recent research into the boll weevil epidemics. See Deirdre Bloom, James Feigenbaum, and Christopher Muller, "Tenancy, Marriage, and the Boll Weevil Infestation, 1892–1930," *Demography* 54, no. 3 (2017): 1029–49). In sections of the South that switched to wage labor agriculture due to an abrupt, exogenous collapse of cotton sharecropping, Black marriage rates similarly fell.

33. Rose Stremlau, "'To Domesticate and Civilize Wild Indians': Allotment and the Campaign to Reform Indian Families, 1875–1887," *Journal of Family History* 30, no. 3 (July 2005): 265–86, 276.

34. David Wallace Adams. *Education for Extinction: American Indians and the Boarding School Experience, 1875–1828.* (Lawrence: University Press of Kansas, 1995), 344.

35. Stemlau, "To Domesticate and Civilize," 268.

36. Alyosha Golstein, "On the Reproduction of Race, Capitalism, and Settler Colonialism," from "Race and Capitalism: Global Territories, Transnational Histories" Symposium, UC Los Angeles, 2017.

37. Mark Rifkin, *When Did Indians Become Straight? Kinship, the History of Sexuality, and Native Sovereignty* (New York: Oxford University Press), 153.

38. I return briefly to King's account in chapter 10.

39. Daniel Heath Justice, "'Go Away Water!' Kinship Criticism and the Decolonization Imperative," in *Reasoning Together: The Native Critics Collective*, eds. Craig S. Womack, Daniel Heath Justice, and Christopher B. Teuton (Norman: University of Oklahoma Press), 147–68.

40. Kim TallBear, "Caretaking Relations, Not American Dreaming," *Kalfou* 6, no. 1 (April 2019): 24–41.

41. Kim TallBear, "Identity Is a Poor Substitute for Relating," in *Routledge Handbook of Critical Indigenous Studies,* eds. Brendan Hokowhitu, Aileen Moreton-Robinson, Linda Tuhiwai-Smith, Chris Andersen, and Steve Larkin (New York: Routledge, 2020), 467–78.

42. Kim TallBear, *Native American DNA: Tribal Belonging and the False Promise of Genetic Science* (Minneapolis: University of Minnesota Press, 2013).

43. Lou Cornum, "Desiring the Tribe," *Pinko* 1 (2019): 34–45, 45.

CHAPTER 6

1. Gay L. Gullickson, *Unruly Women of Paris: Images of the Commune* (Ithaca, NY: Cornell University Press, 1996), 37–38.

2. Marx, *The Civil War in France* (*MECW*, vol. 22, 1871), 334.

3. Pamela Stewart, "'Taking One's Part in the Revolution': A Comparison of Women's Labor as Tools of Revolutionary Change in France, Viet Nam, and Poland," *WorkingUSA: The Journal of Labor and Society* 11 (2008): 499–522, 515. See also Eliza Guinn's "'A Spectacle of Vice': Sex Work and

Moralism in the Paris Commune of 1871" (Oberlin College, Honors Paper).

4. Stewart, "'Taking One's Part in the Revolution,'" 515.

5. "Proletarianization" is a term from Marxist theory referring to people's life circumstances changing so that they become proletarian and are forced to work for wages. The following two sections draws from John D'Emilio in "Capitalism and Gay Identity," in *Powers of Desire: The Politics of Sexuality*, eds. Ann Snitow, Christine Stansell, and Sharon Thompson (New York: Monthly Review Press, 1983). This argument was developed further in Peter Drucker, *Warped: Gay Normality and Queer Anticapitalism* (Chicago: Haymarket, 2014), and Chris Chitty, *Sexual Hegemony: Statecraft, Sodomy, and Capital in the Rise of the World System* (Durham, NC: Duke University Press, 2020).

6. Neil McKenna, *Fanny and Stella: The Young Men Who Shocked Victorian England* (New York: Faber, 2013). McKenna estimates the number of brothels employing male-assigned sex workers to be two thousand, a number otherwise difficult to verify.

7. Judith Walkowitz, *Prostitution and Victorian Society* (Cambridge: Cambridge University Press, 1982).

8. Chris Chitty, *Sexual Hegemony: Statecraft, Sodomy, and Capital in the Rise of the World System* (Durham, NC: Duke University Press, 2020).

9. Saidiya Hartman, *Wayward Lives, Beautiful Experiments: Intimate Histories of Riotous Black Girls, Troublesome Women, and Queer Radicals* (New York: W.W. Norton & Company, 2019).

10. Katherine Franke, *Wedlocked: The Perils of Marriage Equality* (New York: NYU Press, 2015), 80.

11. Ibid., 78.

12. Charles Fourier, *The Theory of the Four Movements*, eds. Gareth Stedman Jones and Ian Patterson (Cambridge: Cambridge University Press [1808] 1996), 275.

13. Ibid., 111.

14. Ibid., 176.

15. Jonathan Beecher and Richard Bienvenu, eds., *The Utopian Vision of Charles Fourier* (Boston: Beacon Press, 1971), 340.

16. Ibid., 346.

17. Ibid., 390.

18. Ibid., 390.

19. Ibid., 306.

CHAPTER 7

1. Other important elements of communization theory, including its name, are outlined in chapter 11.

2. In TC's words: "At this point capital, in its relation to labor, poses itself as an external force. For the proletariat, to liberate itself from capitalist

domination is to turn labor into the basis of social relations between all individuals, to liberate productive labor, take up the means of production, and abolish the anarchy of capitalism and private property. The proletariat's liberation is to be founded in a mode of production based upon abstract labor, i.e. upon value." Théorie Communiste, "Much Ado About Nothing," *Endnotes* 1 (2008): 155–207, 156.

3. This particular paradox—that the emancipation of labor was conceived of imposing the tyranny of work on everyone—is best explored in "A History of Separation," *Endnotes* 4 (2015): 70–193. This essay presents an accessible and comprehensive outline of the history and theory of the workers' movement, as understood in this book.

4. TC, "Much Ado About Nothing," 159–60.

5. My primary reference for understanding the consolidation of a male-breadwinner norm is Seccombe's *Weathering the Storm*. Also see the debate on the "family wage" from early 1980s Marxist feminist literature, including Heidi Hartmann's "The Unhappy Marriage of Marxism and Feminism," in *Women and Revolution*, ed. Lydia Sargent (Montreal: Black Rose Books, 1981); Michèle Barrett's *Women's Oppression Today: The Marxist/Feminist Encounter* (New York: Verso, 1980); Johanna Brenner and Maria Ramas, "Rethinking Women's Oppression," *New Left Review* I, no. 144 (March–April 1984), 33–71; and Martha May's "The Historical Problem of the Family Wage," *Feminist Studies* 8, no. 2 (Summer 1982), 399–424. For statistics about women's labor market participation, see Claudia Goldin, *Understanding the Gender Gap: An Economic History of American Women* (New York: Oxford University Press, 1990).

6. Goldin, *Understanding the Gender Gap*, 45.

7. Karl Kautsky, *The Class Struggle* (1892). https://www.marxists.org/archive/kautsky/1892/erfurt/cho4a.htm.

8. Rosa Luxemburg, "Women's Suffrage and Class Struggle," in *Selected Political Writings of Rosa Luxemburg*, ed. Dick Howard (New York: Monthly Review Press, 1971), 216–22.

9. Clara Zetkin, "Only in Conjunction with the Proletarian Woman Will Socialism Be Victorious," in *Clara Zetkin Selected Writings*, ed. Philip S. Foner (Chicago: Haymarket, 2015), 72–83.

10. Joan W. Scott and Louise A. Tilly, "Women's Work and the Family in Nineteenth-Century Europe," *Comparative Studies in Society and History* 17, no. 1 (1975): 36–64.

11. For a rich account situating Southwest migration and Mexican captivity in the politics of American coerced labor, see Mary Pat Brady, *Scales of Captivity: Racial Capitalism and the Latinx Child* (Durham, NC: Duke University Press, 2022).

12. My account here, unfortunately, does not engage the white supremacist family politics imposed on Latinx and Asian American migrants, often through immigration restrictions. Other research is needed on topics

255

such as the exclusion of Chinese women, the prevention of Chinese migrant men from being able to marry or form families, and the history of US policy toward Mexican migration, all clearly shaping the racial politics of US family formation.

13. Allan Bérubé, *Coming Out Under Fire: The History of Gay Men and Women in World War II* (Chapel Hill: University of North Carolina Press, 2010).

14. Alexandra Kollontai, "Theses on Communist Morality in the Sphere of Marital Relations," in *Selected Writings*, ed. Alix Holt (New York: Norton, 1977), 225–31, 226.

15. Alexandra Kollontai, "Communism and the Family," in *Selected Writings*, 250–60, 256.

16. Ibid., 258.

17. Ibid., 258.

CHAPTER 8

1. Sylvia Ray Rivera, "Sylvia Rivera's June 2001 Talk at the Lesbian and Gay Community Services Center, New York City," http://www.historyisaweapon.com/defcon1/riverarisingandstronger.html.

2. See Women of the Weather Underground, "A Collective Letter to the Women's Movement," in *Sing a Battle Song: The Revolutionary Poetry, Statements, and Communiqués of the Weather Underground, 1970–1974*, eds. Bernardine Dohrn, Bill Ayers, and Jeff Jones (New York: Seven Stories Press, 2006),199–207.

3. Third World Gay Revolution, "16 Point Platform and Program," *Come Out!*, NYC Gay Liberation Front Newsletter 1, no. 7 (1970).

4. For a historical account of radical feminism, see Alice Echols, *Daring to Be Bad: Radical Feminism in America, 1967–1975* (Minneapolis: University of Minnesota Press, 1989). The classic anthology *Radical Feminism*, eds. Anne Koedt, Ellen Levine, and Anita Rapone (New York: Quardrangle/The *New York Times* Book Co., 1973), offers several critiques of the family: see Sheila Cronan, "Marriage" (213–21); Jo Freeman, "The Building of the Gilded Cage" (127–50); Judy Syfers, "Why I Want a Wife" (60–62); and Betsy Warrior, "Housework: Slavery or Labor of Love" (198–207).

5. Betty Friedan, *The Feminine Mystique* (New York: Norton, 1963).

6. Sophie Lewis, "Shulamith Firestone Wanted to Abolish Nature—We Should Too," *The Nation*, July 14, 2021.

7. Sophie Lewis, *Abolish the Family: A Manifesto for Care and Liberation* (New York:Verso, 2022), 57.

8. Third World Women's Alliance, "Women in the Struggle," *Triple Jeopardy* 1, no. 1 (Sept.–Oct. 1971), 8.

9. Daniel Patrick Moynihan, "The Negro Family: The Case for National Action (1965)," *African American Male Research* (1997): 1–35. United States Department of Labor, History eSources, http://www.dol.gov/dol/aboutdol/history/webid-meynihan.htm.

10. The Black sexual freedom offered by urbanization is best captured by Saidiya Hartman's *Wayward Lives, Beautiful Experiments* (2019). Hartman traces trajectories of pleasure and survival by African American women in Philadelphia and New York at the beginning of the twentieth century. Young proletarian Black women, newly moved to major industrial cities and working as wage workers far from their families, wrestled against social expectations, criminalization, and horrified social workers to seek fulfilling lives of sex, romance, and friendship. Saidiya Hartman, *Wayward Lives, Beautiful Experiences: Intimate Histories of Social Upheaval* (New York: Norton, 2019).

11. Francis Beale, "Double Jeopardy: To Be Black and Female," in *The Black Woman: An Anthology*, ed. Toni Cade Bambara (New York: Washington Square Press, 2005), 109–22, 111.

12. Quoted in Tiffany Lethabo King, "Black 'Feminisms' and Pessimism: Abolishing Moynihan's Negro Family," *Theory & Event* 21, no. 1 (2018): 68–87, 75.

13. Hortense J. Spillers, "Mama's Baby Papa's Maybe: An American Grammar Book," *Diacritics* 17, no. 2 (1987): 64–81; Kimberle Crenshaw, "Demarginalizing the Intersection of Race and Sex: A Black Feminist Critique of Antidiscrimination Doctrine," *University of Chicago Legal Forum* 139 (1989): 139–67; King, "Black 'Feminisms' and Pessimism"; Cathy J. Cohen, "Punks, Bulldaggers, and Welfare Queens," *GLQ* 3 (1997): 437–65; Ta-Nehisi Coates, "The Black Family in the Age of Mass Incarceration," *The Atlantic*, October 2015; Tressie McMillan Cottom, "Race Is Always the Issue," *The Atlantic*, September 2015.

14. For accounts of the racial politics of the New Deal, see Steve Valocchi, "The Racial Basis of Capitalism and the State, and the Impact of the New Deal on African Americans," *Social Problems* 41, no. 3 (1994): 347–62; Jill Quadagno, *The Transformation of Old Age Security* (Chicago: University of Chicago Press, 1988).

15. The extensive historiography of NWRO almost entirely ignores this key feature of the movement. The exception, to which the analysis presented here is entirely indebted, is Wilson Sherwin, "Rich in Needs: Revisiting the Radical Politics of the Welfare Rights Movement" (Doctoral dissertation, City University of New York, Graduate Center, New York).

16. Mariarosa Dalla Costa, "Women and the Subversion of the Community," in *Women and the Subversion of the Community: A Mariarosa Dalla Costa Reader*, ed. Camille Barbagallo (Oakland: PM Press, 2019), 17–49, 30.

17. Ibid., 28.

18. Ibid., 34.
19. Ibid., 42.
20. Sylvia Federici, "Wages Against Housework," in *Revolution at Point Zero: Housework, Reproduction, and Feminist Struggle* (Oakland: PM Press, 2012), 15–22, 18.
21. Federici, "Wages Against Housework," 20.
22. Understanding Wages for Housework as an anti-work movement and a provocation draws from revisionist historiography from Kathi Weeks, *The Problem with Work: Feminism, Marxism, Antiwork Politics and Postwork Imaginaries* (Durham, NC: Duke University Press, 2011), and the thinking of Wilson Sherwin.

CHAPTER 9

1. Melinda Cooper, *Family Values*, 7.
2. *Endnotes*, "A History of Separation," 163.
3. Manufacturing fell from 14.4 percent of the global workforce in 1991 to 11.1 percent in 2016. UNIDO, "Industrial Development Report 2018," quoted in Aaron Benanav, "Automation and the Future of Work–I," *New Left Review* 119 (Sept/Oct 2019): 5–38. Benanav also shows that since the mid-2010s, even China has shown a decline in its workforce share in manufacturing. With less explicit data, the political implications of this point are made in *Endnotes*, "A History of Separation," 154.
4. This analysis is offered over several texts in *Endnotes*, most extensively in "A History of Separation."
5. Karl Marx, *Capital, Volume III* (*MECW*, vol. 37, 1894).
6. US Census Bureau and Bureau of Labor Statistics, https://ourworldindata. org/female-labor-force-participation-key-facts.
7. Specifically in member nations of the Organization for Economic Co-operation and Development (OECD).
8. OECD data, https://ourworldindata.org/female-labor-force-participation-key-facts.
9. For some of the history of marriage bars, see Goldin, *Understanding the Gender Gap*; and Claudia Golden, "Marriage Bars: Discrimination against Married Women Workers from the 1920s to the 1950s," in *Favorites of Fortune: Technology, Growth and Economic Development Since the Industrial Revolution*, eds. Henry Rosovsky, David Landes, and Patrice Higonett (Cambridge, MA: Harvard University Press, 1991), 511–36.
10. Göran Therborn, *Between Sex and Power: Family in the World 1900–2000* (New York: Routledge, 2004), Table 5.18, 190. Rates based on per thousand of population aged over fifteen years.
11. Stephanie Coontz, "The World Historical Transformation of Marriage," *Journal of Marriage and Family* 66 (November 2004): 974–79.

12. Therborn, *Between Sex and Power*, Table 8.7, 293.
13. Therborn, *Between Sex and Power*, Table 6.1, 199.
14. Nicola Yates, "Global Care Chains: A State-of-the-Art Review and Future Directions in Care Transnationalization Research," *Global Networks* 12, no. 2 (2012): 135–54.
15. Margaret Thatcher, "Interview for *Woman's Own*," Margaret Thatcher Foundation, 1987, https://www.margaretthatcher.org/document/106689.
16. Ibid.
17. Bill Clinton praised Charles Murray's *Losing Ground* in an NBC News interview on December 3, 1993, Clinton Digital Library, National Archives, https://clinton.presidentiallibraries.us/items/show/32114.
18. For an account of the consequences of US welfare austerity on Black life, see Jane L. Collins and Victoria Mayer, *Both Hands Tied: Welfare Reform and the Race to the Bottom of the Low-Wage Labor Market* (Chicago: University of Chicago Press, 2010).
19. Sentencing Project, "Prison Population Over Time, US Total," Online tool, https://www.sentencingproject.org/research/.
20. Sarah K. S. Shannon et al., "The Growth, Scope, and Scope of People with Felony Records in the United States, 1948–2010," *Demography* 54 (2017): 1795–1818.
21. For example, see Amber Hollibaugh, "2, 4, 6, 8: Who Says That Your Grandmother's Straight," *The Scholar & Feminist Online* 10, no. 1 (2012).

CHAPTER 10

1. I document this history in New York in "The Influence of Donors on Cross Class Movements: Same Sex Marriage and Trans Rights Campaigns in New York State," *Social Movement Studies* 19, no. 5 (2019): 586–601.
2. These and other critiques are detailed in Ryan Conrad, ed., *Against Equality: Queer Revolution, Not Mere Inclusion* (Oakland: AK Press, 2014).
3. Beyond Same-Sex Marriage Collective, "Beyond Same-Sex Marriage: A New Strategic Vision for All Our Families and Relationships," *Studies in Gender and Sexuality* 9 (2008): 161–71. Originally published online in July 2006.
4. Cathy J. Cohen, "Punks, Bulldaggers, and Welfare Queen," 458.
5. Ashley Nellis, "The Color of Justice: Racial and Ethnic Disparity in State Prisons," *The Sentencing Project*, October 13, 2021, https://www.sentencingproject.org/reports/the-color-of-justice-racial-and-ethnic-disparity-in-state-prisons-the-sentencing-project/.
6. Frank Eduards, Michael H. Esposito, and Hedwig Lee, "Risk of Police-Involved Death by Race/Ethnicity and Place, United States, 2012–2018," *American Journal of Public Health* 108, no. 9 (2018): 1241–48.

7. Nick Miroff, "'Kids in Cages': It's True That Obama Built the Cages at the Border. But Trump's 'Zero Tolerance' Immigration Policy Had No Precedent," October 23, 2020, https://www.washingtonpost.com/immigration/kids-in-cages-debate-trump-obama/2020/10/23/8ff96f3c-1532-11eb-82af-864652063d61_story.html; Jordyn Rozensky, "The Biden Administration Routinely Separates Immigrant Families," *National Immigrant Justice Center*, January 19, 2022, https://immigrantjustice.org/staff/blog/biden-administration-routinely-separates-immigrant-families.

8. Kathryn Edin, "What Do Low-Income Single Mothers Say About Marriage?" *Social Problems* 47, no. 1: 112–33.

9. State-provided social benefits leading people to be able to leave bad relationships is substantiated by research emphasizing that heterosexual women had "better sex" in state socialist societies. Kristen R. Ghodsee, *Why Women Have Better Sex Under Socialism: And Other Arguments for Economic Independence* (New York: Bold Type Books, 2018).

10. Carol B. Stack, *All Our Kin: Strategies for Survival in a Black Community* (New York: Basic Books, 1983).

11. Alexis Pauline Gumbs, "We Can Learn to Mother Ourselves: The Queer Survival of Black Feminism, 1968–1996" (Doctoral dissertation, Duke University, 2010). I return to her work in chapter 10.

12. Alexis Pauline Gumbs, China Martins, and Mai'a Williams, eds., *Revolutionary Mothering: Love on the Front Lines* (Oakland: PM Press, 2016). See particularly "m/other ourselves: a Black queer feminist genealogy for radical mothering," 19–31.

13. Gumbs, "m/other ourselves," 22.

14. Ibid., 23.

15. Ibid., 26.

16. Ibid., 28. Capitalized in original.

17. For an extensive account of queer chosen family, see Kath Weston, *The Families We Choose: Lesbians, Gays, and Kinship* (New York: Columbia University Press, 1991). For a thoughtful critique of anti-family and family-abolitionist politics by the same author, see "The Politics of Gay Families" in *Rethinking the Family: Some Feminist Questions*, edited by Barrie Thorne and Marylin Yalom (Boston: Northeastern University Press), 119–39.

18. For some writing on Ballroom and chosen family, see Marlon M. Bailey, *Butch Queens Up in Pumps: Gender, Performance, and Ballroom Culture in Detroit* (Ann Arbor: University of Michigan Press, 2013) and Marlon M. Bailey, "Performance as Intervention: Ballroom and the Politics of HIV/AIDS in Detroit," *Souls* 11, no. 3 (2009): 253–74.

19. Nancy Fraser, "Feminism, Capitalism, and the Cunning of History," *New Left Review* 56 (2009): 97–117.

20. Though I would differ from its moments of overpopulation anxiety, for a collection of recent work, see Adele Clarke and Donna Haraway, eds., *Making Kin Not Population* (Chicago: University of Chicago Press, 2018). See also the excellent new book with far-reaching implications for my work, Patty Krawec, *Becoming Kin: An Indigenous Call to Unforgetting the Past and Reimagining Our Future* (Minneapolis: Broadleaf Books, 2022).
21. Published in Assata Shakur, *Assata: An Autobiography* (Chicago: Lawrence Hill Books, 2001), 52; capitalized in original.

CHAPTER 11

1. J. J. Gleeson and K. D. Griffiths, "Kinderkommunismus: A Feminist Analysis of the 21st-Century Family and a Communist Proposal for Its Abolition," *Ritual*, 2015. A New Institute for Social Research, https://isr.press/Griffiths_Gleeson_Kinderkommunismus/index.html.
2. Madeline Lane-McKinley, "The Idea of Children," *Blind Field*, 2018, https://blindfieldjournal.com/2018/08/02/the-idea-of-children/.
3. Some of King's thinking on the Moynihan Report, and her readings of Spillers and Lindsay, are discussed in prior chapters.
4. King, "Black 'Feminisms' and Pessimism," 70.
5. Ibid., 71.
6. Ibid., 84.
7. Kathi Weeks, "Abolition of the Family: The Most Infamous Feminist Proposal," *Feminist Theory*, 2021, 6.
8. Ibid., 16.
9. For works by Sophie Lewis, see *Full Surrogacy Now: Feminism Against Family* (New York: Verso, 2019); "The Family Lottery," *Dissent*, 2021, 61–63; "Shulamith Firestone Wanted to Abolish Nature—We Should, Too," *The Nation*, July 14, 2021; "Covid-19 Is Straining the Concept of the Family. Let's Break It." *The Nation*, June 3, 2020; "The Satanic Death-Cult Is Real," Commune, August 28, 2019.
10. Sophie Lewis's excellent short book and its relationship to the present text deserves a lengthy comment. The present book should be read as a companion volume to Lewis's work. Our frameworks, references, politics, and arguments have many similarities. We each developed our work in tandem and ongoing dialogue. Most of this book was written before Lewis's *Abolish the Family* became available, and I was only able to incorporate their thinking in late-stage editing. Their work is excellent in addressing some of the anxieties and concerns provoked by family-abolitionist language. They also offer a compelling, accessible entry point for readers, linking family abolition to present and popular concerns. Unlike *Abolish the Family*, the present book clearly locates the history of family abolition in the dynamics of capitalist development and the

changing role of the working-class household. As well, the present book offers more speculative engagement with the future of family abolition. Our works should be read as complementary and mutually supportive.

11. Ibid., 105–6. Lewis cites articles by Katie Stone, Alva Gotby, Sophie Silverstein, Alyson Escalante, Jules Joanne Gleeson, and others.

12. Sophie Lewis, *Abolish the Family: A Manifesto for Care and Liberation* (New York: Verso, 2022), 87; emphasis in original.

13. Among notable critiques of anti-family politics, see Hazel V. Carby, "White Woman Listen! Black Feminism and the Boundaries of Sisterhood," in *The Empire Strikes Back: Race and Racism in 70s Britain*, ed. The Centre for Contemporary Cultural Studies (London: Hutchinson, 1985), 212–38. I am sympathetic to elements of this argument, explored briefly at the end of chapter 5.

14. For an account of one such online debate, see Richard Seymour, "Abolition: Notes on a Normie Shitstorm," *Salvage*, January 27, 2022.

15. Engels, *The Origin of the Family, Private Property and the State*, 189.

16. The most extensive articulated is by Engels, *Socialism Utopian and Scientific* (*MECW*, vol. 26, 1880), but also reflects many commentaries by Marx.

17. Marx, "Afterward to the Second German Edition," *Capital, vol. 1* (*MECW*, vol. 36, 1873), 17.

18. Théorie Communiste, "Much Ado About Nothing," *Endnotes*, v. 1.

19. Engels, "Programme of the Blanquist Commune Refugees" (*MECW*, vol. 24, 1874), 14.

20. Speculative visioning was integrated into movement work through workshops at the Allied Media Conference, and in publications including adrienne maree brown and Walidah Imarisha, eds., *Octavia's Brood: Science Fiction Stories from Social Justice Movements* (Oakland: AK Press, 2015); adrienne maree brown, *Emergent Strategy: Shaping Change, Changing Worlds* (Oakland: AK Press, 2017); and fiction by adrienne maree brown and Alexis Pauline Gumbs. For my own coauthored attempt at the utopian impulse, see M. E. O'Brien and Eman Abdelhadi, *Everything for Everyone: An Oral History of the New York Commune 2052–2072* (Brooklyn: Common Notions, 2022). *Everything for Everyone* offers a fictional depiction of one potential revolutionary trajectory, illustrating many of the points theorized here.

21. In recent conversations with Griffiths and Gleeson, they have presented the universal crèche not as an institution separated from the social body nor a state function. Though this remains ambiguous in their original formulation, their political practice and writing as a whole moves against the reification of the capitalist state.

22. Marx, "Critique of the Gotha Programme" (*MECW*, vol. 24), 87.

23. Much of the argument explored in this section appears in other forms in the excellent edited volume by Jules Joanne Gleeson and Elle O'Rourke, *Transgender Marxism* (London: Pluto Press, 2021).

24. Sandy E. James, Jody L. Herman, Mara Kiesling, Lisa Mottet, and Ma'ayan Anafi, *The Report of the 2015 US Transgender Survey*, 2016, Washington, DC: National Center for Transgender Equality.
25. Make the Road NY, *Transgender Need Not Apply: A Report on Gender Identity Job Discrimination*, 2010, New York.

CHAPTER 12

1. Elizabeth M. Hoover, "Feeding a Movement: The Kitchens of Standing Rock Camps," From Garden Warriors to Good Seeds, December 6, 2016, https://gardenwarriorsgoodseeds.com/2016/12/06/feeding-a-movement-the-kitchens-of-the-standing-rock-camps/. Collective kitchens are similarly essential to feed workers on strike. During 1936 sit-down strikes in Detroit auto plants, mass kitchens cooked food for strikers and their families. They were staffed by Communist Party women. They gathered their ingredients from garden farms by factory workers and others in surrounding towns. Susan Rosenthal, "Genora (Johnson) Dollinger Remembers the 1936–37 General Motors Sit-Down Strike," *History Is a Weapon*, http://www.historyisaweapon.com/defcon1/dollflint.html.
2. Alana Romain, "Are There Kids at Standing Rock? Protestors Are Fighting for Their Future." *Romper*, November 2, 2016, https://www.romper.com/p/are-there-kids-at-standing-rock-protesters-are-fighting-for-their-future-21745.
3. The Kino-nda-niimi Collective, *The Winter We Danced: Voices from the Past, the Future, and Idle No More Movement* (Winnipeg: ARP, 2014).
4. Anna Feigenbaum, Fabian Frenzel, and Patrick McCurdy, *Protest Camps* (New York: Zed Books, 2013), 206.
5. Frantz Fanon, "The Algerian Family," in *A Dying Colonialism* (New York: Grove Press, 1965), 99–120. For an excellent commentary on the text, see Lara Sheehi's presentation through the Parapraxis Seminar on the Problem of the Family: https://youtu.be/wd8xMPF4frc.
6. Nico and Winter, "At Cloverlick: An Interview with the Blackjewel Miners' Blockade," *Pinko* 1 (2019).
7. Feigenbaum, Frenzel, and McCurdy, *Protest Camps*, 215–16.
8. Saul Elbe, "Standing Rock Protestors React to Life Under Trump," *Rolling Stone*, November 23, 2016, https://www.rollingstone.com/politics/politics-features/standing-rock-protesters-react-to-life-under-trump-125430/.
9. This critique is outlined in *Endnotes*, "A History of Separation."
10. Critique developed by Amadeo Bordiga, *The Science and Passion of Communism: Selected Writings of Amadeo Bordiga (1912–1965)*, edited by Pietro Basso, Historical Materialism Book Series (Boston: Brill, 2020).
11. *Endnotes*, "What Are We to Do?," in Benjamin Noys, ed., *Communization and its Discontents* (Brooklyn: Autonomedia, 23–40), 27.

12. Ibid., 26.
13. Ibid., 26.
14. Leon de Mattis, "What Is Communization?" *Sic* 1 (2011): 11–30.
15. Realistically, this would only be possible after a protracted crisis of breakdown in the ability of capitalist markets and the capitalist state to be able to provide for the basic needs of the vast majority of the population. This potential revolutionary scenario—along with extensive depictions of family abolition—is detailed in my coauthored book, M. E. O'Brien and Eman Abdelhadi, *Everything for Everyone: An Oral History of the New York Commune, 2052–2072* (New York: Common Notions, 2022). The next chapter is largely an effort to theorize the structure of the future that Eman and I depict in *Everything for Everyone.*
16. Angry Workers, "Insurrection and Production," 2016, https:// subversionpress.files.wordpress.com/2016/10/insurrection-and-production1.pdf.
17. Only in extreme conditions of global crisis of the state and capital would communization have much chance of being successful. In other conditions, it would be quickly crushed by the forces of capital and the state. At the present time, the progressive anti-family reforms explored in chapter 10 and the many ongoing movements for survival and solidarity offer more realistic avenues for activism and organizing.

CHAPTER 13

1. Angry Workers, "Insurrection and Production."
2. I tried to depict one such transformative justice process in *Everything for Everyone*, 214–16.
3. My thanks to Eman Abdelhadi for helping me clarify this point.
4. This is an extensively debated point. For research on childhood development focused on Romanian orphanages, see Sandra R. Kaler and B. J. Freeman, "Analysis of Environmental Deprivation: Cognitive and Social Development in Romanian Orphans," *Journal of Child Psychology and Psychiatry* 35, no. 4 (1994): 769–81; Kim Maclean, "The Impact of Institutionalization on Child Development," *Development and Psychopathology* 15 (2003): 853–84. However, such research conflates institutionalization and neglect; parsing the effects of high-quality institutional care is more difficult. The research on childhood development in Kibbutzes, some of which sought to minimize mother-child interaction, is significantly more mixed. See Benjamin Beit-Hallahmi and Albert I. Rabin, "The Kibbutz as a Social Experiment and as a Child-Rearing Laboratory," *American Psychologist* 32, no. 7 (1977): 532–41; David Oppenheim, Abraham Sagi and Michael E. Lamb, "Infant-Adult Attachments on the Kibbutz and Their Relation to

Socioemotional Development 4 Years Later," *Developmental Psychology* 24, no. 3 (1988): 427–33.

CONCLUSION

1. Relevant for the discussion of *Aufhebung* in chapter 3, King was also a scholar of Hegel. Dr. King writes: "This two-fold activity of the synthesis is expressed by Hegel by the word *aufheben*, which is sometimes translated 'to sublate.' The German word has two meanings. It means both to abolish and to preserve." Martin Luther King, Jr., "An Exposition of the First Triad of Categories of Hegelian Logic—Being, Non-Being, Becoming" (*The Martin Luther King Jr. Research and Education Institute*, 1953). Thank you to Max Fox for pointing this out.
2. The references to this phrasing are too numerous to list in detail. They can all be found in *The Papers of Martin Luther King Jr.* (hereafter *The Papers of MLK*), volumes 4–6. The first mention chronologically comes in February 1957 (vol. 4, 190), the last in February 1959 (vol. 5, 234). See also vol. 5, 141 and 233; vol. 6, 324. He continues to use the phrase through 1960 but begins to vary his wording. Earlier, King used "beloved community" in a 1956 speech not included in the papers.
3. King, "Revolt Without Violence—The Negroes' New Strategy," March 21, 1960, *The Papers of MLK*, vol. 5, 393.
4. King, "Interview by Inter-American University Students and Faculty," February 14, 1962, *The Papers of MLK*, vol. 7, 402.
5. King, "Statement to the Press at the Beginning of the Youth Leadership Conference," April 15, 1960, *The Papers of MLK*, vol. 5, 427.
6. Ibid.
7. King, "Address Delivered at the Montgomery Improvement Association's 'Testimonial of Love and Loyalty,'" February 1, 1960, *The Papers of MLK*, vol. 5, 360.
8. King, "To Percival Leroy Prattis," April 26, 1960, *The Papers of MLK*, vol. 7, 209.
9. bell hooks, *Killing Rage: Ending Racism* (New York: Henry Holt, 1995), 265.
10. Ibid., 264.
11. bell hooks and George Brosi, "The Beloved Community," *Appalachian Heritage* 40, no. 4 (2012): 76–86, 76.
12. Deborah N. Archer, "Creating Dr. King's 'Beloved Community,'" *Symposia* 66, no. 5 (2011): 8868.
13. Jafari Sinclaire Allen, "For 'the Children' Dancing the Beloved Community," *Souls* 11, no. 3 (2009): 311–26.
14. King, as quoted in Joshua F. J. Inwood, "Searching for the Promised Land: Examining Dr Martin Luther King's Concept of the Beloved Community," *Antipode* 41, no. 3 (2009): 487–508), 494.

15. King, quoted in Ibid., 496.
16. Ibid., 505.
17. Some of this argument is drawn from a forthcoming piece of collective writing to be published by *Pinko*.
18. Miranda Joseph, *Against the Romance of Community* (Minneapolis: University of Minnesota Press, 2002), 73.
19. Marx, "Critical Notes on the Article: 'The King of Prussia and Social Reform, By a Prussian'" (*MECW*, vol. 3): 204–5, as quoted in "The Passion of Communism," *Endnotes* 5 (2019): 249; emphasis in original.
20. Jacques Camatte, "Marx and *Gemeinwesen*," from *Revue Invariance* (1977), translated in *Endnotes* 5 (2019): 275–89.
21. Ibid, 287.
22. Ibid., 288. Jacquette Camatte's erstwhile teacher and comrade Amadeo Bordiga explores Gemeinwesen implicitly in his efforts to think through the transformative subjectivity of collective struggle. Loren Goldner titled a canonical essay on Bordiga, "Communism Is the Material Human Community." Here Golder translates *Gemeinwesen* as "material human community." Loren Goldner, "Communism Is the Material Human Community: Amadeo Bordiga Today," 1995, https://libcom.org/article/communism-material-human-community-amadeo-bordiga-today-loren-goldner.

Index

abolition
of culture and nature (for
Shulamith Firestone), 132; of
police, 49, 53–58, 195; of prisons
53, 55, 57–58, 186, 195, 223, 217;
of slavery, 55, 57; of the state, 56,
190–193
see also Aufhebung; family
abolition; prisons, abolition
abuse
and abolitionism, 57, 58; child,
38–39, 41, 45, 81, 248, *see also*
family policing system; constituency for progressive anti-family
reforms, 168; in employment, 44;
enabled by the family, 4, 7, 21, 34,
37–45, 113, 131, 158, 167, 190,
196, 236; and family abolition,
46, 49, 200, 213, 223, 228, 232;
intimate partner, 4, 41–42, 50,
168, 248, 249; at protest camps,
211–213; in residential boarding
school system, 81; of trans
children, 199, 229, 232
see also family, violence
American Indian, *see* Indigenous
ACT-UP NY (organization), 166
AIDS, 148
and caregiving, 165, 175, 260;
movements, 142–143, 166, 178;
and Thatcher, 154
African Americans, *see* Black
allotment policy/Allotment Act of
1907 (US), 78, 87–90, 120, 249
Aufhebung (abolition, Ger.), 56–57,
250, 265
Angry Workers, "Insurrection and
Production," 217, 220, 227, 254

anti-Blackness, 33, 85–93, 155–156,
183
see also white supremacy
Anchando, Paul, 31–35
Asia
anti-Asian racism, 147, 255–256;
Chinese development, 258;
environmental crisis, 50;
economic development, 147; state
socialism, 126
Audre Lorde Project (organization),
166

Barret, Michèle, 247–248, 255
Beale, Francis, "Double Jeopardy: To
Be Black and Female," 135, 257
Bebel, August, *Woman and
Socialism*, 119
"Beyond Same-Sex Marriage: A
New Strategic Vision for All
Our Families and Relationships"
(document), 165, 166, 259
Black (people), 10, 38
and COVID-19, 17; care relations,
35, 174, 178; chosen family,
175, 179; collective joy, 51, 238,
241; critique of family abolition,
185, 262; dependence on family,
5; domestic workers, 18, 26;
enforced heterosexuality, 10–11,
78, 87–89, 91, 126, 253; enforced
kinlessness, 77–78, 85–87, 91, 93;
enslaved labor, 18; exclusion from
family norm, 20, 23, 26, 35, 135,
146; exclusion from the workers'
movement, 114, 120; family
critique and abolitionism, 51, 92,
108, 181–183, 226, 241; feminism,

Fanon, Frantz, 208, 263
fascism, *see* white supremacy
Federici, Silvia, "Wages Against
  Housework" 138–139, 251
feminism
    affects, 237; Black, 12, 51, 143,
    166, 189, 248, 250, 257, 260, 261,
    262; care labor, 238; and chosen
    family, 173; critique of the family,
    131; and Fourier, 105; radical,
    11, 131, 141–142, 256; of the Red
    Decade, 128, 141–142; post-New
    Left, 143; Marxist 25, 131, 191,
    255
    see also Wages for Housework
fertility
    citations, 250; contribution to
    women's labor market participa-
    tion, 150; decline, 150–151; and
    anti-Indigenous violence, 83;
    rates, 150–151; state interventions
    in, 28
FIERCE (organization), 179–180
film, 36, 228
    Birth of a Nation, 80; *Gone with
    the Wind*, 80
First Nations, *see* Indigenous
Floyd, George, 9, 47–49, 52
    Rebellion (2020 protest), viii, 47,
    55, 186, 249
Floyd, Larcenia Jones (mother of
    George Floyd), 47–48
Fernbach, David, 128
Firestone, Shulamith, *The Dialectic
    of Sex*, 132, 256, 261
Florida, 78, 251
Freud, (Sigmund) 143
Friedan, Betty, 132, 256
Fourier, Charles 104–108
    citations, 251, 254; critique of
    the family, 105; influence on
    Marx, 72, 74–75; theory of the
    sexual minimum, 106; theorizing
    the revolutionary commune,

226–229, 231; vision of family
    abolition, 10–11, 104–108; as a
    utopian socialist, 104, 188
France
    child labor, 65; communization
    theory, 216; fascism, 33; gay
    liberation, 128; May '68, 130
Fraser, Nancy, 177, 260

Gay Liberation Front (organization),
    129, 256
gay liberation (movement
    tendency), 10, 11, 128–130, 140,
    142, 148, 165, 173
    see also queer
Gemeinwesen (community, Ger.),
    12, 241–244, 266
    see also Camatte, Marx
gender
    in ballroom, 260; in Black life,
    104; and bourgeoisie, 70, 91; and
    care labor, 207, 236; changing
    norms, 2, 12, 25, 152, 158, 184;
    and the commune, 221, 224, 229;
    conservatism, 122, 159; deviancy/
    transgression, 68, 74, 99–101,
    108; division of labor, 3, 5, 42, 97,
    236; enforcing gender norms on
    Indigenous people, 78; and family
    abolition, 6, 54, 229, 232, 246; and
    family ideal, 36–38; family gender
    regime, 190; family imposition of,
    9, 35, 45, 220; and family politics,
    49, 114, 203, 248; fantasy, 34, 158;
    gender freedom, 6, 54, 171, 173,
    199–201, 229, 232; Indigenous
    nonbinary identities, 82, 252;
    inequality, 23; and labor market
    access, 43, 250; liberation, 10, 232,
    246; nonconformity, 152; and
    peasants, 97; at protest camps,
    211–213; roles in household,
    2, 22–23; policing of, 101; and
    Russian Revolution, 123, 126;

of family, 22; in Engels, 73–74; family ideal, 39; in Fourier, 105; in Jim Crow, 11, 78, 88–89, 104, 120; peasant, 97; and poverty, 169; and Reconstruction, 102–103; same-sex, 163–166, 172; and settler colonialism, 78–80, 82–83; and sex work, 68; as state regulation of family, 45, 155; in Thatcher, Margaret, 154; and welfare reform, 155–156

see also family, housewife

Malcolm X, 238

Marx, Eleanor, 119

Marx, Karl, 9, 12, 27, 80, 253, 258, 262, 266

critique of utopian socialism, 108, 187–189; on Aufhebung, 56–57, 250, 265; on bügerliche Gesellschaft, 72; *Economic-Philosophic Manuscripts of 1844*, 72, 250; *The Eighteenth Brumaire of Louis Bonaparte*, 67; on Gemeinwesen, 241–245; on General Law of Capitalist Accumulation, 147–148; on the Holy Family, 61; on communist revolution, 110–112, 213–215; on capitalist crisis, 145; on family abolition, 61–62, 71–75, 91–93; on the lumpenproletariat, 67–69; *The Manifesto of the Communist Party* (with Engels), 62, 69, 70, 72, 75, 119, 250; on proletarianization, 98; "Theses on Feuerbach," 61–62, 250; on working-class kinship relations, 62–66, 91

Marxist feminism, *see* feminist, Marxist

mass incarceration, *see* prisons

Mexican Americans

border family separation, 168; coerced labor, 255; family politics, 256; labor, 121; racial terror against, 31

see also Latinx, migrants, Southwest

Michel, Louise, 96

Mieli, Mario, 128

migrants/migration

Black migration 88–89, 99, 101–102, 122, 133–134, 156, 174; border policy, 38, 168; in capitalist development, 64, 152; care relations, 35, 51, 66; Chinese American family politics, 255–256; citations, 255–256; 260; and COVID-19, 17; domestic labor, 18; exclusion from family form, 20, 66, 77, 146; and eugenics, 45; European (American) immigrant identities, 121; and family policing system, 4, 169; and the future commune, 225, 230; global care chains, 151; immigration enforcement, 92, 163, 168; in insurgent reproduction, 207; preventing Black migration, 88; protests, 204, 207; targeted by white-supremacist violence, 31–33, 50; unconventional family structures, 165, 173; women's workforce participation, 149

see also Chinese Americans, family policing system, Mexican Americans, state violence

mission system (of colonial California), 82–84, 252

mothering (concept of Alexis Pauline Gumbs), 52, 174, 180, 260

Moynihan Report/Daniel Patrick Moynihan, 134–135; 155, 248, 257, 261

mutual aid

Black, 156; care, 237; chosen family, 175, 178; citation, 247;

of Red Decade, 148; limits to
reforming the private household,
176–178; Paris Commune, 95–96;
progressive anti-family reforms,
12, 170–173, 186; settler colonial,
89; Universal Basic Income (UBI),
171; Wages for Housework, 139;
welfare reform, 155–155; workers'
movement, 112, 114
respectability
absence in Russia, 123; alternatives to, 108; and Black politics,
104, 135, 226; of family, 3, 11, 34,
113–114, 116–117; and poverty,
197; and whiteness, 10, 118; working-class divisions, 112, 115, 117
Rivera, Sylvia Ray, 129, 256
Roberts, Dorothy, 38, 168, 248
see also family policing system
Romania (orphanages), 264
Russian Revolution, 109, 123–126

schools
compulsory, 11, 37, 115, 172;
COVID-19, 17–19; family ideal,
37, 113; household decision-making, 22; overcoming, 182, 197; at
protests, 205; residential boarding
school system, 39, 77, 81–84,
192–193, 251–253; socialist,
120; struggle around, 138; state
provision, 28
Seccombe, Wally, *Weathering the
Storm*, 250, 255
Second International, 11, 111,
118–120, 214
Seminole Wars, 78
service industry
and communization, 217; contrast
to family, 44; and COVID-19,
18–20; employment growth,
147, 151; as feminized, 151; in
the future commune, 221–222;
low-wages, 19, 147, 194; for

social reproduction labor, 18–21,
149–151, 199, 206, 235; sexual
harassment in, 153, 199
see also housework, work
Seventies (1990s), *see* Red Decade
sex
in anti-Indigenous genocide,
81–84; as care, 235; criminalization, 28; desire of the family, 245;
distinction, 132; changing norms
of, 158; and divorce, 150; normative regime of, 12; in the future
commune, 197, 223, 227–229;
at protests, 1; pro-sex feminism,
143; radical feminist hostility to,
142; in right wing ideology, 34,
37, 39, 159; sex-class theory, 130,
141, 143; "sex love," 70–71, 73; sex
radicals, 128–130; in state socialism, 260; struggles over, 25; and
urbanization, 99–102
see also heterosexuality, gay, gay
liberation, queer, sexual/sexuality,
sex work
sex work
citations, 253, 254; as commodified care, 235; and communist
emancipation, 104; Contagious
Disease Acts, 101; during the
Red Decade, 129; in Engels,
66–69; exclusion of, 117; links
with broader working class,
101; Marxist-Feminist theory,
26; in nineteenth century cities,
11, 97–104, 192; in the Paris
Commune, 96; queer youth, 153;
Radical Feminist hostility to,
142; state regulation of, 28, 37,
192; Street Transvestite Action
Revolutionaries, 129; transfeminine, 100, 129; trans women of
color, 129, 133; urbanization, 117
see also lumpenproletariat, sex,
sexual/sexuality

Tiqqun/Invisible Committee (orga-
nization/theory tendency), 216
see also communization
trans/transgender/transfeminine
accessibility of, 12, 52, 146; and
alienated care under capitalism,
236; attack on gender-affirming
care, 39; ballroom culture, 175;
care relations, 179; citation,
263; Black and Latinx, 129,
133, 175, 179; changing family
dynamics of, 12, 52, 146; children
challenging parental bigotry, 50;
chosen family, 52, 174–175, 179;
as constituency for progressive
anti-family reforms, 167–168,
173; family abolitionism, 10,
181–183; familial judgment, 42;
in the future commune, 199–201,
229; within gay rights, 163–165;
gender freedom and communist
reproduction, 199–201; gender
transgression in the Red Decade,
128–129; group housing, 133;
homelessness among youth, 172;
Indigenous nonbinary identities,
82, 252; and poverty, 129; 163;
proletarian resistance, 11, 100,
108; protest, 211; racial violence,
129, 163–165; trans liberationists,
11, 129; radical thought, 12, 143,
181; radical feminist hostility
towards, 141; sex work, 100,
129, 133; struggles recently,
143; transfeminine identities in
nineteenth century Europe, 100,
108; trans women of color, 129,
133, 175; and urbanization, 99
see also gender, queer
Trump, Donald
child separation policy, 168;
citations, 248, 260; family as
perverse bourgeois ideal, 41–42;
45; family as racial terror 31–35

Trump, Melania, 31–35

Ulrich, Karl (nineteenth century
homosexual militant), 74
United Kingdom, *see* England
Universal Basic Income (UBI), 136,
170–171
urban/urbanization
Black struggle, 47, 127, 135; and
Black freedom, 102, 257; Black
urbanization, 88–89, 101–102,
133–134; as capitalist tendency,
9, 27, 64, 98; diversity of, 197; and
the future commune, 217; Engels
studying, 9, 63–64, 67–68, 71; and
the future commune, 222; and
gender variation, 100, 129; and life
expectancy, 65; and the lumpenproletariat, 67–68; marketization
of services, 193; overcrowding, 91;
pathologizing Black life, 133; and
poverty, 64, 68, 71, 127, 135; and
proletarianization, 97–99; protests,
47, 96, 203–205; racial violence,
242; and respectability, 121; and
sexual freedom, 96, 99–101, 134,
142; sex work, 99–101, 129, 192;
staggered timing, 98–99; and
surplus populations, 101; trans
women of color, 129
see also suburbs
utopian socialism
citations, 254, 262; and colonialism 188; contrasted with protest
camps, 208; Fourier as 104, 188;
Marxist critique of, 108, 187–189,
201; planned communities,
208–210; value of, 189–190, 237
see also Fourier
utopianism, 187–190

violence
against children, 38–39, 41, 45,
81; against women, 3, 41–42,

gender discipline, 200; Moynihan Report, 135; National Welfare Rights Organization, 136–140; racial discipline, 128; and the Red Decade, 164–171, 177; in the Russian Revolution, 124; state efforts to intervene in family life, 28; Universal Basic Income, 171; welfare rights struggle, 127–128, 135–137, 140, 164–171
see also family policing system, National Welfare Rights Organization, Universal Basic Income
women
Black domestic workers, 18; Black radical, 10–11, 133–137, 148; Black women and family, 134–135, 156, 166, 174; Black women in the Moynihan Report, 134; Black women and slavery, 85–86; bourgeois, 69–70; and care labor, 236; changing expectations, 152; dependency on the family, 153; in Dalla Costa, Mariarosa, 138; dependency on the wage, 153; domestic workers, 18; "double shift," 25; employment, 10, 25–26, 114–120, 125, 131, 148–151; equality, 26, 118–120, 123–126, 148; exclusion from public, 86, 98; fantasies of, 159; in Fourier, 105; "free community of women," 75; in the future commune, 225, 229; heading households, 134, 174, 230; housework, 25; Indigenous women, 83; isolation of, 40, 132; in Marx and Engels, 65–71, 74; in the National Welfare Rights Organization, 136–137; in the Oaxaca Commune, 1–3, 203, 219; in the Paris Commune, 95–97; and progressive anti-family reforms, 168, 173; in radical

feminism, 131–133, 140–141; rebellion of, 1–3, 139, 148, 229; rolling back gains of, 148, 158; in the Russian Revolution, 123–126; in the Second International, 118–120; sex-class analysis, 141; sexual assault, 211–213; sex work, 66, 101; slave-owning, 77, 80; sterilization, 38; suburban housewife, 132; trans women, 129, 175; urbanization, 100–102; violence against, 41–42, 168, 211–213; in Wages for Housework, 137–139; welfare, 156; white women in settler colonialism, 78–79; during World War II, 122; working-class, 10, 64–66
see also feminism, gender, housewife, sex work, trans
work
anti-work, 58, 128, 132, 136–137, 140, 146; Black, 79, 87, 89, 91, 102, 135, 257; care, 235, 236; citations, 250, 255, 258; and COVID-19, 17; and community, 242, 245; and communization, 217, 219; domination of, 125–126, 194, 195, 196, 255; excluded from, 4, 43, 51, 89, 167, 190, 191; and family abolition, 6; in fascist ideology, 33; in Fourier, 106; gay, 163, 165; freedom from, 194–196, 172; as gender discipline, 199; household dependence on 27–28; peasant, 97; proletarianization, 98–101, 254, 257; remote, 17; and sex, 99–100; in socialism, 123–126, 192; shaping family forms, 27; slavery, 79, 85, 86, 91; stress of, 4
see also housework, industrialization, putting-out system, service industry, sex work, social

Thanks to our Patreon subscriber:

Ciaran Kane

Who has shown generosity and comradeship in support of our publishing.